Approaches to
Teaching the Novels of
Toni Morrison

Approaches to Teaching
World Literature

Joseph Gibaldi, series editor

For a complete listing of titles,
see the last pages of this book.

Approaches to Teaching the Novels of Toni Morrison

Edited by

Nellie Y. McKay

and

Kathryn Earle

The Modern Language Association of America
New York   1997

©1997 by The Modern Language Association of America
All rights reserved
Printed in the United States of America
Second printing 1999

For information about obtaining permission to reprint material from
MLA book publications, send your request by mail (see address below),
e-mail (permissions@mla.org), or fax (212 477-9863).

Library of Congress Cataloging-in-Publication Data

Approaches to teaching the novels of Toni Morrison / edited by
Nellie Y. McKay and Kathryn Earle.
p.   cm. — (Approaches to teaching world literature, ISSN 1059-1133 ; 59)
Includes bibliographical references (p.   ) and indexes.
ISBN 0-87352-741-0 (cloth). — ISBN 0-87352-742-9 (pbk.)
1. Morrison, Toni—Study and teaching. 2. American fiction—Afro-
American authors—Study and teaching. 3. Women and literature—
United States—Study and teaching. 4. Afro-American women in
literature—Study and teaching. 5. American fiction—Women authors—
Study and teaching. 6. Afro-Americans in literature—Study and
teaching. I. McKay, Nellie Y. II. Earle, Kathryn, 1960–
III. Series.
PS3563.08749Z54   1997
813'.54—dc21   97-26867

Cover illustration for the paperback edition: Verlena Johnson,
Warrior Woman #2, 1995, mixed media, $10\frac{1}{2}$" x 3".
Used with permission of the artist

Set in Caledonia and Bodoni. Printed on recycled paper

Published by The Modern Language Association of America
10 Astor Place, New York, New York 10003-6981

CONTENTS

PREFACE TO THE SERIES

In *The Art of Teaching* Gilbert Highet wrote, "Bad teaching wastes a great deal of effort, and spoils many lives which might have been full of energy and happiness." All too many teachers have failed in their work, Highet argued, simply "because they have not thought about it." We hope that the Approaches to Teaching World Literature series, sponsored by the Modern Language Association's Publications Committee, will not only improve the craft—as well as the art—of teaching but also encourage serious and continuing discussion of the aims and methods of teaching literature.

The principal objective of the series is to collect within each volume different points of view on teaching a specific literary work, a literary tradition, or a writer widely taught at the undergraduate level. The preparation of each volume begins with a wide-ranging survey of instructors, thus enabling us to include in the volume the philosophies and approaches, thoughts and methods of scores of experienced teachers. The result is a sourcebook of material, information, and ideas on teaching the subject of the volume to undergraduates.

The series is intended to serve nonspecialists as well as specialists, inexperienced as well as experienced teachers, graduate students who wish to learn effective ways of teaching as well as senior professors who wish to compare their own approaches with the approaches of colleagues in other schools. Of course, no volume in the series can ever substitute for erudition, intelligence, creativity, and sensitivity in teaching. We hope merely that each book will point readers in useful directions; at most each will offer only a first step in the long journey to successful teaching.

Joseph Gibaldi
Series Editor

PREFACE TO THE VOLUME

Confirmation of the importance of Toni Morrison's work, if it were needed, came in 1993, when she received the Nobel Prize in literature. But preparation of this volume began several years earlier. Although it is difficult now to remember that recognition of Morrison was slow in coming, many teachers struggled with her novels in the classroom for years, having little secondary literature to assist them. Now Morrison has become a veritable industry. This volume aims to help instructors digest the burgeoning mass of materials and to provide strategies for tackling a writer who is complex, controversial, and challenging to read and teach.

The volume presents background materials on Morrison, which are followed by essays outlining strategies that teachers have successfully employed in a cross section of institutional settings and over a wide range of courses. The essays' approaches should benefit those teaching Morrison's work for the first time, but they have much to offer experienced instructors as well. It is an unusual challenge for any teacher to bring to the fore Morrison's charged issues of racial and social injustice while at the same time underscoring their complicated genesis. The ethnic diversity of the classroom can be significant in shaping discussion and may allow for a free and lively exchange, as Morrison's treatment of contentious issues is egalitarian and multifaceted rather than polemical. But instructors must be aware of potential sensitivities in a way not demanded by the established canon, where blacks are conspicuous by their absence and "ignoring race is understood to be a graceful, even generous, liberal gesture" (Morrison, *Playing* 9–10).

The first part of the volume serves as a guide to editions, audiovisual aids, and background materials. But recommendations on background materials may be found in part 2 as well: Terry Otten's essay on Morrison's interviews provides essential information on the most authoritative source on Morrison— the author herself.

The essays in part 2 are divided among four sections. The first is entitled "'Out There, in the World': Race and Identity in the Classroom." Commenting on permanence and time in *Beloved*, Sethe says: "If a house burns down it's gone, but the place—the picture of it—stays, and not just in my rememory, but out there, in the world" (36). The novel is historically fixed, but the issues it raises relating to race and identity have endured, though they are transformed. This section appears first because it is designed to orient readers to Morrison's position in the world of the classroom.

The second section, "'The Thing out of Which I Come': Morrison Contextualized," situates Morrison canonically. Morrison has stated:

> I am not experimental, I am simply trying to recreate something out of an old art form in my books—the something that defines what makes a

book "black." . . . [S]tories [in the black community] are constantly being retold, constantly being imagined within a framework. And I hook into this like a life-support system, which for me, is the thing out of which I come.   (Mason 564)

Morrison also freely acknowledges the importance of other writers to her art. This section should be of special interest to those teaching Morrison in surveys of American or African American literature.

The third section, "Colors and Sounds: Language, Style, and Technique," addresses students' difficulties with Morrison's prose style and narrative techniques, which can initially alienate readers. The force of the writing derives not just from what Morrison says but from how she says it. In an interview with Claudia Tate, Morrison commented, "I must use my craft to make the reader see the colors and hear the sounds" (120). Those who have read and taught her know that lines, even whole passages, from her work linger in the mind and continue to resonate. It is therefore essential that students learn to deal with her difficult and complex style and language so that these elements enhance rather than impede appreciation of her work.

The final section, "'Holes and Spaces': Interpretive Strategies," attempts to encourage sophisticated theoretical approaches in the classroom. As Morrison once stated, "[M]y language has to have holes and spaces so that the reader can come into it" (Interview with Tate 125). While the three preceding sections aim to resolve particular problems students may have in reading Morrison, this section seeks to reveal how rich and multifaceted her work is. There is considerable overlap among sections. We have avoided organizing the essays in the obvious way—chronologically by novel—because several of them discuss multiple works. Moreover, since we believe that many of the difficulties in teaching Morrison persist throughout her work, we think the present structure is most useful, for we hope that instructors will look at all the essays before ruling any out as irrelevant and will see that they may apply particular approaches to other works with equal success. However, the volume features an index of the novels for those who wish to read on specific works, as well as a list of works cited.

This book has been shaped by many colleagues, students, and friends. We would like to thank, first, each of the contributors who worked so hard to see that the aims of this volume were met and who bore all delays patiently. While we still feel that a book on the body of Morrison's work is preferable to one on a single novel, this decision made the selection of essays deeply frustrating, since we received many more proposals of merit than we could choose. We would also like to thank the other survey respondents, listed at the end of the book; we found their input invaluable in compiling the materials section. In addition, several respondents sent reams of literature connected to their courses, which proved a most valuable resource. We would like to acknowledge the support given by Joseph Gibaldi, from conception to manuscript, and by Alicia

Mahaney and Adrienne Ward, both formerly of the MLA staff, who brought enthusiasm and constructive advice to the project in its early stages. We are also grateful to James Poniewozik, currently of the MLA staff, for his careful copyediting of the manuscript. Special thanks go to Donia Allen, Keisha Bowman, Akua Brath, Nanci Calamari, and Lisa Woolfork. Finally, we would like to thank Graham Farrant for all his support and assistance.

Nellie Y. McKay
University of Wisconsin, Madison

Kathryn Earle
Berg Publishers, Oxford, England

Part One

MATERIALS

Introduction

The writings of black women in America have recently gained great visibility in college and university classes in this country and abroad as many more teachers than ever, of various races and both genders, have become aware of the special qualities of these works. This trend began with the emergence in the 1960s and 1970s of writers like Maya Angelou, Toni Cade Bambara, Paule Marshall, Toni Morrison, and Alice Walker and the recoveries of Gwendolyn Brooks, Zora Neale Hurston, Nella Larsen, and Ann Petry, among others. This effect on contemporary literature was evident by the late 1970s. Initially helped by the black and women's movements, black women writers have accrued not only popular appeal but also scholarly and academic prestige as a result of the more recent interest in multicultural education and diversity in the humanities curriculum. Also important is the influence of black women scholars who taught and wrote about many of these women long before critics in other groups did. For an accurate assessment of this historical background, teachers can consult the early criticism of such black women critics as Toni Cade Bambara, Hazel Carby, Barbara Christian, Frances Smith Foster, Gloria Hull, Deborah McDowell, Andrea Rushing, Barbara Smith, Hortense Spillers, and Mary Helen Washington, whose work made possible the subsequent full recognition of black women writers.

Most prominent among the black women's writings now used in classes are the novels of Toni Morrison. The survey that preceded preparation of this volume confirmed our hunch that Morrison is taught in a wide range of courses: from freshman composition to graduate seminars; from surveys of American, African American, and women's literature to single-author courses; and in thematic courses in contemporary literature at all levels of instruction.

The survey asked teachers of Morrison's novels to identify the works they assign to their students and the works they use in preparing to teach Morrison. The discussion below outlines their responses.

The Novels

As of this writing, Toni Morrison has published the following novels: *The Bluest Eye* (1970), *Sula* (1973), *Song of Solomon* (1977), *Tar Baby* (1981), *Beloved* (1987), and *Jazz* (1992). Each work presents challenges to the student and the instructor. *The Bluest Eye*, not terribly well-received in the early 1970s, is now widely used in introductory and women's literature courses. It is perhaps Morrison's most accessible novel, though its nonlinear structure, graphic rape scene, poetic style, and female-bildungsroman form can make it difficult to teach, especially to male students. *The Bluest Eye* was followed by *Sula*, another female bildungsroman, whose eponymous heroine subverts convention and forces students to question their value systems. *Sula's* female-centered world can make male students uncomfortable. Although this novel rejects facile interpretation, students often try to impose a simplistic dichotomy of good and evil on it. With *Song of Solomon* Morrison proved that she could capably re-create male as well as female milieus. It is a rich and rewarding novel, but again it is demanding because of its multiplicity of cultural allusions and mixture of literary forms. The ending of *Song* always presents a problem for students, as it defies convention and frustrates the need for closure. *Tar Baby*, set in the Caribbean and prominently featuring whites as well as blacks, is atypical of Morrison's work. This novel invites questions of race, heritage, and identity through the contrasts it depicts. Although students may find its plainer style more accessible, it appears to be almost nobody's favorite. Many critics consider it Morrison's most undervalued work. *Beloved* is arguably Morrison's most complex novel, as Sharon Holland and Michael Awkward, among others, point out in this volume. *Beloved* forces students to accept the impossible as commonplace, and most find it a challenge to grapple with the palimpsest quality of the narrative. Finally, *Jazz* reconfigures fictional boundaries and represents a departure into a type of interdisciplinary fiction that incorporates many fields besides history. Its integration of a jazz style and jazz themes demands a familiarity with a musical realm far removed from the experience of most students and therefore presents a particular challenge to instructors.

All the novels remain available in the United States and Canada in paperback. In 1993 Random House published a six-volume set in hardcover. The complete text of *Sula* is in *The Norton Anthology of Women's Literature* (Gilbert and Gubar), and *The Norton Anthology of African American Literature* carries it as well (Gates and McKay). In addition, the novels all have appeared in British editions and in numerous translations. *The Bluest Eye* and *Jazz* are on audiotape and in large print, and some books are available in braille.

Other Works

Articles and Essays

Toni Morrison is one of a handful of creative writers who also produce successful nonfiction prose. She began to publish review articles and essays in 1971. These writings appear in academic and popular periodicals and as book chapters. Like her fiction, her nonfiction engages a broad spectrum of complex ideas and makes it impossible for readers to see her through narrow ideological or political lenses. For instance, although she makes clear in the essays that her experiences as a black person and a woman in a Western society shape her intellectual perspective and her artistic vision, she does not subscribe to traditional feminist ideology. Similarly, she rejects a black nationalism that dispenses easy answers to difficult questions regarding the human condition. Even so, she writes passionately in the defense of black women and the heritage of black people, she excoriates racism and other forms of injustice, and she revels in her love of great literature. Unfortunately, space considerations prevent a specific mention of most of Morrison's nonfiction titles; what follows is a brief summary of three of her most cited essays and of one that is too recent to have built up a wide reputation but that we believe will soon join the other three.

Toni Morrison's three most cited essays are "Unspeakable Things Unspoken: The Afro-American Presence in American Literature" (1989), "Rootedness: The Ancestor as Foundation" (1983), and "Memory, Creation, and Writing" (1984). Scholars applauded "Unspeakable Things" as a major statement on the influence and presence of blackness in the life of the country and in the American literary tradition. Morrison suggests that a more general conscious embrace of blackness by nonblack writers would facilitate a better understanding of the richness of the national literature. In "Rootedness," originally an interview and expanded into an essay, Morrison defines the qualities inherent in "authentic black literature," the writer as individual and as representative of the "tribe," and the role of the black novel as culture-bearing artifact. In "Memory," one of the earliest works to document Morrison's commitment to an intrinsically black art, Morrison discusses her responsibilities to the creative process and to her readers. The more recent essay that is especially noteworthy is "Introduction: Friday on the Potomac," in *Race-ing Justice, En-gendering Power: Essays on Anita Hill, Clarence Thomas, and the Construction of Social Reality* (1992), a volume she edited. While the book may appear too topically political for the introduction to be closely allied to the more literary essays mentioned above, the essay is another effort to problematize the issues of race and power prominent in Morrison's fiction.

Morrison initiated the *Race-ing Justice* project immediately after the Anita Hill–Clarence Thomas Senate hearings in 1991 that preceded Thomas's appointment to the Supreme Court. Convinced that these "complicated and complicating" proceedings were of major social significance and demanded immediate responses with "perspective, not attitudes, context, not anecdotes, analyses, not postures," she turned to eighteen academicians for their "contextualized and intellectually focused insights" on the event (xi). The book, she hoped, would serve as one opening to a new conversation, a "thoughtful, incisive, and far-ranging dialogue" between black women and men, who, although their opinions often differ, need to establish an honest interchange on the contentious issues of blind race loyalty and gender (xxx). The collection includes provocative essays by a racially mixed group of scholars, men and women, from widely diverse disciplines. Her brilliant piece addresses how the black bodies of Hill and Thomas were transformed into, inscribed on, and became in the eyes of millions of television viewers the "site of the exorcism of critical national issues . . . situated in the miasma of black life" (x). Examining the not-too-well-hidden subtext of the well-known Robinson Crusoe–Friday saga, Morrison focuses on language. On the one hand, the master disregards all but his own language, just as he disregards all but his own humanity; on the other, Friday, who loses his mother tongue, is left to speak in the master's tongue, which is the only adequate payment to the master for having rescued him from his own people. Morrison concludes that "both Friday and Clarence Thomas . . . [who] aligned himself with, the foot, as it were, that he had picked up and placed on his head, accompany their rescuers into the world of power and salvation [from blackness]. But," she notes, "the problem of rescue still exists: both men . . . are condemned first to mimic, then to internalize and adore, but never to utter one single sentence understood to be beneficial to their original culture" (xxix). While *Race-ing Justice* reconfirms Morrison's commitment to broad social concerns beyond literary studies and situates her as a leader in the academy in this area, "Friday on the Potomac" offers another illuminating and widely useful discussion on race and language in black and white America.

We strongly advise those who teach the novels of Toni Morrison to familiarize themselves with as many of her essays as they can. Among the best not mentioned above are "City Limits, Village Values: Concepts of the Neighborhood in Black Fiction," "The Site of Memory," and "On the Backs of Blacks," a brief piece that examines current United States immigration policies.

Playing in the Dark

Morrison extends ideas she raised in "Unspeakable Things" in *Playing in the Dark* (1992), her only book of nonfiction prose, in three chapters. She describes her project here as the creation of "a map of . . . a critical geography . . . [intended] to open . . . space for discovery, intellectual adventure, and close exploration . . . without the mandate for conquest" (3). She explains in the preface that she seeks reasons for and meanings behind "the way black people ignite critical moments of discovery or change or emphasis in literature not written by them" (viii). Over time, her literary observations led her to curiosity about three related issues: the pervasive use of black images and people in the expressive prose of whites; the nature of the taken-for-granted assumptions implicit in the use of these images; and the sources of such images and their effects on the literary imagination and the products of that imagination (x). Black writers like her, she says, have less access to traditional constructs of blackness than whites do. Instead, they struggle with language that evokes and reinforces hidden signs of racial superiority, cultural hegemony, and the dismissive "othering" of people and language outside the mainstream. Black writers must work at not romanticizing blackness, at not vilifying whiteness but not reifying whiteness either. They search vigilantly for ways to free language from its "sometimes sinister, frequently lazy, almost always predictable employment of racially informed and determined chains" (xi). The preface concludes with critical questions that inform the three essays in the book, questions on the construction and consequences of "literary whiteness" and "literary blackness" in a race-conscious culture (xii).

In the first chapter, "Black Matters," Morrison announces the goal of her project: a head-on address of the meticulously scripted exclusion of the black presence in American literature despite that presence's prominent role in shaping the body politic, the Constitution, and the history of American culture. Although literary production has long been regarded as the preserve of white male views, genius, and power, with no relation to the presence of black people in this country, she insists that "the black presence is central to any understanding of our national literature" (5). To prove her point, she analyzes the influence of certain agents of criticism that rob literature of its ideology and ideas; the effects of racism on those who perpetuate racial hierarchy and exclusion and racial vulnerability; and the way in which "[e]xcising the political from the life of the mind is . . . a kind of trembling hypochondria always curing itself with unnecessary surgery" (12). The chapter concludes with an analysis of Willa Cather's last novel, *Sapphira and the Slave Girl*, as a book that "describes and inscribes its narrative's own fugitive flight from itself" (19). In this novel of racial and gender betrayal "that faces the void of racism," Cather uses an improbable relationship between a slave woman and her daughter to "dream" and "redream" "[Cather's] problematic relationship with her mother" (27). Through Sapphira, the white character, who uses black female bodies at no risk to her power, Cather experiences "a *safe* participation in loss, in love, in chaos, in justice" (28). Although the novel has many flaws, Morrison gives Cather credit for attempting consciously to make the journey toward the unspeakable.

Chapters 2 and 3 of *Playing in the Dark*, "Romancing the Shadow" and "Disturbing Nurses and the Kindness of Sharks," explore related themes in the works of Edgar Allan Poe, Mark Twain, Ernest Hemingway, and others, focusing on the romance that is "[never] free of what Herman Melville called 'the power of blackness,'" the unacknowledged Africanist presence in all aspects of American life, and the inextricable connections between Africanism and Americanness (37). Morrison returns time and again to examine the subtle ways in which the presence and language of blackness, though the presence was stubbornly ignored and the language was often unspoken, influence American literature from the eighteenth century on. Her objective, she tells readers, is to "avert the critical gaze from the racial object to the racial subject; from the described and imagined to the describers and imaginers; from the serving to the served" (90). Her concern is to subvert a polite literary criticism that refuses to see the richness and complexities in American literature and to activate another that will not be afraid to face "the disrupting darkness" of the Africanist presence in its midst (91).

Morrison is not the first black writer to advance the theory of interconnections between the African presence in America and the language and literature of white American writers. Many of the most notable black writers, including

Ralph Ellison and James Baldwin, made it a central aspect of their criticism of American cultural production. But Morrison is the first to gain substantial critical support on the issue. Recently interest in reinterpreting the founding texts of American literature has grown, especially among a younger generation of cross-racial literary scholars. *Black and White Strangers: Race and American Literary Realism* (1993), by Kenneth W. Warren, argues that there are strong relations among black and white nineteenth-century canonical texts. In *Criticism and the Color Line: Desegregating American Literary Studies*, edited by Henry B. Wonham, more than twenty contributors respond to Morrison's call to breach the conspicuous silence regarding the role of race in nineteenth-century American literature. Morrison is a major influence in this area of critical inquiry.

Interviews and Nobel Prize Lecture

Morrison is a favorite interview subject for scholars, writers, and journalists (including television reporters).[1] Danille Taylor-Guthrie's 1994 paperback collection, *Conversations with Toni Morrison*, provides an excellent representative selection. Compiled from interviews conducted between 1974 and 1992 that appeared in academic and popular journals, newspapers, and anthologies, the collection gives teachers and students access to an often neglected medium of Morrison's thoughts and ideas. "The Art of Fiction CXXXIV," in the *Paris Review*'s fortieth anniversary issue (1993), is Morrison's most comprehensive discussion of her art and ideals, especially concerning black art. Everyone who teaches her work needs to become acquainted with this interview.

In 1993, Toni Morrison became the first African American to receive the Nobel Prize in literature. Not surprisingly, her Nobel lecture and acceptance speech focused on language. At the Swedish Academy, Morrison, whose childhood was full of stories, noted that she had always seen narrative as not merely a means of entertainment but rather a conduit for knowledge. And so she told them a story: Once upon a time there was an old, blind black woman, the daughter of slaves, who lived alone in a small house outside of the town, revered for her wisdom and without peer among her people. One day the old woman was visited by a group of young people from the nearby city, who came to mock her and expose her as the fraud they believed her to be. Their performance was a demonstration of power over her seeming helplessness. However, she turned the tables on them, shifting the center of the discourse away from their mockery of her, onto them and the instruments through which they exerted their power. Her behavior and her words reprimanded them. They listened and learned of their responsibilities from her (*Nobel* 9–30).

The speech addresses the responsibility of readers, writers, and speakers to keep language alive and regenerative. A dead language, one that fosters only its exclusivity and dominance, Morrison calls dangerous, subjugating, and oppressive. Such a language stifles the development of ideas, of intellect, and of all human potential. A living language is vital, continually renewing itself in the imagination of those who use it. In the speech Morrison declares her continuing commitment to and acceptance of the responsibility of language, as reader, writer, and speaker: her lecture is an act of consequence and a call to all to reconsider their responsibilities in using language. In this spirit, mindful of the writers who went before her, and those who will follow her, and of all within her circle of affection, she accepted the award in what she called "a moment of grace" (33). The Nobel lecture was published as a small book and an audiotape in 1994 by Knopf.

The Black Book

Morrison's affinities to black history are nowhere better demonstrated than in *The Black Book*, in which her name does not appear but which she edited in 1974. This coffee-table-book-sized collage volume of texts on black life and culture is partly her response to the political rhetoric of the black power movement of the 1960s. Morrison disagreed with much of that rhetoric because of what she considered its lack of respect for what African Americans had been forced to do to survive in America. "The Making of *The Black Book*," a 1974 essay in *Black World*, she describes the 198-page work as a "genuine Black history book" that recollects black life as lived (89). "I was scared that the world would fall away before somebody put together a thing that got close to the way we really were. . . . It was a true labor of love," she writes (90). The book has no chapters or stated themes, so that one does not have to read its parts in order. It includes "old, old newspaper articles" (89), gossip, rumors, songs, photographs, engravings, and prose excerpts. There are items on sports figures, entertainers, and cowboys; pictures of utensils and handicrafts; accounts of lynchings; and stories of many nameless persons. There are maps of the Underground Railroad and documents relating to the slave trade, as well as recipes, dream analyses, soap ads, anecdotes on the lives of black people, and instructions on making voodoo dolls. While she worked on *The Black Book* Morrison came across an old newspaper report of a runaway slave woman who tried to kill her children to save them from recapture and reenslavement. Almost a decade later the account would become the nucleus of her fifth and most celebrated novel, *Beloved*. The size of *The Black Book* and the variety and arrangement of its contents make it a volume that students enjoy leafing through; by passing around a copy in class, teachers can leave students with the feeling of literally holding history in their hands.

Further Readings for Students

Our survey showed that many teachers do not assign background readings on Morrison or African American literature to their undergraduate students. For many teachers, time constraints may limit the amount of background reading they can assign while still covering the desired primary material. A teacher may decide to cover major background information in an overview lecture and integrate necessary supplementary information into subsequent lectures or discussions. At institutions that have strong multicultural and ethnic studies programs or that emphasize mainstreaming nontraditional writers into the traditional humanities curriculum, students have incrementally greater opportunities to acquire background information on African American literature, history, and culture. This is especially true of students beyond the freshman year who are interested in nontraditional writers.

Among the background readings that respondents do recommend are Frances Smith Foster's *Written by Herself: Literary Production by African American Women, 1746–1892* (1993), Deborah E. McDowell's *"The Changing Same": Black Women's Literature, Criticism, and Theory* (1995), Hazel V. Carby's *Reconstructing Womanhood: The Emergence of the Afro-American Novelist*, Barbara Christian's *Black Women Novelists: The Development of a Tradition, 1892–1976*, and essays from the journals *African American Review* (formerly *Black American Literature Forum* or *BALF*; see, e.g., B. Bell; Coleman; Demetrakopoulos; Krumholz; Lee; Sale; Sitter; Wilentz), *Callaloo* (see, e.g., special section in 1990), and *CLA* [College Language Association] *Journal* (see, e.g., Berret; Hovet and Lounsberry). Some respondents noted that they like to assign Morrison's critical work, particularly her essay "Rootedness," and two interviews conducted with her: Robert Stepto's "'Intimate Things in Place': A Conversation with Toni Morrison" and Bessie Jones's interview in *The World of Toni Morrison*. The following section and the works-cited listing in this volume also include titles instructors may find useful sources of background readings.

The Instructor's Library

Our survey asked instructors what reference works, critical studies, background readings, and audiovisual materials they use that can better familiarize new teachers with Morrison's work. We have space to list only a small selection of items we consider among the most important: books and collections of essays on the novels and a selection of Morrison's critical writings.

Teachers must bear in mind the special problems associated with teaching and writing about living authors, especially very productive ones. The recognition of Morrison's nonfiction writings on American literature makes Morrison a major critical writer as well. On the one hand, critics cannot examine her work as a static whole, since she continues to write: one always writes in the shadow of the forthcoming book. On the other hand, as a critic of the tradition to which she contributes, she also shapes the interpretive framework through which her fiction is judged. Morrison is hardly the first black creative writer to cross the boundary between literary criticism and literature, but she is the most influential and visible black writer to date.

Reference Works

More than seventy dictionaries and encyclopedias on American, world, and African American history and literature carry entries on Tony Morrison. They range from brief biographical accounts to substantive summaries of her life and works. One of the most frequently cited, although it appeared before *Beloved* and *Jazz*, is Susan Blake's piece in volume 33 of the *Dictionary of Literary Biography: Afro-American Fiction Writers after 1955* (1984). Blake's essay remains useful for its succinct evaluation of Morrison's place in the literary world. More recent reference works that offer valuable introductory materials on Morrison include *African American Writers*, edited by Valerie Smith et al. (1991), *Black Women in America: An Historical Encyclopedia*, edited by Darlene Clark Hine (1993), and *Notable Black American Women*, edited by Jessie C. Smith (1991). The last two are important for their positioning of Morrison in the context of black American history, particularly the history of black women and of black institutions from slavery to the present.

The two best bibliographic sources on Morrison, through 1986 and 1988, are David L. Middleton's *Toni Morrison: An Annotated Bibliography* (1987) and Craig H. Werner's "Toni Morrison," in his *Black American Women Novelists: An Annotated Bibliography* (1989). Deborah Mix's "Toni Morrison: A Selected Bibliography" (1993), in a special issue of *Modern Fiction Studies* on Morrison, makes a valuable contribution in identifying much of the post-1987 criticism. Middleton's bibliography of primary and secondary sources includes lengthy annotations of Morrison's essays and reviews, of interviews with her, and of criticism of her work. It also lists prizes she won between 1975 and 1987, the anthologies in which her writings appear, the audiotape recordings of her work, and her special appointments. Werner's bibliography has a lengthy and useful introduction to black women novelists and a general-studies section that offers a historical overview of critical commentary on black women novelists and their most important works. The volume includes separate annotated listings on thirty-two novelists, including Morrison. Each entry consists of three parts: a short biography, general commentary on the writer's work, and a discussion of specific items in her bibliography. Although Mix's bibliography includes no annotations, it is significant because it confirms the rapidity with which Morrison criticism has appeared worldwide since 1986. Without doubt *Beloved* receives the most attention from critics. Given the burgeoning criticism on Morrison, instructors wishing to stay abreast of new work should examine the bibliographies in new articles, journal essays, essay collections, and book-length critical studies on Morrison, African American literature, and contemporary women and American writers.

Book-Length Critical Studies

There are nine published book-length studies of Toni Morrison's novels. They range from works most useful to beginning teachers with little knowledge of Morrison or the black literary tradition to studies suitable for more advanced readers. Taking the writers in alphabetical order, we offer a brief assessment of each.

The Novels of Toni Morrison: The Search for Self and Place within the Community (1992), by Patrick Bryce Bjork, is suited for those who are not well acquainted with the novels. That the central theme appears in several other Morrison studies does not make this volume less useful. Bjork provides a close reading of the first five novels, making his work especially useful for undergraduate students and general readers. However, discussions of important background materials, particularly those pertaining to Morrison, are scanty, and the bibliography omits many of the most important critical discussions of the novels. For a book published in 1992, these are major faults, but they do not render it useless.

Toni Morrison's World of Fiction (1993), by Karen Carmean, is a clearly written and comprehensible overview of Morrison's novels that teachers unfamiliar with the full body of Morrison's work should find useful. The introduction includes a helpful discussion of process in the artist's writings. Carmean stresses that Morrison's fundamental concern is language, especially the distinctive language of black people in relation to other aspects of black cultural aesthetics; Carmean notes, for example, that there are musical moments in each novel. In addition, Carmean writes, Morrison's pervasive use of orality and her meticulous attention to detail suggest a similarity between her novels and Greek tragedy. Carmean reads *The Bluest Eye* as a story of love and survival: how one survives as a whole person in a world where one's identity depends on others. In *Sula*, readers learn to discard conventional expectations as they enter a deliberately inverted fictional world of complex reality, in which good and bad lose their traditional meanings. The protagonist in *Song of Solomon* recovers a rich cultural history that connects him to people, places, values, and the meaning of his past; in the narrative Morrison makes imaginative use of the language of folk and fairy tales, magic, root medicine, and history. In *Tar Baby*, even more dramatically than in her previous works, Morrison brings together myth, legend, and folklore to African concepts of nature as a conscious entity and extends the "village" to the Caribbean and beyond. Carmean concludes that the novel contains some of Morrison's best writing. *Beloved* challenges readers to recall and confront their past, however traumatic, rather than be held captive to it, Carmean writes; Morrison makes use of the storytelling strategies of the African griot to achieve a vision of organic unity. *Jazz*, the second in what Morrison promises to be a trilogy, picks up at roughly the historical point in black history where *Beloved* leaves off. The novel, writes Carmean, documents some progress for blacks over a half century in the move from wretched plantation existence to self-sufficiency in the city. Following a fast beginning that establishes its dominant tone and theme, the narrative breaks into different parts: stories, voices, motifs, images, and relative themes that always return to the issue of human passions. We find Carmean's book useful as an overall substantive introduction to Morrison's novels.

In *Fiction and Folklore: The Novels of Toni Morrison* (1991), Trudier Harris locates Morrison's art at the center of the black literary tradition. For more than a hundred years, many of the most renowned black writers, including Charles Chesnutt, Zora Neale Hurston, Langston Hughes, and Ralph Ellison, have used the rich African American expressive culture as a creative source. The writers were fully aware that although literacy was denied to Africans and their descendants in America until well past the middle of the nineteenth century, an oral literature flourished among earlier generations in songs, folk rhymes, jokes, riddles, and tales. These black writers recognized the significance of the earlier forms by relying on them to give integrity to their written works. Morrison also makes extensive (although not exclusive) use of folklore as sources. Harris's book opens with a reminder that in 1984 Morrison commented that she was struggling to fashion an intrinsically black literature, one requisite of which is its combination of black oral and written expressions. She wants her work to cause the reader to listen to as well as read the words. Morrison has often spoken of seeking to effect a connection between the writing and the reader, somewhat like the connection between the audience and the black preacher when they participate in a sermon.

But Harris argues that Morrison does not consistently create parallels to historical black folklore materials in her work. More often, she transforms them into what the critic calls literary folklore: material that "can be incorporated into literary texts without compromising its original quality" (7). In Harris's opinion Morrison, more than any other writer, uses folklore in a way that leaves "no dichotomy between form and substance, theme and character" (7). Morrison's achievement raises a number of questions that Harris attempts to address in her study of the novels, for example, "Can a literary author 'create' folklore within a text? . . . Can a literary text 'create' materials that will subsequently enter the oral tradition and be passed down by word of mouth?" (8). Harris concludes that Morrison's mastery of her craft enables Morrison to create materials that so closely resemble the original forms that it is almost impossible to detect where communal memory ends and the artistic imagination takes over.

Harris studies Morrison's first five novels in meticulous detail, carefully delineating the techniques that Morrison employs to incorporate folkore into her fiction. The book opens with the section "Literary History and Literary Folklore," which sets the stage perfectly for what follows. Harris's insights into the novels are penetrating, and she raises new questions for readers to contemplate. Her study, informed by close, careful readings and a sound knowledge of the folklore of Afro-America and other cultures, is the best overall critical text to date for those who teach these novels. One of the strengths of this book is

Harris's ability to position herself at a critical distance and present an unbiased appraisal of Morrison's work, even as she acknowledges the writer's genius. *Fiction and Folklore* should be on the shelves of everyone interested in Morrison or in the literary uses of black folklore.

In a treatment of the six novels, *The Dilemma of Double Consciousness: Toni Morrison's Novels* (1993), Denise Heinze argues that Morrison seeks to resolve the tensions embedded in the double consciousness that W. E. B. Du Bois identified at the turn of the century as the heritage of all black people in America. The central issue for Heinze is Morrison's success as a great American writer who also preserves the integrity of blackness. On the one hand, a basher of many myths of Western culture, on the other, a new mythmaker who creates meaning out of connections to the past and to spiritual love, Morrison has created novels that transform and embody two warring literary selves. Morrison's vision, writes Heinze, combines political consciousness with aesthetic sensibility and elevates the beautiful and reclaimable in humanity. This book is useful for teachers interested in the conflicts black writers face as they engage their bicultural status and in the writers' responsibility to the white and black communities.

In *New Dimensions of Spirituality: A Biracial and Bicultural Reading of the Novels of Toni Morrison* (1987), a study of Morrison's first four novels, the coauthors Karla F. C. Holloway (who is black) and Stephanie A. Demetrakopoulos (who is white) demonstrate some of the problems that Americans face in negotiating differences in their biracial, bicultural experiences. The seven feminist essays by each author are at once contradictory and complementary; the authors seek to uncover the differences between them that result from race, and the elements of the bonding between them. Holloway grounds her work in black women's survival, Demetrakopoulos in the universal feminine in Morrison's novels. The volume is an interesting study of cross-racial dynamics in literary criticism that highlights feminist perspectives.

Dorothea Drummond Mbalia's *Toni Morrison's Developing Class Consciousness* (1991), a Marxist interpretation of the novels that is influenced by Kwame Nkrumah, is the most controversial critical work on Morrison. Mbalia contends that in the first five novels Morrison demonstrates a continuously growing consciousness of capitalism as the most powerful and destructive of Western forces that oppress all peoples of African heritage and a movement toward Marxian ideology. Mbalia traces that development from Morrison's "mistaken" explications of racism (*The Bluest Eye*) and gender (*Sula*) to a discovery of the importance of knowing family, community, and heritage (*Song of Solomon*) to class consciousness (*Tar Baby*) and finally to finding solutions to class exploitation and racial oppression (*Beloved*). The novels connect to one another through the "African principles of collectivism, humanism, and egalitarianism" (22). But while Mbalia accurately defines many central themes of Morrison's novels, Mbalia's approach does not adequately take into account the breadth of Morrison's imaginative powers. It is undeniable that Morrison is interested in black peoples across the globe and that she seeks to expose the racial, sexual, and class oppressions they suffer; but she also insists, explicitly and implicitly, orally and in her writings, that although her novels are political they are not prescriptive or ideologically bound. They are not sociological studies. For instance, it is not accurate to suggest, as Mbalia does, that Morrison derives her source material entirely from African and African-diaspora culture. Careful readings of Morrison's novels reveal her vast knowledge and use of African, American Indian, Oriental, and Euro-American cultural material. In all her writings Morrison successfully transcends the boundaries of an either-or framework in favor of the both-and framework that frees her imagination. An inflexible Marxist interpretation trivializes the scope of her accomplishments and contributions to black literature. Nevertheless, there are useful insights in this book, and those who teach Morrison's novels should not overlook it.

In *The Crime of Innocence in the Fiction of Toni Morrison* (1989), Terry Otten traces the evolution and the varied uses of the Fall motif in Morrison's first five novels. He examines the complex imagery of the garden in her work and uses that myth to depict the fall and transcendence of her black protagonists in a white world. The novels share several themes: "the passage from innocence to experience, the quest for identity, the ambiguity of good and evil, the nature of the divided self, and especially, the concept of a fortunate fall" (95). These themes make Morrison's works universal and endow her characters with symbolic dimensions inside an integrating pattern. Doubtless, teachers interested in the Fall motif will find reasons in this book to apply it to *Jazz* as well.

Barbara Hill Rigney's *The Voices of Toni Morrison* (1994) is a potentially controversial postmodernist reading of Morrison's first five novels. Rigney claims that Morrison, while not completely exempt from "phallocratic law" (no writer is), writes consciously from and about a peripheral zone, thus gaining a degree of autonomy from that law (1). Informed by the writings of Hélène Cixous, Catherine Clément, Julia Kristeva, and others, Rigney maps Morrison's use of language, her rendering of history, her reinscription of identity, and her articulation of female desire. To discover the magnitude of the political and artistic revolution in Morrison's works, Rigney identifies key elements in the author's storehouse: her use of history as time and space; the relation between silence and language and between absence and presence; her blurred oppositions; and the primacy of a maternal space that is much less ambiguous and problematic than the maternal space in many other feminist critics' work. In Morrison's world African mothers are not merely figures of dread to African American women; they are ancestors who are necessary to survival. This relation stands in contrast to the portrayal of white mothers in many works by white feminist women writers. Rigney suggests in her conclusion that by disrupting patriarchal prescriptions, Morrison produces a history of female desire that, defined in terms of contemporary feminist and African American critical theory, constitutes a black feminine-feminist aesthetic. Although some critics will take exception to Rigney's heavy reliance on the French theorists in describing this aesthetic, the analysis is interesting and will raise intriguing questions for teachers regarding theory, criticism, and culture.

Toni Morrison (1990), by Wilfred D. Samuels and Clenora Hudson-Weems, is a volume in the Twayne's United States Authors Series that covers Morrison's first five novels. Like other books in the series, it begins with a chronology of the subject's life and a biographical chapter. Each of the next five chapters is devoted to a novel, and the sixth concludes the book. The authors focus their discussion on a theme from each novel and provide subheadings for smaller topics within each chapter. The subtitle "Communities of Women" recurs constantly. Samuels and Hudson-Weems make clear that one cannot read Morrison's novels without recognizing the centrality of her concerns for black women.

Essay Collections

There are four essay collections on Toni Morrison. *Toni Morrison*, edited by Harold Bloom (1990), collects eleven essays and reviews as well as Morrison's essay "Unspeakable Things Unspoken." Although every essay but one was originally published elsewhere, the quality of each makes the collection worthwhile. In addition, the collection is the only book that reprints "Unspeakable Things," Morrison's most cited essay. *Toni Morrison: Critical Perspectives Past and Present*, edited by Henry Louis Gates, Jr., and K. A. Appiah (1993), is a larger collection that includes previously printed reviews, essays, and interviews; a chronology of Morrison's life; and a more comprehensive bibliography than the one in Bloom's book. There are two reviews each of the first five novels and three of the last, fifteen essays on the first five novels, and four interviews. The pieces were originally published between 1970 and 1992. The reviews in particular demonstrate how different many perceptions of Morrison's work were twenty years ago. The essays are consistently good, while the interviews permit Morrison to speak herself, a fitting conclusion to this section of the volume. An additional asset of the book is the bibliography's emphasis on post-1985 citations. Even though some of the essays are otherwise easily accessible, the collection is worthwhile for Morrison scholars and teachers. Nellie Y. McKay's *Critical Essays on Toni Morrison* (1988) has an introduction, book reviews, interviews, and twelve original essays. While the volume does not cover Morrison's last two novels, it continues to be widely cited by Morrison scholars and teachers. *New Essays on* Song of Solomon (1995), edited by Valerie Smith, is the first volume to address a single Morrison novel. Appearing in Cambridge University Press's American Novel Series, Smith's collection explores one of the author's most popular and most often taught books. Its introduction and four new essays by established Morrison critics focus on issues of orality and literacy, call and response, familial relationships, and the novel's subversion of postmodernism through vernacular structures.

Modern Fiction Studies' special issue on Toni Morrison's novels (1993), edited by Nancy J. Peterson, contains some of the best essays to appear on

Morrison. Also of interest is the special issue of *d'AFRAM Newsletter* (1993), "*Beloved, She's Mine*": *Essais sur* Beloved *de Toni Morrison*, edited by Genevieve Fabre and Claudine Raynaud and published in Paris. This collection of thirteen essays by American and European scholars is another useful (though difficult to obtain) addition to the Morrison shelf. A casebook of some of the best essays on *Beloved*, edited by William L. Andrews and Nellie Y. McKay, is forthcoming from Oxford University Press.

Uncollected Critical Essays

There are dozens of uncollected critical essays on Toni Morrison in anthologies and in journals, too many to list in this volume. Again, we advise teachers to search computer databases for publications on individual novels or special topics on Morrison and to keep abreast of the journals that most frequently publish articles on her, such as *African American Review*. Volume 26, number 1 (Spring 1992) includes excellent essays on *Beloved* by Bernard W. Bell, Deborah Ayer Sitter, Maggie Sale, and Stephanie A. Demetrakopoulos and one equally as good by Gay Wilentz on *Song of Solomon*; volume 26, number 3 (Fall 1992) contains a superb piece on *Beloved* by Linda Krumholz. Other journals that regularly publish criticism of Morrison's novels include *Callaloo*, *CLA Journal*, *Contemporary Literature*, and *MELUS* (*Multi-Ethnic Literatures of the United States*).

Background Readings

Toni Morrison is extremely well-read, as evidenced by the breadth of the allusions in her novels and other writings. She is steeped not only in African and African American folklore and cultures but also in Western, Native American, and some Eastern cultural traditions. In many of her interviews she speaks powerfully of her love of reading and its effects on her writing. At the same time, Morrison insists that she writes out of her background as a black American, a black woman, and an American. Two major concerns of hers are language and history (which are reflected, respectively, in the style and content of her novels), and one needs to keep those concerns in mind when reading her fiction.

The background readings that teachers of Morrison's work should be familiar with include standard overviews of black literary and cultural history; the works of past black writers, including women; histories of black women writing in America; and at least one standard nineteenth-century American literary history. In addition to books already mentioned, we suggest the following: John Hope Franklin and Alfred A. Moss's *From Slavery to Freedom*, Charles T. Davis and Henry Louis Gates's *The Slave's Narrative*, Nathan Huggins's *The Harlem Renaissance*, Eileen Southern's *The Music of Black America*, Alain Locke's *The New Negro*, Lawrence Levine's *Black Culture and Black Consciousness*, Gates's *The Signifying Monkey*, Houston A. Baker's *Blues, Ideology, and Afro-American Literature*, Werner Sollors and Maria Diedrich's *The Black Columbiad: Defining Moments in African American Literature and Culture*, Bernard Bell's *The Afro-American Novel and Its Tradition*, W. E. B. Du Bois's *The Souls of Black Folk*, the writings of Zora Neale Hurston, especially *Their Eyes Were Watching God* and *Mules and Men*, Ralph Ellison's *Invisible Man* and *Shadow and Act*, James Baldwin's *Go Tell It on the Mountain*, Pauli Murray's *Proud Shoes*, and Margaret Walker's *Jubilee*; Ann Allen Shockley's *Afro-American Women Writers, 1746–1933*, Cheryl A. Wall's *Changing Our Own Words*, and Anna Julia Cooper's *A Voice from the South*; the classic slave narratives by Frederick Douglass, Harriet Jacobs, and Booker T. Washington; William L. Andrews's *To Tell a Free Story*, Frances Smith Foster's *Witnessing Slavery*, Robert B. Stepto's *From behind the Veil*, Deborah Gray White's *Ar'n't I a Woman?* and Valerie Smith's *Self Discovery and Authority in Afro-American Narrative*; Robert Farris Thompson's *Flash of the Spirit*, Herbert Gutman's *The Black Family in Slavery and Freedom*, Vincent Harding's *There Is a River*, C. Eric Lincoln's *Race, Religion, and the Continuing American Dilemma*, Lincoln and Lawrence H. Mamiya's *The Black Church in the African American Experience*, and Albert J. Raboteau's *Slave Religion*. This list is clearly not exhaustive, and these books themselves suggest many others.

Audiovisual Materials

As mentioned above, Morrison's novels are available on audiotape. Some teachers also enrich lectures and discussions by showing videotapes that feature the author. Morrison has appeared in such television series as *In Black and White: Conversations with Afro-American Writers*, *Writers in Conversation*, *A World of Ideas*, *Profile of a Writer*, *The Writer in America*, and *Great American Writers*. In these programs she engages in interviews, reads from her novels, and discusses such issues as the contributions by blacks to American literature, the African American presence in American literature, slavery and its legacy, the definition of the self as a writer, writing as a political activity, and the process of writing.

NOTE

[1] In the works-cited list for this volume, interviews with Morrison are grouped together under Morrison's name.

Part Two

APPROACHES

Tracing and Erasing:
Race and Pedagogy in *The Bluest Eye*

Rafael Pérez-Torres

The Bluest Eye is not only a poignant and beautiful novel but also a text that raises critical questions about identity construction. Because facing such issues can be painful, threatening, or alienating, the book can touch non–European American students who have had to live within a culture that consistently devalues their aesthetics, and it can alienate students who feel kinship with dominant social values. Ultimately, instructors can turn the thematic difficulties the novel presents to good use by addressing them explicitly.

For a class of predominantly white students, the novel can help highlight the deracialized status of Caucasians. The book focuses incessantly on the "ugliness" of Pecola Breedlove, an ugliness fostered by a society that values blond hair and blue eyes as standards of beauty. *The Bluest Eye* can be unsettling because it traces the racial identity American society has erased for many of our students. It can also crystallize some of the conflicts students of color consciously or unconsciously have felt in developing a sense of identity. To make the book speak to all students no matter what their ethnic or racial backgrounds, it should be treated as a text that scrutinizes the complex dynamics of identity formation that involve everyone.

In addition to race, the novel takes as a primary issue the position of women within marginalized cultures. The "double marginalization" experienced by the characters is due to the emphasis on standards of beauty and the exploitation of their budding sexuality. This marginalization has its source in a community's internalization of oppressive systems of value, which fragments both individual psyches and the community as a whole.

The Bluest Eye illustrates some potentially destructive practices that can go into identity formation. While the novel suggests that Claudia McTeer has survived the traumas of growing up black in America, it is not wholly affirmative or celebratory. *The Bluest Eye* looks critically at both a dominant Euro-American society and an African American community complicitous in its own oppression. As such, it is a wonderfully complex narrative that lends itself to a fruitful and highly nuanced classroom discussion. I focus below on a pedagogy addressing race because that is often one of the most delicate problems in teaching *The Bluest Eye*.

While I try to take into account a diversity of classes and situations, the reality remains that postsecondary education serves primarily white and middle-class students. Similarly, most college instructors are white (though I am not), just as most instructors are middle-class (as I am). This issue needs to be addressed here and in the classroom since *The Bluest Eye* examines the harmfulness of taking one type of identity as a universal standard. Rather than hide and elide the sensitive and controversial issues *The Bluest Eye* introduces, a successful discussion of the book should confront issues of identity (both within the text and within the classroom) as honestly and intelligently as possible.

One of the first issues I raise in class about the text is not terribly advanced, but I think it is necessary. I emphasize that the book is a fiction and that Pecola, Claudia, and Frieda exist only in the imagination. Further, I make clear that the novel is not just about individuals. As Chandra Mohanty has pointed out, race in academic institutions is often treated as an individualized and personalized issue (174–76). If students perceive works like *The Bluest Eye* as just stories of individuals caught in desperate circumstances—even if beautifully and painfully rendered—the representational power of the novels as analyses of racial identity in the United States vanishes.

But the novel cannot be taught as a representative portrait of the black experience in America either. Once in class I was discussing the phrase that opens *The Bluest Eye*: "Quiet as it's kept" (Washington Square, 9). I referred to an interview with Thomas LeClair in which Morrison said, "That [phrase] is a piece of information which means exactly what it says, but to black people it means a big lie is about to be told. Or someone is going to tell some graveyard information, who's sleeping with whom. Black readers will chuckle. There is a level of appreciation that might be available only to people who understand the context of the language" (28). After class, a black student told me he had never heard the phrase. I tried to explain as best I could that for a particular community at a particular time this phrase must have had currency (I could only take Morrison's word for it). The incident reminded me to tread carefully when suggesting that particular representations are "representative."

Important too is the history of the novel's publication. Not withstanding the recuperation of minority texts undertaken by some of our best scholars, cultural self-representation among multicultural groups—even a representation as pained and agonized as *The Bluest Eye*—is relatively new and empowering. The ability to name and describe one's own experience and the experiences of the community was hard-won. The historical conditions of the novel's production should be addressed. After all, though Morrison wrote the novel in the wake of the civil rights movement, she had a difficult time finding a publisher for it. Students should understand that, until recently, stories about racial and personal identity like *The Bluest Eye* were not on many people's bookshelves, let alone on syllabi. The issue of mimesis, which much avant-garde theory considers passé, cannot be dismissed as old-fashioned when it comes to the representation of experiences marginalized by or erased from the national consciousness.

The illusion that Pecola, Frieda, and Claudia are real produces a feeling of connection in readers and makes the narrative urgent and affecting. In this sense, it is useful to talk about the text as representational. Nevertheless, a successful pedagogy that focuses on the thematization and construction of race must also read *The Bluest Eye* as an analysis of systems: of racialized identity, of racial construction, of gender roles, of disempowerment, of oppression. The issue of racialized identity provides one connection to all students' life experiences. Everybody has a race. *The Bluest Eye* is a useful book through which to explore this issue because it makes explicit the function of race and color in establishing a sense of self and self-worth. The trope of color—associated with the flowers that never bloom, the eyes that are never really blue—runs throughout the text and highlights the function of color within a system of racial distinction and valuation.

An early scene in the novel is emblematic of these issues: the adoration of the Shirley Temple cup. The primary narrator, the adult Claudia, recounts how Frieda and Pecola adulate the figure of pristine white beauty: "I couldn't join them in their adoration because I hated Shirley. Not because she was cute, but because she danced with Bojangles, who was *my* friend, *my* uncle, *my* daddy, and who ought to have been soft-shoeing it and chuckling with me" (19). The dispossession and exclusion, Claudia finds, turn to violence against pretty white dolls given to her at Christmas. The adults who give these gifts teach her to value "the single-stroke eyebrows . . . the pearly teeth stuck like two piano keys between red bowline lips . . . the turned-up nose . . . the glassy blue eyeballs . . . the yellow hair" (20). Gradually, the violence against white dolls becomes violence against white children. The adult Claudia reconsiders the significance of her actions:

> When I learned how repulsive this disinterested violence was, that it was repulsive because it was disinterested, my shame floundered about for refuge. The best hiding place was love. Thus the conversion from pristine sadism to fabricated hatred, to fraudulent love. It was a small step to Shirley Temple. I learned much later to worship her, just as I learned to

> delight in cleanliness, knowing, even as I learned, that the change was
> adjustment without improvement.   (22)

The embrace of dominant aesthetic values becomes an escape from the madness of disinterested violence, itself caused by adults imposing values bound up as much with economic exchange as with cultural exchange. Given the unrelenting poverty that surrounds Claudia and Frieda, it is obvious that the adults buy their children such emblems of perfect white beauty at great cost. The novel examines the social conventions within a black community that equates white aesthetics with beauty and the possession of wealth. While Claudia comes to white aesthetics as a process of "adjustment without improvement," Pecola does so as a preliminary step toward the madness of complete self-absorption.

The novel thus scrutinizes how white most often is considered not a racial category in the text (or in our society) but, rather, a nonrace, a norm, a universal standard. White in *The Bluest Eye* is not a race but an ideal, a natural state to which Pecola most strenuously aspires. The madness this desire engenders manifests itself in varying degrees among the characters who most closely associate white with a natural state. Cholly feels that association in his need and failure to express his sexuality lovingly as a form of affirmation; he is denied this expression by his humiliation before the eyes of white men as a youth. Mrs. Breedlove finds order and a sense of self-worth only in the world of her white employers. Her madness manifests itself in her inability to comprehend and address her family's needs. Pecola, of course, perceives worth and beauty as linked to whiteness and can attain these qualities only in the barren madness of her imaginary world of bluest eyes.

When the instructor highlights the systemic function of whiteness, a class on *The Bluest Eye* can move away from simplistic discussions of mimesis—How true is the book?—and from reading the novel as a representative story about an experience that students of all colors may or may not find relevant. One unstated issue in teaching texts ostensibly representative of racialized experiences can be understood by white students to be their duty to realize the destructiveness of racism. This then leads to a mere descent into guilt. Somehow, the white students, as privileged members of a nonracialized group, are being blamed for conditions that they may not have caused. (That they are the beneficiaries of these oppressive conditions is an issue they must eventually confront, but only over time.)

To avoid unproductive student guilt, instructors should state explicitly the purpose for including *The Bluest Eye* in a course. An engaging and ultimately fruitful discussion may develop if there is less emphasis on the book as a representation of a disempowered, underrepresented, or minority experience and more emphasis on it as a critical scrutiny of racialized identity construction. This perspective allows both student and instructor to highlight their relation to and experiences with the vexing issue of race.

Students of color may respond in any number of ways to *The Bluest Eye*: they may appreciate the factors that caused them turmoil and doubt, or they may revalue the strategies of identity construction they learned from their communities and families that have helped them avoid the kind of madness represented in the novel, or they may respond in other unthought ways. In any event, the dynamics laid bare by the book may appear familiar to them.

White students may respond in different ways too. Certainly some will demonstrate the type of white liberal guilt familiar to anyone who has taught works by authors of color. Even the compulsion of some white students who know little about black writing to celebrate these works rather naively can ultimately be productive. By focusing on how *The Bluest Eye* analyzes the construction of race, these students can understand more fully the insidiousness of racialized oppression. Other white students may see that their good intentions must go beyond laissez-faire arguments for a color-blind society. Erasing color erases a history of disempowerment and repression that *The Bluest Eye* carefully and painstakingly traces. Raising the problems of racial construction to the class and to the discussion of *The Bluest Eye* may help lead to an engaged and inclusive pedagogy that does not blame or assign guilt to any member of the class.

As with all literary texts, there can be no fixed approach to teaching this book suitable to every class situation. The class's makeup (size, racial and gender distribution, age) partly determines the instructor's approach to any text. The way students perceive the intent of the course syllabus will especially determine their reception of and relation to a text as complex as *The Bluest Eye*. I have always tried not to marginalize Morrison's novel by making it the only work by a woman or an African American on the syllabus. Moreover, the text's placement during the semester can be a vital signal. Teaching the book first or last may send a message to students about the novel's relative importance. If one teaches the book first or last, discussion of its position could be useful.

Especially in the introductory courses, I tend to use the book late in the semester because it helps encapsulate thematically and formally many issues I raise earlier. The structure of the novel, for example—the juxtaposition of the culturally biased Dick and Jane story with the natural seasons that divide the book into four parts—shows students the interrelation between narrative structure and thematic development. After all, the book highlights the destructive effects of culture on such natural phenomena as the growing up of little girls and the coming into sexuality of little boys. Through course evaluations and discussion with students, I have learned that the novel works well in making visible to them a culture that constantly effaces itself. Working from the margins, so to speak, students who engage the complexities of *The Bluest Eye* can begin to identify for themselves cultural practices being erased so busily elsewhere.

The Bluest Eye is a good read, a skillful rendering of characters and a moving tale of dissolution and growth, but it is also a story about race and exploitation, persecution and violation, and violence and the oppressive discrimination practiced by society. The issues I raise and strategies I propose here cannot make *The Bluest Eye* any less explosive. But the blast can, I believe, be channeled, so that students of diverse backgrounds and experiences can learn to use the text (and literature in general) as a critical tool with which to reimagine the dread and promise of their worlds.

Teaching Controversy: *The Bluest Eye* in the Multicultural Classroom

Kathryn Earle

> Her hair was parted, plaited, and greased close to the
> skull, and she had a flat and quiet face. There was only
> one thing wrong about Berenice—her left eye was bright
> blue glass. It stared out fixed and wild from her quiet,
> coloured face, and why she had wanted a blue eye
> nobody human would ever know.
> —Carson McCullers, *A Member of the Wedding*

An instructor teaching a racially charged book such as *The Bluest Eye* can understand how black students can see white liberalism as merely convenient, fundamentally insincere, or at worst self-serving, much as male feminism can seem inappropriate. Given this understanding and the certainty that racism exists within as well as outside the classroom, a white instructor teaching this explosive book can be effectively paralyzed, especially in a multicultural classroom. While I hope this essay will help anyone approaching the novel for the first time, in the main it offers advice to white instructors tackling the novel's racial issues in multiethnic settings. It also aims to provide strategies on managing what is arguably the novel's most pivotal scene—Cholly's rape of Pecola—which can be alienating and discomfiting for students and teacher alike.

Teachers who mask their emotional responses to texts to maintain a semblance of objectivity may find *The Bluest Eye* deeply troubling because it is difficult to maintain a neutral pose when teaching the novel. Yet without that neutral appearance white instructors in particular risk seeming apologetic, defensive, or, worse, offensive. One of *The Bluest Eye*'s principal themes—that black women's absorption of white standards of beauty perpetuates a destructive value system—is crucial to framing any discussion of the novel, but that statement can sound patronizing if it seems as though it is the instructor's opinion rather than the author's. While we cannot teach if we are consumed with worry that what we say might hurt or offend, any sensitive white instructor should be aware that it is reasonable for black students to ask how a white person can know what it feels like to be assaulted with countless cultural signs that devalue or even erase their identity. Barbara Smith asserts:

> When Black women's books are dealt with at all [in criticism], it is usually in the context of Black literature, which largely ignores the implications of sexual politics. When white women look at Black women's works they are of course ill-equipped to deal with the subtleties of racial politics. (170)

How, then, can a white instructor effectively teach a novel dealing explicitly with charged racial and sexual politics within the black community to black students?

I hoped to answer this question when I first conceived of an Approaches volume on Morrison. At the time I was working at the MLA and in the evenings teaching a composition course to adults at Baruch College of the City University of New York. The student population at Baruch, a business college, is ethnically diverse. Because the literature reader I was using did not adequately reflect this diversity, I decided to redress the imbalance in part by teaching *The Bluest Eye*.

But once I had scheduled it, I was plagued with doubts, many of which I traced to my situation as a young white instructor. While I had had no qualms about speaking ex cathedra on Russian peasantry or French aristocracy (two subjects I know equally little about), the prospect of teaching *The Bluest Eye* to a largely black class daunted me. Had my class been entirely white, I would have had no such reservations. I needed to assess the reasons for my hesitancy and to find a way of overcoming it.

I was, to some degree, concerned about discussing in the classroom racial issues that were being expressed violently in the streets just outside. Many of my students were living in neighborhoods that have entrenched racial tensions—not only between whites and blacks but also among various minority and religious groups, nearly all of whom were represented in my class.

But that wasn't the whole picture. I'd had fewer qualms about teaching *Sula*, *Song of Solomon*, or the "Battle Royal" chapter from Ralph Ellison's *Invisible Man*, all of which address the problematics of race relations. The reason, I think, was that there is something uniquely disturbing about the sexual element in *The Bluest Eye*. The obvious minefield one encounters in class discussion is the rape scene, but also troublesome is that the value system resulting in Pecola's obsession with blue eyes manifests itself as well in assorted perversions: Soaphead Church's and Mr. Henry's sexual peccadillos and the determination of the women from Mobile, Aiken, and Newport News to eradicate any trace of "Funk" (Washington Square, 68).

I suspect that, because of these sensitive subjects, other teachers are reluctant to assign the novel. When we canvassed the academic community before writing the outline for this book, for example, we discovered that *The Bluest Eye* is not taught as frequently as some of Morrison's other novels, even though it is short, has been anthologized, and is one of her most accessible works. Another possible and compelling explanation for the reluctance is that the hierarchy implicit in the student-teacher relationship (no matter how democratic the teacher) is overturned if students speak with greater authority on certain aspects of a work, as may happen when a white instructor teaches the novel to black students. Unlike Morrison's other novels, *The Bluest Eye* cannot cleanly be separated historically or geographically from the here and now, because the novel's principal themes have such currency and Claudia's "voice-over" reinforces its contemporaneity.

Whatever the reasons for my hesitation, the first time I taught *The Bluest Eye*, wary of alienating students, I sidestepped controversy. This is without doubt the worst way to teach the book. At the time I felt that evading painful subjects would be easier for my students, and possibly for me as well. I was worried that Morrison's unflinching portrayal of conflicts within the black community might have alarming repercussions in the classroom. For example, it seemed apparent from the novel that, within the black community, light-complected women were generally regarded as more attractive than darker-complected women. Was this perception of attitudes in the community just a stereotype, reinforced by the media, or was it true? As an outsider, I could only make an educated guess, and the prospect of discussing the subject with students who might respond with hurt, anger, or scorn was disabling. I focused instead on neutral topics—the novel's poetic language, its structure, the narrative frame. While all these matters should be discussed, my class was clearly aware that they were not central. I had hoped that my students might broach more-sensitive issues, and in doing so I had abdicated my responsibility and had done them a disservice.

But although I had not taught the book well, my students had been genuinely moved by it. So, ignoring persuasive evidence that I should abandon the folly of assigning a book I was ill-equipped to teach, I altered my strategy and tried again. In approaching the particularly charged issue of skin tone, I relied on the familiar ploy of bringing fashion magazines to class, which allowed us to discuss how the media affect the image of black women. This device deflected the focus from the black community itself and enabled us to discuss the difficulty of constructing a positive self-image in a culture where clichéd standards of beauty continually erode the confidence of black and white women alike. From there we were able to move to the novel—to Geraldine and Maureen Peal—and a number of students, mostly women, became vocal participants.

I had also hoped to bring in a Dick and Jane reader because, in all the years I taught *The Bluest Eye*, only a handful of students had known what one was. Many of my students came from outside the United States—from Ecuador, Nigeria, Cambodia—and so naturally had not been exposed to the readers, but even many of my American students did not know. As the Dick and Jane device is crucial to an understanding of how white standards are disseminated and assimilated, I had to explain what these readers were and their relevance to the novel and to such scenes as Pecola's admiration of the Shirley Temple mug and Claudia's chilling dismemberment of the white baby doll. This approach too allows for a relatively uncharged entrée into the text and goes some way toward explaining how the refrain relates to various incidents. (It was virtually impossible to find a Dick and Jane reader; a children's librarian at the New York Public Library told me the books were considered rare and could not be checked out.)

This example brings me to another fundamental problem with teaching *The Bluest Eye*—one easy to overlook. Morrison employs a number of cultural touchstones of varying degrees of importance, and younger students or students reared outside the United States are often unfamiliar with them. The Maginot line and Bojangles generally need explaining, and while the students will probably know that Shirley Temple, Jean Harlow, Greta Garbo, and Ginger Rogers were actresses, the names won't resonate for them. Students won't necessarily know what the actresses looked like or understand their cultural relevance—important factors in advancing the idea that Hollywood inundated (and continues to inundate) people's lives with artificial and entirely white images of feminine beauty. Maureen Peal, significantly, mentions the film *Imitation of Life*, which in many ways mirrors the plot of *The Bluest Eye* and is well worth viewing. (Several survey participants mentioned that they show the movie in class.) While I have not been able to locate the Claudette Colbert version, there is a remake starring Lana Turner available on video, and, if time permits, a showing could spark lively discussion. (It is, however, a long film.) Like Pauline, Annie becomes an "ideal servant" (100) in the house of a white woman (Turner) and her daughter. Annie's daughter, who is very light-skinned, passes for white. The pressure on Annie's daughter to be part of white society has obvious similarities to the tensions in *The Bluest Eye*, but more interesting, perhaps, is that, after years of ostensibly excellent relations with the white family, Annie is all but invisible at one level. Her life contrasts graphically with the charmed life of her self-absorbed employer. When toward the end of the film Annie's "employer-friend" expresses surprise at her having other friends, Annie replies, "You never asked." Despite some heavy-handed 1950s sentimentality, *Imitation of Life* makes incisive statements about race relations and bigotry.

With time, I learned that another of the most accessible routes into *The Bluest Eye* is through the theme of guilt and blame, which Claudia and Frieda mistakenly believe they share: "It was a long time before my sister and I admitted to ourselves that no green was going to spring from our seeds. Once we knew, our guilt was relieved only by fights and mutual accusations about who was to blame" (9). Like a kind of original sin, it has stained them, even in their innocence, and it renders the reader complicit as part of the larger social structure that leaves two little girls feeling responsible for an evil only because they were powerless to prevent it. The need to blame and understand is instinctive, and it is natural to want to locate the novel's culprit—to find a clear and simple explanation for the tragedy, because the sense of closure would enable us to move on, forget, and possibly clear our consciences. But Morrison's works resist unilateral interpretation, and students blind to the novels' ambiguities will have an enriched appreciation if they are carefully pointed out.

I have found that one controversial way to animate students is to offer a "professional" defense of Cholly. Incest and rape are dangerous topics in the classroom, as there is always a chance that a student has been the victim of an assault. Therefore it is useful to frame the defense neutrally—that is, by setting the scene for a professional courtroom defense or by asking students to imagine how they would perceive the situation if Cholly were someone they knew and cared about. The one persistent difficulty I have had with teaching Morrison's novels has been getting the men to participate as actively as the women, and this is no doubt because they perceive her works, with the exception of *Song of Solomon*, as "women's novels." But this approach is effective in drawing them in.

Students tend to ignore factors that mitigate the enormity of Cholly's violation of Pecola, and a close examination of the rape scene will show them just how complex his emotional state is before he commits the rape. Morrison continually undercuts the atrocity: "The sequence of his emotions was revulsion, guilt, pity, then love. . . . He wanted to break her neck—but tenderly," and so on (127). Students should be shown that Cholly is not a heartless villain but a product of circumstances that are explicitly stated—he has been abandoned, emasculated, and rejected. They also need to see that the rape is motivated not by a perverse desire to destroy his daughter but by sweet memories of Pauline and Pecola's fragility—that is, by love, no matter how disturbed. In fact, the actual rape reads more like a love scene:

> The tenderness welled up on him, and he sank to his knees. . . . Crawling on all fours toward her, he raised his hand and caught the foot in an upward stroke. Pecola lost her balance and was about to careen to the floor. Cholly raised his other hand to her hips to save her from falling. He put his head down and nibbled at the back of her leg. His mouth trembled at the firm sweetness of the flesh.   (128)

Someone reading this passage out of context would interpret the scene completely erroneously. I have found it useful to show the students excerpts before they read the novel to see if they can tell what is going on. The near impossibility of the assignment makes them realize in later discussions that the situation is not as straightforward as they might want it to be. Morrison has created a multifaceted character who is emotionally, psychologically, and sexually confused and scarred, but not inherently evil. Yet while it is important not to simplify Cholly's actions, it is equally important not to sanction them. Like Sethe in *Beloved*, Cholly has broken the rules of the community and must pay for his transgression.

When students become outraged by something less than a blanket condemnation of Cholly, as some invariably do, I ask if they can find a more appropriate target for their anger. Most of them are so repulsed by his behavior that they cannot look beyond it to its roots—just as, I point out, the gossiping women at the end of the story implicate Pecola, without stopping to consider if there is a larger issue at stake or where the fault really lies, and just as Claudia displaces her aggression by dismembering the doll. Males typically respond in one of two ways to the rape: either they are appalled and virulently condemnatory, or they are defensive and may even see the scene as an attempt to malign their gender. (The latter is especially likely if feminist issues have informed class discussion considerably and if the course is required.) It is difficult to explain the rape and its antecedents in such a way as to condemn the act without wholly condemning the perpetrator, but to stop short of examining Cholly's motivations is to elide the real tragedy of the book.

While the rape at first glance begs for a feminist reading, that Cholly's mother threw him on a junk heap when he was just four days old must give pause and illustrates that Morrison has depicted Cholly as both victim and victimizer. It also raises the question of why his mother behaved as she did, and asking students this question encourages them to conceive of alternative explanations for an act that seems unconscionable. Was she really not "right in the head" (105)? Had she been beaten with a razor strap *before* she abandoned him, possibly for getting pregnant? In speculating, students should see that Pecola, who ironically ends up searching the garbage, discarded and reviled just as Cholly was, inherits this legacy of disinheritance. The novel depicts a vicious cycle of pain, degradation, and victimization, and it defies any simple interpretation that will enable the reader to put it to rest.

It is from this inability to find an outlet for our anger that the novel derives its power. It is not satisfactory that "the earth itself might have been unyielding," but this conclusion is as viable as any other (9). And while Cholly can be read one-dimensionally through willful misinterpretation, perhaps in part because he confirms pernicious stereotypes of the wayward black man who abandons his family to a life "outdoors" (18), the "somebody" who "done-gone-and-left" (24), Pecola forces us to acknowledge the devastating effects of our complicity as part of the unseeing society that allows families in the Breedloves' situation to spiral wildly out of control. Teaching New York City students is an advantage in this respect because they know firsthand that urban life anesthetizes people to suffering and understand how someone like Pecola could slip through the cracks.

Because I usually schedule *The Bluest Eye* for the end of the semester, I can compare it with other works we have studied and mention some of my initial reservations about teaching the book. While several of my (less diplomatic) students have said that they think white instructors cannot teach the novel with the understanding black teachers might bring to it, they all have said that it should be part of the curriculum, even if that means it is taught by a white instructor. This sort of discussion has enabled us to raise the larger questions of what books should be part of the curriculum and why and whether some of the literature regarded as unimpeachably great is socially relevant. Students have pointed remarks on this subject that beg reconsideration of traditional notions of excellence. One could argue that critical agreement on the canon becomes meaningless—at least pedagogically—when students have become disaffected.

A discussion of the curriculum can provide a meaningful segue back to *The Bluest Eye*. Once students realize that the superstructure mandating standards of worth, beauty, and social consequence does so not only through advertising, television, and film but also through education, they see just how ubiquitous and sly the dissemination of monolithic white ideals is. And they can make the logical connection back to the Dick and Jane reader.

The Bluest Eye speaks to the black community in questioning a demeaning value system. Black students bombarded with images that undermine their sense of self-worth can be vicariously empowered through Claudia. Though her refusal to credit false standards results in misplaced animosity toward the white baby doll, Shirley Temple, and Maureen Peal, it is nonetheless a bold affirmation of self. It is not, she comes to realize, the doll, Shirley, and Maureen Peal she should reject but the culture that values them only because of the way they look.

I have repeatedly come away from *The Bluest Eye* both enriched and frustrated—enriched by the experience of (re)reading and sharing this moving and eloquent book but frustrated by the social implications of its lack of resolution. As teachers we often assign literature that exposes and seeks to ameliorate injustice, which allows us to crusade from positions of privileged complacency. By depicting insoluble social problems in all their complexity, thereby denying closure, Morrison grimly illustrates the naïveté of such grand notions.

"Raked with Wonder":
A White Instructor Teaches *Sula*
Toni A. H. McNaron

The students I teach *Sula* to are overwhelmingly white and predominantly female. I myself am a transplanted white southerner who has lived and worked
in Minnesota for thirty years. Loaned to me in 1974 by a white graduate student who felt pretty sure I'd like it, *Sula* was my first taste of Toni Morrison's
work. Not only did I like the novel, but I found it an incandescent prose poem,
and it never fails to move and challenge me. Since then I have included *Sula*
in syllabi for any courses where it might conceivably fit.

Students encountering this slim but powerful book in my courses usually
come from middle-class or solidly working-class backgrounds and often still live
at home, working part-time to help their parents pay college expenses. Their
religious background is usually Lutheran; Roman Catholic comes in a weak second. Never blasé about higher education, they are eminently teachable—something that has always seemed an advantage at the University of Minnesota.

Most of these students have not had personal relationships with African
Americans and, though they view themselves as liberals, know little about the
complex cultural origins of novels like *Sula*. When I first began including Morrison and her peers in my courses, I mistakenly thought it would be enough to
ask students to read them alongside Marge Piercy, Margaret Atwood, and Virginia Woolf. Student response quickly convinced me that I was wrong, since
the students most likely fell into one of two common traps that await poorly informed white readers of literature by people of color. They elided racial and
class differences in their zeal, or they told themselves (and me) that the characters were too foreign for them to identify with and so they felt distant from
or alienated from the texts.

Setting out to become a better teacher of the novels that I considered the
most exciting fiction being written, I soon found multicultural theorists who in-
sisted on contextualizing the works of writers of color. This approach made immediate sense to me as a scholar of the English Renaissance, since I knew I
needed to provide background information in Shakespeare and metaphysical
poetry classes. However, I soon discovered that it was much easier for me, a
product of white Anglo-European culture, to contextualize products from that
same milieu than to do the same for Morrison's work. I had to admit my own
relative ignorance of African American culture beyond what I knew about the
damaging effects of slavery from reading William Faulkner and from growing
up in Alabama.

I relate my experience here to point out to other white instructors that it is
simply not enough to "add and stir" when we formulate syllabi. We have to familiarize ourselves with the cultural terrains of writers of color before we can
hope to achieve academic rigor in teaching or researching their work. New

Criticism by any more current name does particular disservice to representational fictions that portray cultures different from our own; indeed, some of us believe it might be better not to teach such literature at all than merely to insert it between productions by white writers whose context is (perhaps falsely and dangerously) taken for granted.

I ask my students to write both textual and personal responses to *Sula* in journals. Meanwhile I present background commentary about the institution of slavery and its vestigial influence on whites and blacks today; historical information about the intimate ties between patterns of land distribution and race and class; analysis of the possible meaning of motherhood in African American culture, in which mothers and children were systematically separated by slave masters; examination of the history of friendship between women in African American societies; discussion of the primacy of the family and the broader community in African American literature and life; and a reminder that *Sula* is about white culture as surely as it is about African American culture. Many students resist parts of these lectures, trying to retain their older framework for reading contemporary literature—that is, the heroic but isolated individual can triumph over circumstances if "he" is just strong-willed enough.

Before we open general discussion, I offer suggestions about how to read texts by African American women writers. To avoid students' romanticizing or expropriating the work along gender lines and "othering" it along race or class lines, I encourage them to perceive the characters in *Sula* as simultaneously like and unlike them. I also ask them to bring to the next class a list of three parts in the novel in which they find themselves drawn into the text and three in which they feel distinct resistance or distancing occurring.

We discuss the lists during the next class. Points where they identify with Morrison's work most often include descriptions of Nel and Sula's magical and sensual friendship, Morrison's description of Sula as an artist with no medium of expression (105), and the convincing, rhapsodic presentation of the heterosexual relationship between Sula and Ajax and the equality between the two lovers (108–15). Points where the students feel like throwing the book across the room most often include Eva's burning of Plum (39–41), Nel's mother's cowering behavior on the train south (17–21), and Sula's casual sex with Nel's husband (89–91).

Once we have identified these moments, we try to reach a fuller understanding of the complexity of both kinds of scenes by examining the text around each incident. In particular, we revisit the scene where the two girls dig holes in the ground with their sticks (49–50). Here it is Nel who ups the ante; she breaks Sula's idle pleasure in being with her by digging faster and, fatally, by throwing the first debris into their lovely communal cuplike hole. Students see that it is Nel who is unable to suspend herself in her friendship with Sula, Nel who seems to have less self-knowledge because she is more involved in attaining middle-class standards of living. She is, in other words, her mother's daughter, and, like her mother facing the train officials, Nel bows to convention. She wants a clean house and a proper husband. Students are encouraged to think about whether she and her mother are not more acculturated toward dominant white values than Sula and her family are. Nel cannot possibly understand Sula's value system, in which friendship with her matters far more than some man who happens to be in the house on a sultry afternoon.

Focusing on possessiveness, about which Morrison has much to say in this novel, we learn that Sula is genuinely surprised at Nel's violent rejection of her and of their long-lived alliance, when all she did was play around on the kitchen floor for a little while with Jude. Students come away from the discussion with new perspectives on Nel's mother and on Sula's interaction with Jude. They also seem clearer about the intensity of Sula's love for Nel; it helps to point out how crestfallen Sula is at Nel's wedding and to note that she is exiled from Medallion after losing her friend to conventional heterosexuality.

To deepen our discussion of this central bond, we examine Nel's recognition scene after Sula's death. Given our previous analysis, students can comprehend much more fully the import of Nel's coming to awareness about the ball that has floated just outside her reach ever since Sula and Jude had sex on the kitchen floor (93). Nel has assumed its coming was tied to her husband's leaving her and has not wanted to look at it. At the end of the novel, however, she declares:

> "All that time, all that time, I thought I was missing Jude." And the loss pressed down on her chest and came up into her throat. "We was girls together," she said as though explaining something. "O Lord, Sula," she cried, "girl, girl, girlgirlgirl."
>
> It was a fine cry—loud and long—but it had no bottom and it had no top, just circles and circles of sorrow.   (149)

Having worked through their heterosexist readings that parallel Nel's original ideas about the ball, the class can apprehend the profound significance of Morrison's ending.

Before leaving the subject of Nel and Sula's friendship, I present students with a summary of Barbara Smith's landmark article "Toward a Black Feminist Criticism." Smith uses *Sula* as an example of how reader-response theory can work. As a lesbian-feminist reader, Smith responds to Morrison's portrayal of the intense connection between the two little girls, which originates, Morrison tells us, with their meeting in dreams, long before their first meeting in person. Smith calls the relationship lesbian, even though Morrison has denied having such an intention when she wrote their story. This discrepancy between reader and writer enables students to see how much our own histories and contexts determine what we find in the literature we study or read casually.

Morrison's representation of motherhood is too major a theoretical issue to overlook, and we turn to it next. A brief overview of Morrison's repeated handling of the theme in her novels is followed by an in-class exercise. Students imagine what they believe themselves capable of doing should motherhood demand it of them. We discuss the shibboleth "I'd do anything for the good of my children" as a measure of mother love in white middle-class culture. Students then write anonymous responses to several scenes: Eva's reputed placement of her leg in the path of a train to receive insurance benefits with which she can continue to support her family; Eva's using her last bit of lard to break open baby Plum's dangerously clogged bowels; Mrs. Helene Wright's response to white racism on the train ride south with Nel; Hannah Peace's declaring that while she loves Sula she does not like her much; Eva's burning Plum with kerosene to end his hopeless life.

These in-class responses form the basis for discussion at our next meeting. Every time I read over the students' honest responses, I am struck by their biased judgment of behavior in cultures whose ethical boundaries vary from those of their own. They are often skeptical or mildly moralistic about Eva's heroic sacrifice of her leg, vaguely repulsed by the lard scene, flatly disapproving of Mrs. Wright for not standing up to train officials, censorious of Hannah for ruining her daughter's life, and shocked beyond all romanticism at the thought of a mother's burning her own son, "to whom she hoped to bequeath everything" (38).

I believe that an instructor's principal role at this stage is to help students contextualize each of these powerful scenes, thereby resisting their usual individualized psychological reading of human interactions. We discuss how all human exchanges will be unavoidably affected by something as pervasively dehumanizing as slavery; I remind them that slave owners routinely raped slave women into pregnancy and brutally denied them the right to rear their children. Coping with such a legacy will of necessity produce new definitions of "love" and "sacrifice" beyond the imaginative reach of many students. To help students see that even such brutality can have constructive repercussions, I focus with them on Eva's strange but unquestioning nurturance of the deweys once they settle in town.

We also examine the work of cultural theorists like Henry Louis Gates and Abdul JanMohamed to see how, for African Americans shadowed by slavery, taking a life might in some extreme instances be the only agential possibility. Referring to *Beloved* and Sethe's central act of saving her child from a return to slavery by slitting the child's throat jars students out of their ethnocentric thinking so that they may more intelligently judge Morrison's mothers. Though some students are simply unable in the time we have to unloose their thinking from years of cultural conditioning, many come to appreciate Eva as the devoted mother I take her to be. Further, we discover, though it requires holding seemingly opposing ideas simultaneously, that Morrison may also be exploring the danger motherhood can pose for African American women. In such a context being a good mother as defined by others often entails the loss of more than a leg. Referring again to *Beloved*, we read passages in which Sethe becomes paler and thinner as Beloved gains strength and color. (Since we have often already studied Gloria Naylor's *The Women of Brewster Place*, students are frequently reminded of Mattie Michael's inability to maintain a separate self in relation to her son.) In this regard, Morrison and others serve as beacons for white women trying to walk the treacherous line between responsible love for children and responsible love for self.

Before concluding our work on the novel, we consider its men. Many white feminists, my students included, find it much easier to decry our oppression as women than to acknowledge our role in oppressing others. Discussing Plum and Shadrack encourages a broader view of social reality. These two black men risked death serving their country in World War I but returned to find that country just as unwilling to admit them to its halls of power and success as it had been before they went away. Students first tend to disapprove of these men as weak and immature. It is important to offer a theoretical framework for examining the effects of slavery on the African American men as well as women who survived it and to encourage students to relinquish their usual readings, which depend on individual psychology and end in individual blame. It is helpful for students to see that such readings can perpetuate racism as surely as comparable readings of women characters can lead to blaming the victim. When extending sexist victimization theory into nonwhite contexts, I usually meet with resistance. Particularly as midwesterners, my students do not easily admit an active part in the systemic discrimination against African Americans by virtually every American institution.

At this point, we look back to the consciousness-raising exercises the students completed early in the term. These questionnaires attempt to begin a process of self-examination in relation to several kinds of prejudice, for example, racism, sexism, homophobia, anti-Semitism, and classism. Each exercise had asked the principally white students to recall messages given to them about various minority groups that have contributed to the unexamined biases they hold and to consider whether they have ever had a member of one of the groups as a doctor, friend, classmate, child, household worker, lover, colleague, or parent. Most of them cannot check "yes" for any category—which I seize as fertile ground for exploring the negative effects of lack of exposure to people who are perceived as different from us and our families.

After the students refer back to the assignments, many are more open to my interpretation of Plum's drug addiction and Shadrack's mental instability as the mediated consequences of their shattering experiences as returning black soldiers. From this more informed position, they are even able to reexamine their initial rejection of Eva's runaway husband, BoyBoy. A side benefit of this work is that students begin to understand that contextualizing does not require them to excuse behavior that genuinely offends them; it merely means that they will be able to see the object of their judgment more fairly and three-dimensionally—a desirable way to read all literature.

Part of our last class is devoted to the incredibly vivid metaphors Morrison uses to underscore her ideas. It is important that white English majors not ignore the sheer artistic strength of writers of color in their preference for a political or sociological reading. Some of the images I call attention to include the following: "[l]ike moonlight stealing under a window shade" (11); "deeper than the pits of plums, steadier than the condor's wing; more tranquil than the curve of eggs" (12); "like the keloid scar of the razored man who sometimes played checkers with her grandmother" (45); "like old promises nobody wanted kept" (64); "like steel shavings drawn to a spacious magnetic center" (106); "[a] crease of fear touched her breast" (128); and the amazing comment on Nel's long-unused sexuality, "But it was a love that, like a pan of syrup kept too long on the stove, had cooked out, leaving only its odor and a hard, sweet sludge, impossible to scrape off" (142). But even when we relax into a consideration of Morrison's genius for language, I urge students to consider the cultural context behind these powerful metaphoric expressions, which suggests that even our poetic language is class-, race-, and gender-specific.

Days spent in rigorous discussion of *Sula* yield benefits far beyond an understanding of the novel itself. Through Morrison's carefully crafted story students can begin to work on their unexamined racism and to learn more about how the institution and practice of slavery still shadows the lives and emotions of contemporary Americans. If I can assist white midwestern undergraduates in such a journey, then any amount of uncertainty I may once have experienced about the wisdom of a white southern transplant's presuming to teach such literature seems misplaced if not mischievously self-centered. The novels exist; the work and pleasure of teaching them lie before us all.

Beyond the Bitterness of History:
Teaching *Beloved*

Carolyn C. Denard

This essay addresses a series of responses that I have received from students over the past few years while teaching Toni Morrison's *Beloved*. I must explain at the outset that most of the students to whom I have taught the novel have been white. And what has struck me and created a moment of pedagogical pause, as a black woman professor, has been the students' seemingly paralyzing responses of guilt, embarrassment, and hurt. Students have said quietly to me after reading this novel, "How can you even *look* at me after reading this novel?" As some students have accepted personally the blame for the atrocities in this novel, others have expressed everything from cavalier rejection of the awful ways of the whites in *Beloved* to tearful and apologetic "I didn't know"s as they have claimed contemporary distancing from their ancestors.

Black students, too, have been caught up in the horrifying historical events of this text, and while they have not expressed guilt or apology, they have had equally paralyzing responses of anger and disbelief—at the treatment of the slaves and at both the ghost and the killing of the child. In my decision to address these responses from students pedagogically, I am not trying to minimize them or smooth over the awful history unfolded in this text: good literature should change our vision and call on us to speak out; good literature should elicit passionate response.

But what I have worried about as a teacher of *Beloved* is the obstacle these apologies, this fear, this guilt, and this anger present for students—if they do not move beyond these emotional responses to get at the larger message of the novel. I do not want students to walk away from the novel, as some are prone to do when confronted with the historical realities it presents, and to translate it into a pathological rendering of slavery, told to inform them of the barbarity of the slave masters and the slave mothers. And while I believe some guilt-ridden or angry revelations are healthy and necessary, I am troubled by the cowering deference of mostly white students to these first responses: they lie down for their beating, they shut up, they agree. They don't dare question or challenge me or the text. I am concerned that by adopting this posture toward the racial history, which is certainly a true and major part of the story, they will not learn that it is on the back of this horrifying history of slavery that Morrison makes her eloquent and hopeful thematic statement in the novel. I am concerned that they will be too consumed with nursing their wounds to see how the text sets straight the record of black life and black humanity during slavery.

A novelist addresses a question similar to that of the cultural anthropologist. If history is what happened, then literature—or, for the anthropologist, ethnography—is what what happened *means*. There are many documentable historical facts in *Beloved*: the story of Margaret Garner, the cruelty of life on slave plantations, the inhumanity of the Middle Passage, and the trials and triumphs of the Underground Railroad (see app. for sources of further information on these subjects).

But that history is not the sum total of the story Morrison tells in this novel. She seeks to get at the interior of that history, to see how these awful experiences, historically lumped into statistical summaries of the slave experience, affected slaves one by one. Students need to be reminded that their initial discomfort is a response to the historically based facts of the text—or, as Clifford Geertz would say, to the "thin description" of the text (6). They must understand that Morrison's rendering of that history in human terms—the enhancing, imaginative interpretation of that history—is the real test of the merit of the novel. In an interview with Mervyn Rothstein, Morrison says:

> The novel is not about slavery. Slavery is very predictable. There it is and there's [information] about how it is, and then you get out of it or you don't. [The novel] can't be driven by slavery. It has to be the interior life of some people, and everything that they do is impacted on by the horror of slavery, but they are also people.

What Morrison is after and what thick description seeks to articulate, then, is the meaning of history on a human level for those who experienced these horrors one by one.

To get at that interior life, Morrison relies on a sensitive and trusting imagination, on her kinship with other human beings, and on a haunting ancestral memory (see Morrison, "Memory"). Sethe's killing of her child in *Beloved* is based on the story of a slave woman, Margaret Garner, who killed one of her children and tried to kill the rest to prevent them from being returned to slavery. Morrison said that after reading Garner's story

> I didn't do any more research at all about that story. I did a lot of research about everything else in the book—Cincinnati, and abolitionists, and the Underground Railroad—but I refused to find out anything else about Margaret Garner. I really wanted to invent her life.   (qtd. in Rothstein)

In teaching *Beloved*, then, I try to help students focus not so much on the historical background of the novel (slavery) as on the human, interactive foreground of the novel (how people survived). Students find it easiest to concentrate on the historical background in this aesthetically and thematically complex novel because that is what they are most familiar with, even if only in a cursory way. They know that slavery existed, that it was wrong, and that it was a scourge on individuals and the nation. As teachers, we must help students to look beyond that history and to focus more carefully on the black men and women trying to carry out meaningful, human lives after slavery, which bruised and bloodied their humanity but did not destroy it. We must give students the tools—questions, sensitive analyses, role-playing exercises—that they need to change their perception of the novel.

I discuss here two tools I have used to help students change their angle of vision in reading *Beloved*. The first tool is a cultural analysis of the characters' responses to history. Analyzing these responses foregrounds the community of ex-slaves and helps students focus on the values held by the blacks themselves as agents of their own humanity rather than as resigned victims of the values of their white enslavers. The second tool is a series of questions in which students analyze their responses to historical events and compare them with the characters'. The questions allow the students to address the history outright, but also the questions lead the students to examine the individual human responses to history. In my classes I always begin with the questions, but I offer the analysis here first so that readers will better understand the context and the thematic direction of the questions.

The largest portion of the self-defining humanity of the black characters in *Beloved*, surprisingly enough in a world filled with hatred, is their manifestations of love—thick love, tiny love, jealous love, thirty-mile love, self-love, family love, community love—the modification of it, the protection from it, the overindulgence in it, the guardedness of it, the insistence on it. Loving the self, the family, the friend, the child, the natural world becomes a balm for the horror of slavery. In the foreground of this text is a story of the varying ways in which a people tries to impart human love in inhuman times.

Sethe's motivation before and after the killing of her child is a desire to love:

> I was big, Paul D, and deep and wide and when I stretched out my arms all my children could get in between. I was *that* wide. Look like I loved em more after I got there. Or maybe I couldn't love em proper in Kentucky because they wasn't mine to love. But when I got here, when I jumped down off that wagon—there wasn't nobody in the world I couldn't love if I wanted to. (Knopf, 162)

Paul D is also motivated by love. He keeps his sanity and his humanity intact when confined to a chain gang in Alfred, Georgia, by continuing and protecting, if only in a small way, his ability to love: "[Y]ou protected yourself and loved small. Picked the tiniest star out of the sky to own; lay down with head twisted in order to see the loved one over the rim of the trench before you slept" (162).

Baby Suggs, because of her knowledge of the power of love and her insistence on imparting that knowledge to others, takes it as the text for her memorable sermon in the clearing:

> "Here," she said, "in this place, we flesh; flesh that weeps, laughs; flesh that dances on bare feet in grass. Love it. Love it hard. . . . Love your hands! Love them. Raise them up and kiss them. Touch others with

them, pat them together, stroke them on your face 'cause they don't love that either. *You* got to love it! . . .   (88)

There are other examples: Denver's love for Beloved, Sixo's love for the Thirty-Mile Woman, Halle's love for Baby Suggs. The novel progressively becomes a story about the ability, the willingness of those who were not beloved, to love.

The other manifestation of the characters' humanity, and to my mind the bravest and most remarkable example of Morrison's ability to represent her characters on their own terms, is their ability to claim their own guilt and in turn seek their own forgiveness with one another. Their sense of guilt is not put forth in language dependent on or relative to the destructive and immoral slave system that whites leveled against blacks daily. It is established according to the codes of behavior that blacks, despite this system, set forth as right and acceptable for themselves.

If *Beloved* were written just to criticize a system that subjected a group of human beings to inhuman treatment, Morrison would not need to show the code of ethics among the oppressed group. But Morrison does, and though the horror of slavery seems a reasonable cause for a violation of ethics, it does not exempt from punishment the violators of the community's code. Nor does it exempt them from their personal need to repent and ask for forgiveness. Indeed, much of the present-time focus of the story concerns the characters' working out, or facing the consequences of violating, their own codes.

The community, feeling Baby Suggs is too prosperous, too prideful, does not warn her and the others of the coming of strangers:

> Nobody warned them, and [Stamp Paid had] always believed it wasn't the exhaustion from a long day's gorging that dulled them, but some other thing—like, well, like meanness—that let them stand aside, or not pay attention, or tell themselves somebody else was probably bearing the news already to the house on Bluestone Road. . . .   (157)

Believing Sethe's actions are too extreme and her response to the deed irreverent and arrogant, the community ostracizes her for "trying to do it all alone with her nose in the air" (254). Ella, Sethe's most vocal critic in the community, "understood Sethe's rage in the shed twenty years ago, but not her reaction to it, which Ella thought was prideful, misdirected, and Sethe herself too complicated" (256). Even Paul D believes that Sethe's killing of the baby was beneath her: "'You got two feet, Sethe, not four'" (165). And Baby Suggs is depressed to her death by the overwhelming contradiction of Sethe's action: "[S]he could not approve or condemn Sethe's rough choice. One or the other might have saved her, but beaten up by the claims of both, she went to bed" (180). And finally Sethe herself risks self-destruction as she repents and seeks forgiveness from the ghost of her daughter: "I won't never let her go. I'll explain to her. . . .

Why I did it. How if I hadn't killed her she would have died and that is something I could not bear to happen to her. When I explain it she'll understand. . . . I'll tend her as no mother ever tended a child . . ." (200).

The community members must not only face their guilt over the death of the baby but also work out their terms for forgiveness—for themselves and for Sethe. Denver comes to realize that even the ghost has gone too far in violating a daughter's respect for her mother and finally brings the conflict to a halt with a cry for help: "Somebody had to be saved. . . . Nobody was going to help her unless she told it—told all of it" (252–53). And when Ella hears Denver's story, she too agrees that Beloved's actions have surpassed what is reasonable and acceptable in the community—even for a ghost:

> Whatever Sethe had done, Ella didn't like the idea of past errors taking possession of the present. Sethe's crime was staggering and her pride outstripped even that; but she could not countenance the possibility of sin moving on in the house, unleashed and sassy. . . . She didn't mind a little communication between the two worlds, but this was an invasion.
>
> (256–57)

Determined to restore the moral order in the community, Ella leads a group of thirty neighborhood women in prayer to the house on Bluestone Road to exorcise the ghost and offer Sethe forgiveness (257).

All these characters are motivated in their anger, their guilt, and their forgiveness by the black community's code of ethics. Slavery gets none of them off the hook, and they must answer to themselves and their community before they finally achieve forgiveness and are able to move forward.

This is the powerful subject of the novel: How a people try to keep their humanity intact in a world whose morality and humanity is turned upside down— and how they succeed. If students are too consumed with abhorring the history revealed in the text and, thus, do not pay attention to the novel's depiction of the power and endurance of the effort to claim one's humanity, then they miss the larger, more important message.

I initially developed the following list of hypothetical questions to sensitize students to the human meaning behind the historical facts of this novel, and I suggest it now as an early discussion exercise to encourage students to respond not only to the history but, more important, to the characters' responses to that history.

> You have a choice of killing your baby or allowing it to grow up in a system that defines it as chattel and freely sells, rapes, beats it without allowing it any opportunity for defiance. What do you do? (Because some students find this situation hard to imagine, I sometimes use the following one instead: You are a political prisoner. You have been subject to the worst, most inhumane treatment imaginable. You escape

with your young child. You are captured. You can either kill the child or have the child live the life that you have lived. What do you do?)

A woman in your community kills her children to save them from what, in her opinion, is a living hell. How do you, as a community member, respond?

You are on the jury in Sethe's trial. Given the circumstances of the death as described in the novel, how do you judge her? Why?

You are an adult heterosexual male deprived of normal, healthy sexual relationships with women year after year after year. You cannot leave your situation, and you are only in the company of other men. What do you do? What do you do to the persons who impose this life on you?

You are sent away to a work camp where you receive treatment worse than slavery, and you are at the mercy of the overseer's sexual and physical whims. What do you do?

You are chained and a heavy iron bit is placed in your mouth, strapping your tongue and keeping you open-mouthed yet silent for days or weeks. What do you do? How do you feel after the ordeal is over?

I get a full range of answers: "I would kill my child." "I would fight back." "I would try to help her." "I would acquit the woman." "I would run away." "I would just die." "I would pray for deliverance." "I don't know what I would do." It is a good role-playing exercise, even with its inherent role-playing limitations of pretense. It allows the students to respond immediately to the historical issues that bother them. It also allows for an instructive comparison of their responses with the characters' when we discuss the novel later.

I try to keep the responses and the ensuing discussion as serious and focused as possible. Some students overstate their responses for laughs, but I always take them back to the point of the question, trying to elicit their most basic human responses.

The only student response that is usually similar to a character's involves the killing of the child. Many students disagree with this option, but most see it as heroic. What is interesting is that this response is precisely the one for which Sethe has to pay and of which the community disapproves. Even though Morrison, as the "defense," presents a case that seems to justify the action, it is also the action for which Sethe pays throughout most of the novel. Herein lies the complexity of the novel, a complexity that this role playing allows students to ponder.

This exercise also boosts serious character analysis; it pushes students closer toward making thematic statements about the meaning of the novel on many levels. For both black and white students the history becomes more a means of understanding the development of strength and complexity of character than an end in itself.

One thing that becomes clear to students after this exercise is how the killing of the baby affects Sethe. Even though she is glad to have saved her daughter from slavery, her grief and guilt nearly destroy her as she seeks forgiveness. The students come to realize the complexity of Sethe's decision. They have argued about it; they have put themselves in her place. They have seen Sethe save her children from Sweet Home and understand the protective logic of her action, but they also understand that she pays for the decision on a personal, moral level. They understand that Morrison has not allowed slavery to destroy Sethe's human ability for love *or* for guilt. They better understand Morrison when she says of Sethe's action: "[Sethe] did the right thing but she didn't have the right to do it" (qtd. in Rothstein). It is a powerful moment for students when they begin to reflect on the political and moral implications of Sethe's decision.

What also becomes clear to students, once they have been encouraged to focus on how individuals respond to their historical circumstances rather than just on the history itself, is the enduring and indomitable nature of the human spirit. Morrison's imaginative re-creation here is not just her fantasy. She is trying to explain in human terms what did exist. How a people subjected to the most inhuman form of treatment, the most hateful, love-defying existence, kept their human potential for both love and guilt intact. That is why despite hundreds of years of bestial, inhumane treatment blacks are still living basically humane, loving lives. Morrison tells us this history to show us the power of love in spite of it. She wants her readers to understand that while blacks were often driven to excess by the cruelties of slavery, slavery was not allowed to excuse those actions.

Both black and white students can use the code of ethics revealed in the development of the black community in this text as a representative example of the best that is human in the individual. As students are made to examine the lives of these "victims" of history within the moral and spiritual structure of the lives that the characters determined for themselves, students might begin to see this novel not as an exercise in self-flagellation or an opportunity to rekindle anger but as a call to triumph over the misery, the unfairness, the bitterness of history in their own lives and bring forth their "best thing[s]" (273), their best human selves. For as Morrison has shown in the writing of *Beloved*, what lies beyond the bitterness of the history revealed in this novel is a people trying desperately, triumphantly, dangerously even, to forgive and to love.

APPENDIX

For a summary of the Margaret Garner case, see Gerder Lerner, ed., *Black Women in White America: A Documentary History* (New York: Random, 1972) 60–63. See also P. C. Bassett, "A Visit to the Slave Mother Who Killed Her

Child," *The Black Book: A Pictorial History of Black America*, ed. Middleton Harris, Morris Levitt, and Roger Smith (New York: Random, 1973) 10.

For accounts of life on slave plantations, see John W. Blassingame, *The Slave Community: Plantation Life in the Antebellum South* (New York: Oxford UP, 1972); Eugene Genovese, *Roll Jordan Roll: The World the Slaves Made* (New York: Random, 1972); and Ulrich B. Phillips, *American Negro Slavery: A Survey of the Supply, Employment, and Control of Negro Labor As Determined by the Plantation Regime* (Baton Rouge: Louisiana State UP, 1966).

For background on the treatment of slaves during the Middle Passage, see Elizabeth Donnan, ed., *Documents Illustrative of the History of the Slave Trade to America*, 1930–35, 4 vols. (Washington: Carnegie Inst. of Washington, 1962); Herbert Klein, *The Middle Passage: Comparative Studies in the Atlantic Slave Trade* (Princeton: Princeton UP, 1978); and Daniel P. Mannix and Malcolm Cowley, *Black Cargoes: A History of the Atlantic Slave Trade, 1518–1865* (New York: Viking, 1962).

For history of the Underground Railroad, see Charles Blockston, *The Underground Railroad* (New York: Prentice, 1987); Henrietta Buckmaster, *Let My People Go: The Story of the Underground Railroad and the Growth of the Abolitionist Movement* (Boston: Beacon, 1959); and Homer Johnson, *From Dixie to Canada: Romance and Realities of the Underground Railroad*, 1896, vol. 1, 2nd ed. (Westport: Negro Universities, 1970).

Editor's Note   The author prefers to capitalize the terms *black* and *white* in reference to groups of people; the terms are lowercased here in accordance with MLA house capitalization style.

Marginality and Community in *Beloved*

Sharon P. Holland and Michael Awkward

When we set out to identify some of the most difficult aspects of teaching Morrison's fifth novel, it occurred to us that the difficulty lay not so much in the text itself as in our perception of its events and characters. Teaching *Beloved* involves an overwhelming contradiction: teachers promise students that what at first appears incomprehensible will eventually become familiar and ascertainable, while as teachers they realize that vast sections of the text elude the critic's touch and give way to revelation only gradually, if not stubbornly. As Morrison's characters make their presence known to us and to one another, we must remember that Beloved is not one of the living, but a manifestation of the living. The question becomes, How do we teach that—how do we demonstrate and uncover the multilayered relations between spirit and flesh, mother and child, lover and beloved in the novel? As readers, we must be aware that each of the characters' interactions with one another represents some aspect of those relations and that our understanding of them as narrative elements depends on how we conceive the levels of existence that Morrison constructs. Moreover, in teaching *Beloved*, we must constantly remind our students that the novel is about not only one woman's figurative Middle Passage during slavery but also the relations outlined above and the attempt to create a community because of and in spite of them; we must encourage students to delve beyond the explicit meanings of the story and into the novel's implicit moments.

From the beginning, it is both fair and wise to caution students that the author intends the opening pages to destabilize the reader, and while it is our job as teachers to explicate the novel's most beautiful moments, we should ensure that students are not reconciled to this sense of displacement too quickly, because it affords them a significant experience. It is important to tell students of Morrison's pronouncement: "[T]he in medias res opening that I am so committed to here is excessively demanding. It is abrupt, and should appear so. No native informant here. The reader is snatched, yanked, thrown into an environment completely foreign, and I want it to be the first stroke of the shared experience that might be possible between the reader and the novel's population" ("Unspeakable Things" 32). Understanding Morrison's purpose in the novel's beginning allows students to participate fully in both the explication of its words and the happening that they are called on to witness and participate in. The experience of working with the novel is never static, as Morrison's idea concerning its opening makes clear. Students not only observe the novel's community but also become part of it, since an understanding of how community functions in *Beloved* is crucial to a reader's development of critical agency with the text itself. After achieving this unique communion, students can begin to explore what kind of community or sense of community thrives in *Beloved*.

Students need to understand the several layers of community that Morrison depicts in *Beloved*, as that understanding is crucial to their unfolding of the text's meanings. While Sethe, Denver, Paul D, and Beloved themselves compose a community of sorts, they each reflect different notions of that community, and their coming together serves as a means of testing these separate but fluid assumptions. At first there appear to be only two communities in *Beloved*—the insular community of 124 Bluestone Road and everything considered to be outside it. We like to encourage students to look closely at how each character views this inside-outside relationship. If readers are to take the characters as simplified representations of their worlds, then Beloved belongs to the community of the dead, of ancestors and spirits who are constantly among us; Denver, born into this world from the womb of a black woman and soothed by the hands of a white woman, represents the tenuous coming together of the community inside 124 and the community outside; Sethe, who confronts both the memory of slavery and the cost of freedom in her efforts to conceive a workable notion of community, brings together the conflictual states of "rememory" (Knopf 36) and forgetfulness; and Paul D, who becomes infatuated with the possibility of family that he believes Sethe and Denver provide, approaches—and abruptly flees from—that possibility for a life with his fellow Sweet Home sufferer and former object of sexual desire. From this description, students begin to see that the inside-outside theory works to a certain extent but is challenged by the characters' ideas of their individual relations to 124, ideas that the outside world influences.

But what environment or space does 124 exist in? Whose world is being represented? Once students get past the first pages, it is usually a good idea to challenge them to remake a Western cosmology that draws a line between living and dead, breaking down their notions of the living world as a landscape where there are no ghosts and therefore no Beloveds or Sethes who struggle with them. Turning to some of the features of Sethe's cosmology helps illustrate the most subtle but important difference between worlds in the text. One must pay close attention to Sethe's notions of "rememory." They provide insight into her sense of the interconnections between the tangible and the intangible, between the world of the living and the world of the spirit, and they facilitate our comprehension of her response to both Paul D and Beloved. For example, in a discussion with Denver early in the novel about Sethe's interactions with the spiritual world—a type of interaction she believes her youngest daughter cannot adequately comprehend—Sethe comments:

> I was talking about time. It's so hard for me to believe in it. Some things go. Pass on. Some things just stay. I used to think it was my rememory. You know. Some things you forget. Other things you never do. But it's not. Places, places are still there. If a house burns down, it's gone, but the place—the picture of it—stays, and not just in my rememory, but out there, in the world. What I remember is a picture floating around out there outside my head. I mean, even if I don't think it, even if I die, the

picture of what I did, or knew, or saw is still out there. Right in the place
where it happened.   (35–36)

In Sethe's theory of spatiotemporal permanence—a belief in the enduring presence and tangibility of the spirit of place—events and objects (and, we might
add here, the dead) are not limited to their duration in time or space or to the
recollections of those who have experienced them. They leave a permanent
record of their existence on the physical plane; they exist not only in imaginative activities such as memory and, on another discursive level, (re)memory's
formulation as history but also as a tangible presence "out there, in the world."
When students grasp these ideas, it is possible to recall the earlier discussion
and remind them that this shift in cosmology, or the presence of things in this
world, opens the door to an understanding of Beloved's reincarnation as a manifestation of the spirit. The murdered daughter becomes, in other words, confirmation of the tangibility, as both spirit and flesh, of that which has passed on.
Beloved embodies living "herstory."

Searching for a counterpart to Sethe's sense of place and the spirit of things,
students might find that Paul D's appearance at 124 Bluestone Road introduces
an alternative, indeed a competing, ontological response. While Sethe's response to the pain of past events and places is described as that of "a greedy
child" whose imagination "snatched up everything" and for whom "[n]o misery,
no regret, no hateful picture [is] too rotten" to refuse (86), Paul D has learned
to limit the scope and therefore the effects of the potentially painful stimuli that
he is willing to confront. After barely surviving the psychically devastating—or,
in gendered terms, the demasculinizing—effects of Schoolteacher's systematic
efforts to undo the work of Mr. Garner, Sweet Home's previous patriarch, Paul
D "had shut down a generous portion of his head, operating on the part that
helped him walk, eat, sleep, sing" (41). One scene that students often struggle
with takes place when Paul D first comes to 124 and disrupts it with his angry
response to the baby ghost. After the discussion about spirit and place, it is easier for students to see why, rather than endure 124's disruptive spirit, Paul D attempts to banish it to make a space for himself in Sethe's life. He "broke up the
place, making room, shifting it, moving it over to someplace else, then standing
in the place he had made" (39). In his efforts to forget the past, Paul D seeks to
disrupt Sethe's ontology by destroying 124's interior space in order to compel a
skeptical Sethe to choose between the living embodiment of the past that he
represents and the enduring spirit of place that has inhabited the residence
since what Stamp Paid terms "The Misery" of Sethe's act of infanticide (171).
Paul D's refusal to recognize the rights of the child's spirit to inhabit its place
apparently necessitates its reembodiment as the mysterious and even more disruptive Beloved. Both readings provide adequate examples of how the text
seeks to depict a cosmology dissimilar to the often dichotomous Western binary
one. Students can begin to understand that Sethe's remaking of her space allows
room for Beloved to enter into the novel. The students' attention is displaced

from the impossibility of this occurrence to its possibility, created by a character determined to discover a new way of seeing the worlds she inhabits—postemancipation America and the community at 124.

Students should be asked to keep in mind that while Sethe needs an alternate worldview to survive in and out of slavery, it can blur her perception of events affecting her approach to living. *Beloved* consistently addresses this sense of paired realities and the choices each person is responsible for making in relation to existing or created space, reality, and time. To illustrate further this tension between physical worlds and perceptions, it might be useful to turn to another difficult section. One of the most striking scenes occurs when, after Paul D's interventionist act and declaration, "We can make a life, girl" (46), Paul D, Sethe, and Denver go to the "less than mediocre" carnival, and Sethe witnesses a "picture" that she believes signals the possibilities of a less pain-filled future. Morrison writes:

> They were not holding hands, but their shadows were. Sethe looked to her left and all three of them were gliding over the dust holding hands. Maybe he was right. A life. . . . All the time, no matter what they were doing . . . the three shadows that shot out of their feet to the left held hands. Nobody noticed but Sethe and she stopped looking after she decided that it was a good sign. A life. Could be. (47)

Here, as Sethe conjures a scene of false possibilities, students can see most vividly the transforming effects of Paul D's presence and of his banishment of the spirit. Swept away by wishful thinking and the spectacle of shadow projection much as the black townspeople are by the carnival's false promises of unnatural wonders, Sethe ignores the radical disunity among Paul D, Denver, and her. She replaces the tangible "picture floating around out there outside [her] head" with intangible images of family that none of the principals are prepared to actualize. This scene illustrates another of the novel's difficult themes: while Morrison gives her characters a way of reordering their place in real events and space, she also includes moments when the freedom to envision is abused. Sethe's act of infanticide and her reordering of that experience outside the movement within 124 demonstrates what can result from this abuse.

The above explication of the worlds created in *Beloved* allows for a complex discussion of how the characters achieve agency or a sense of control over their lives. But another level of discussion can hinge on an understanding that these levels of agency are not free from the effects of the prevailing ideas and economic language of slavery, which defined all black bodies as property. The novel views slavery as a force of white hegemony in discourse and in deed. The effects of the Fugitive Slave Law are evident in the community of 124—it is the thing that Sethe flees from, the reason she commits infanticide, and ultimately a discourse that threatens to spill over into her conception of time and space by making every place a potential space for the capture of black bodies.

Nothing, not even Baby Suggs's clearing, is sacred anymore. Beloved's fleshly embodiment during the walk home from the carnival suggests the impossibility of keeping the past at bay and exemplifies how the characters of 124 cannot escape the dominance of hegemony—the language of slavery. They sometimes see themselves as property or chattel and take on some of the labels through which they are defined. For example, Paul D cannot accommodate Sethe's act of infanticide in his emotionally constricted psyche, despite his willingness to add to her store of thought pictures the image of himself enchained with a bit in his mouth and that of her husband, Halle, "squatting by the churn smearing the butter as well as its clabber all over his face because the milk they [Schoolteacher's assistants] took [from Sethe] is on his mind" (70), and this inability leads Paul D to perceive Sethe as a freak of nature. He speaks to her as a spectacle appropriate for figuration in carnivalesque discourse. Paul D's response to her attempts to protect her offspring from the devastation of Schoolteacher's mastery, which he knows all too well—"You got two feet, Sethe, not four" (165)—is for her apparent confirmation of white hegemony's insistence on the depiction of all blacks as sideshow freaks at a community carnival, as half human and half animal ("put her human characteristics on the left; her animal ones on the right. And don't forget to line them up" [193]). In Sethe's estimation Paul D's cryptic comment demonstrates his inability to comprehend her sense that death was preferable to the physical and discursive abuse she and her children would suffer if they returned to Sweet Home. Here, students should note one of the text's implicit questions: Did Sethe have the right to kill her own child—did she have the right to make that choice for her children?

We must remember that Morrison purposely leaves the most problematic event out of the text. Teachers are constantly called on to emphasize the historicity of the story in *Beloved*, that Sethe's tale is actually an imaginary reshaping of a real event—the story of Margaret Garner, a slave who in 1856 escaped from her owner in Kentucky and fled to Cincinnati. When she realized that she would be captured and returned, she slit the throat of her daughter and was arrested before she could kill her other children. To this day scholars are not certain what became of the real Margaret Garner. Picking up twenty-one years after the killing, *Beloved* asks that Sethe be accountable for her actions and that readers participate in the unmaking of her narrative. This notion of accountability is entwined with ideas of black bodies as less than human and more than animal. Paul D's words show that Sethe's infanticide and suicidal impulses have not protected her from being figured as subhuman (this time by a fellow Sweet Home sufferer who himself employed cows as objects of sexual desire), just as she would have been had she allowed herself to be subjected to the cruel lash and pen of the white patriarch who misrepresents her using ink that Sethe literally made with her own hands. Sethe and Paul D can realize their desire for family and unity only when they move past this discursive impasse of human/animal and Paul D becomes willing to "put his story next to hers" and allow her to recognize her own worth ("You your best thing, Sethe. You are" [273]).

Part 2 of the novel is perhaps its most challenging and puzzling. Students often have trouble reading Beloved's stream-of-consciousness dialogue. One problem in working with this section is that readers seem to come unprepared for its difference. We like to point out to students that there is a scene that foreshadows the individual narratives of the three women left alone at 124— Sethe, Denver, and Beloved. Explication of its nuances is essential to a feminist reading of the text. After Paul D has been banished from the community at 124 to the church's cellar, the three go ice skating.

> Holding hands, bracing each other, they swirled over the ice. Beloved wore the pair; Denver wore one, step-gliding over the treacherous ice. Sethe thought her two shoes would hold and anchor her. She was wrong. Two paces onto the creek, she lost her balance and landed on her behind. The girls, screaming with laughter, joined her on the ice. Sethe struggled to stand and discovered not only that she could do a split, but that it hurt. Her bones surfaced in unexpected places and so did laughter. Making a circle or a line, the three of them could not stay upright for one whole minute, but nobody saw them falling.   (174)

For this mother and her daughters, the meeting by the frozen creek symbolizes their worlds arrested and stationary for the moment; the three women are "falling" into a relationship with one another that will be defined by each of their marginal positions. After this scene, Sethe will succumb to the pain of re-memory and leave behind the forgetfulness encouraged by Paul D's presence and worldview; Beloved will literally claim Sethe as might an ancestor (and, later, an evil spirit); and Denver ultimately moves from this community to seek help from the outside community that had ostracized her and her family since "The Misery."

Moreover, the suspension of their worlds is stressed by the frozen creek, a space as liminal as that which Sethe, Beloved, and Denver occupy. As a tributary of the river, the creek serves as a symbolic extension of their complex relationship. For this discussion of representation it is helpful to view materials that speak to the varying African retentions alive in the Americas, such as Robert Farris Thompson's *Flash of the Spirit*. In a study of Afro-American retentions, John Michael Vlach states that "it is believed in Lower Zaire that deceased ancestors become white creatures called bakulu who inhabit villages of the dead located under river beds and lake bottoms; they may return from this underworld to mingle with the living" (143). Beloved, who appears on the dry bank of the river with lungs enflamed from her journey from another world (or an otherworld), emerges as a bakulu figure who, because of Paul D's exorcism, has had to navigate the space between death and life literally. Because the water is frozen, the narrative is for the moment still, and in this moment Beloved's place of origin is obscured by the cold of winter. Just as Sethe misreads the spectacle of the familial shadows during the carnival scene, she mistakenly heralds her memory of the skating scene as an achievement of psychic tranquility, a peace that, like "[t]he peace of winter stars[,] seem[s] permanent" (176). She forgets that there can be no peace without atonement. Instead of peace, Beloved seeks retribution, not only as a daughter killed by her mother but also as a spirit whose space—whose enduring presence and tangibility—has been violated. Once these clues to Beloved's layers of representation are identified, it is easier for teachers to encourage students to approach each symbolic manifestation as a significant event tied to African retentions on this continent rather than as a peculiar metaphor used for stylistic purposes. Readings from critics like Vlach and Thompson might aid in an understanding of the use of symbolism in many of Morrison's other novels as well.

The introduction of the skating scene at the beginning of part 2 causes community and narrative rupture. A teacher who follows a line of feminist analysis should remind students that this new place-space at 124 is reconfigured into a female space. Paul D, driven from 124 by his inability to deal with Sethe's infanticide, sits in exile through most of part 2. Similarly, when Stamp Paid—who transported a just-escaped Sethe and a newborn Denver to Baby Suggs's house and shared with Paul D the newspaper report of the infanticide—attempts to knock at the door of 124, he is repelled by

> a conflagration of hasty voices—loud, urgent, all speaking at once so he could not make out what they were talking about or to whom. The speech wasn't nonsensical, exactly, nor was it tongues. But something was wrong with the order of the words and he couldn't describe or cipher it to save his life. All he could make out was the word *mine*. The rest of it stayed outside his mind's reach. . . . When he got to the steps, the voices drained suddenly to less than a whisper. It gave him pause. They had become an occasional mutter. . . . Just that eternal, private conversation that takes place between women and their tasks. (172)

Literally outside the language of 124, Paul D and Stamp Paid are left to their own devices. When the individual narratives of the women emerge in part 2 of the novel, the men are at a safe distance. In fact, throughout *Beloved*, Paul D's and Stamp Paid's texts and story making are kept outside the collective voice of 124. To surmise that Morrison is saying that men's narratives always sit outside women's would misrepresent the men's roles in the novel. Instead, we might say that Morrison arrives at a notion of ritual—women's ritual—that must take place for the community to heal and for male and female narratives to rest side by side.

In the end the voices of women wrench the embodied spirit's hold from 124 and return it to its earlier relative peace. These thirty women, mobilized by Denver's journeys outside the community of women in 124, by their dedication to Baby Suggs's memory, and by a belief that "the children can't just up and kill the mama," that "past errors [should not] tak[e] possession of the present"

(256), chant outside the space of Beloved's revenge. In response to Ella's exor-
cising holler, which is motivated by her consciousness of her own unspeakable
sexual and physical violence against her innocent offspring, "[t]hey stopped
praying and took a step back to the beginning. In the beginning there were no
words. In the beginning was the sound, and they all knew what that sound
sounded like" (259). The assembly moves Beloved, the embodied spirit, from
124 with a "sound" that is not rooted in Christianity, though clearly Morrison's
passage refigures John 1.1: "In the beginning was the Word, and the Word was
with God, and the Word was God." This sound, however, moves beyond experience of this new world, beyond narrative—beyond the narratable—and the
margins of the women's existence to connect with and revoice African discursive practices and cosmological states. The vibration from this sound invades
the spirit space Beloved occupies and returns her to the water, which disem-
bodies, as it were, this spirit whose place-space in the lives of Sethe and Denver had not heretofore been questioned.

Her departure becomes folktale and her presence disremembered. But
what we might term "disrememory"—the efforts of the communities inside
and outside 124 Bluestone Road to erase from consciousness signs of the embodied spirit's existence—fails to rob that spirit of its place-space, its permanence in the realm of the physical. In fact, that spirit can be said to continue
to affect the physical world: in the spaces between sleep and consciousness,
when "the rustle of a skirt hushes when they wake," when "the knuckles brush-
ing a cheek in sleep seem to belong to the sleeper," and between the living and
its representation, when "the photograph of a close friend or relative—looked
at too long—shifts, and something more familiar than the dear face itself
moves there" (275). Having atoned for her sins, Sethe (and, by extension, other
members of *Beloved*'s African American community such as Ella, Stamp Paid,
and Paul D, who have inflicted heart-wrenching pain on others) has no need to
bump into Beloved's disembodied spirit or seriously to consider the implications of its presence. And while Beloved's spirit is not at rest, Sethe's brain,
heretofore "greedy" to form pictures of pain, learns not to absorb its machina-
tions into its recesses. As Morrison writes, "Although [Beloved] has claim, she
is not claimed" (274). While Beloved gets and literally is the last word in the
novel, Sethe has learned to banish the spirit not from its place in the outside
world but rather from her interior, from her brain.

The novel's conclusion echoes Sethe's perspectives on the enduring presence and tangibility of the spirit in that Beloved's spirit does not "go," does not
become intangible. However, it ceases to be Sethe's burden or responsibility
and henceforth recedes from her consciousness. But Morrison's rich text
passes at least its interpretive burdens onto its readers, onto those who seek to
confront its complex, haunting story.

Authority, Literacy, and Modernism in *The Bluest Eye*

Thomas H. Fick and Eva Gold

In *Playing in the Dark* Toni Morrison probes the Africanist presence in the white imagination, but her first book has a quite different emphasis. *The Bluest Eye* explores what enables an oppressive white presence in black culture; it is a kind of prolegomenon for the African American aesthetic Morrison develops more fully in her later fiction. In this novel Morrison uncovers the assumptions about authority that allow—and encourage—racism to flourish, even, or especially, in the black community; she does not explore what thrives in spite of and in opposition to racism. It is an angry book, and the controlled anger (as well as the less obvious but equally powerful love) makes it a superb novel to teach. Morrison is angry at the destructive presence of authority, but she firmly grounds this presence in historical contexts and literary traditions. And for those teaching the novel, exploring this anger is more than a cheap way of tapping into youthful rebellion (or facile liberal sentiments).

Teachers can begin to examine Morrison's interest in authority by making students aware of their responses to the book. Both black and white students find it powerfully affecting. But black students notice right away what white students generally do not: that the novel concerns the internalization of white standards within the black community (the culture within the culture). Whites play a relatively small part—insensitive employer, redneck sadist, bleary-eyed shopkeeper. What the students' different responses show is how Morrison focuses attention on the authorizing assumptions of power—the unexamined conditions of most white students' lives—and not on the agents of that power (the employer, redneck, shopkeeper, or college student): cultural authority is located somewhere beyond (or above) the white individual. (The absence of whites also makes white students less defensive, just as the northern setting does in southern classes.) For example, Claudia, the narrator, remarks of a "high-yellow dream child" (Pocket, 52) that the enemy is not the girl but "the *Thing* that made *her* beautiful, and not us" (62). (It is significant that many white students do not realize that Maureen Peal is of mixed race.) And as this language suggests, that *"Thing"* is not a person or a race but a historically grounded belief in absolute and transcendent value. In American literature courses, we look at the novel's exploration of this belief by examining the opening Dick and Jane narrative in the context of African Americans' experiences of literacy, by discussing the way movies and movie technology embody the authority of cultural absolutes, and by looking at modernism as the site of tensions between repressive authority and an authentic (racial) self.

We begin by discussing the opening Dick and Jane narrative. Students easily recognize this familiar text as authoritarian and are eager to condemn it as somehow unrealistic. First, however, we investigate the implications of this preliminary text in the light of the African American experience of writing and literacy. It is useful to remind students that it was illegal to teach slaves to read and that literacy and its acquisition were focal points of many slave narratives. We ask students to recall two slave narratives, Frederick Douglass's *Narrative* and Harriet Jacobs's *Incidents in the Life of a Slave Girl*, and to recall the central place of literacy as a source of both freedom and restriction in these works. Douglass and Jacobs in differing ways write themselves to freedom (as does Claudia); but in the textually oriented South the Bible was used to justify slavery just as the Dick and Jane narrative serves to confirm second-class citizenship. (Most students know Twain's *Adventures of Huckleberry Finn*; we remind them that Tom's insensitivity toward slaves is inseparable from his faith in textual authority.) We see the same ambivalence about writing in *The Bluest Eye*. While Claudia apparently writes her own liberating text, the most joyous moments are associated with oral culture: Mrs. McTeer's neighborly gossip in her kitchen, for example, and the three whores' storytelling. And the one written text (other than the Dick and Jane story) is written by Soaphead Church, a highly educated man who has rejected his black heritage.

Most important, we review the structure of representative slave narratives, which were typically authenticated by white narrative voices: the letters attesting to the "truth" of the narratives by William Lloyd Garrison and Wendell Phillipps for Douglass and by Lydia Maria Child and Amy Post for Jacobs. We ask students if the Dick and Jane narrative has a similar function: Does the white voice validate the truth of the story? In what way? Most will see that this narrative (excerpts of which are epigraphs to the Breedloves' sections) is the antithesis of the authenticating voice of white abolitionists in slave narratives. It "authenticates" the Breedloves' (and Claudia's) narratives ironically through the contrast between its coercive artificiality and the poetic realism of the rest of the novel. Ultimately, we hope students will see that *The Bluest Eye* responds not only to reading primers but also to the broader implications of literacy and textual authority, especially as they are worked out in slave narratives. We want to make the students self-conscious about their own reading and writing. As Dana Nelson has pointed out, students equate literacy with freedom; but she cautions that we must attend not only to reading but also to what is read (142).

After we've discussed the Dick and Jane narrative, we turn to Claudia's story (saving a discussion of the italicized "prologue" until later). We've found one of the best ways to proceed is to focus on the allusions to movies and actors throughout the novel. We discuss how the idea of beauty that Hollywood promulgates excludes African Americans and how the African American community internalizes white standards of beauty. (Claudia first hates Shirley Temple but then learns "to worship her" [25]). Examining the movie references is an effective way to discuss specific forms of repression and to introduce crucial themes and passages. But we also look beyond the content of movies to examine the assumptions and traditions that underwrite the cultural authority of film. The mechanics of movie projection allow Morrison to critique the twentieth-century appropriations of Platonic realism for cultural repression. Platonic realism posits that absolute truth and value are located in a realm of immutable archetypes, which this transient world only imitates, and that only a select few have access to this realm.

We begin by reading Plato's "Allegory of the Cave" (about three pages). We use Francis Macdonald Cornford's translation of *The Republic* because a note points out that "a modern Plato would compare his Cave to an underground cinema" (228n2); we use the note to encourage students to discover connections among Plato's allegory, the cinema, and *The Bluest Eye*. The responses are always interesting. (It may also help to ask students what we should make of Maureen Peal's observation that Pecola is the name of a character in the film *Imitation of Life*: what is the meaning of "imitation"?) We want students to recognize that movie technology reproduces Plato's allegory: celluloid takes the place of Socrates's hand-carried objects, a projector the place of his fire, and a voluntary audience the place of chained captives. In each case the screen shadows forth the "real" world, of which ours is considered an imitation. When Claudia notes that romantic love and physical beauty are "[p]robably the most destructive ideas in the history of human thought" (97), she means destructive for African Americans confronted by Shirley Temples and Jean Harlows. But what makes these ideas or images destructive is the mode of representation. Shirley Temple is much less coercive when she (or her surrogate) can be torn apart in search of the thing that makes her beautiful and others ugly—as when Claudia destroys her baby doll and finds sawdust, a "cold and stupid eyeball," and "a disk with six holes" (21). The locations of authority in some transcendent order, to which only an elite few have access, mystifies power while degrading the physical and individual (a theme central to *The Bluest Eye*, especially in the chapters on Geraldine and Soaphead Church).

It is rewarding, especially in upper-level courses or with an adventuresome class, to examine further how Plato's allegory, and by implication the modern technologies that reproduce it, support specifically racist and sexist assumptions. Since the cave is dark and physically lower than the light of paternal truth, race and class can be seen as implicated in the allegory (DeKoven 67): precisely these paternalistic assumptions were used to justify slavery. And as an image of the womb, Plato's cave may be potentially a place of female power, but it is immediately a place of imprisonment (Gilbert and Gubar, *Madwoman* 93–104). The cave appropriates women's bodies; it is a womb whose physiology is rearranged to promote an androcentric notion of production and reproduction. Plato's allegory, that is, locates reality in the hypothetical, unseen source (paternity), while it presents the sensible shadows (maternity) as unreal (Homans; Irigaray). Thematically, Pauline and Pecola's rejection of mothering reflects this valuation. Pauline chooses to comfort the frightened daughter of her white employer when the visiting Pecola topples a berry cobbler, seriously burning herself. The product of Pauline's womb is less real to her than the surrogate of paternalistic white culture. And of course in her final madness Pecola denies her pregnancy, creating instead an imaginary friend who will give her the blue eyes she wants.[1]

At this point we turn to the relation between *The Bluest Eye* and modernism. Earlier in the course students were introduced to modernism as a historical culture like Victorianism and the Enlightenment; we discussed how modernism can be seen as overturning some categorical distinctions (male/female; human/animal) while maintaining others—most specifically race and class. (Daniel Singal provides a good general introduction to American modernism, though he largely ignores race and gender.) We now return to consider more fully the relation of race and gender to modernism. Until recently, the modernist canon comprised mostly white males; what about people of color?[2] If, as Marianne DeKoven comments, race is "a category of otherness crucial to the formation of modernist narrative" (67), have people of color been positioned as enabling racial others instead of being given space within modernist discourse? Even writers of the Harlem Renaissance have usually been assigned a separate but equal place alongside modernists like T. S. Eliot, William Carlos Williams, and Ezra Pound. Since *The Bluest Eye* was published at about the moment when modernism gave way to postmodernism, it provides a fine opportunity to look back at and raise questions about this literary culture and the practice of criticism.

The literature on modernism is extensive, and it is impossible to survey the range of critical perspectives here (or in class). Useful as *The Bluest Eye* may be in probing modernism and the politics of canon formation, however, we are not interested in whether the novel confirms one view of modernism. Rather, we are interested in modernism as the site of conflict over the type of authority that should prevail (radical vs. elitist; local vs. international; physical vs. transcendent). In other words, the problematic nature of modernism is itself a fertile ground for discussing the issues that resonate powerfully in *The Bluest Eye*.

We focus on works from the traditional modernist canon (the one Morrison seems to have in mind): Eliot's *The Waste Land* and Williams's "To Elsie."[3] Eliot exemplifies the racist, sexist, and authoritarian emphasis in modernism (like that in Plato and in film); Williams's work exemplifies an antiauthoritarian emphasis on personal authenticity and diversity. In our general discussion of the novel we have pointed to a third tradition: the intraracial tradition of African Americans exemplified by Mrs. McTeer's blues and the authenticating presence of Black English. As we remark above, however, this third tradition is much more important in Morrison's subsequent novels; in *The Bluest Eye* it represents a repressed discourse.

We begin by discussing how Morrison both alludes to and revises Eliot's script. We turn to the italicized prologue following the Dick and Jane narrative (9): Claudia remembers when she and her sister Frieda planted marigold seeds in a childish rite they hoped would guarantee the health of Pecola's baby. The seeds don't grow, and the baby dies; only in the postscript does Claudia understand that it is not her fault, that "the entire country was hostile to marigolds that year" (160). Most students are able to make significant connections between this section and *The Waste Land*: *The Bluest Eye* is framed by the narrator's brooding recollection of a wasteland, and the seasonal titles of the major sections—"Autumn," "Winter," "Spring," and "Summer"—delineate a parody of (re)birth and growth. (Pecola is raped in "Spring.") In the novel, however, the problem is caused not by the loss of white Western culture's authority but by its omnipresence and by the concomitant denial of both personal feeling and the value of African American culture. Morrison shows that the transcendent master narrative that Eliot perceives as sick or absent is powerful and ubiquitous (as exemplified by the movie references), and indeed it creates Pecola's own wasteland. (We see her at the end "plucking her way between the tire rims and the sunflowers, between Coke bottles and milkweed . . ." [159].)

Thus a major challenge of teaching the novel is not only to explore the destructive effects of specific white values on (or within) black culture but also to show how Morrison engages issues central to modernism and relates them to the twentieth-century African American experience; in a similar way the Dick and Jane narrative preceding Claudia's wasteland evocation engages issues of literacy and relates them to slave narratives. To explore these issues further we turn to Williams, a modernist who heatedly objected to Eliot's authoritarianism in ways that anticipate Morrison's more pointed anger. (It might be helpful to read some of Williams's responses to Eliot.[4]) Williams's prose and poetry are an extended response to Platonic realism; Williams is the poet of the physical and the local, of body and place (though he largely ignores race). Like Morrison, he traces the loss of personal authenticity that results from an elitist conception of transcendent truth and value.

We focus on "To Elsie," one of Williams's clearest commitments to the immediate and authentic against the transcendent and coercive; it is also a poem that recapitulates the Breedloves' (and especially Pauline's) tragedy and defines Claudia's success. Like Pauline Breedlove, Elsie dismisses her world (and body) as excrement while straining after a transcendent but meretricious ideal. Her condition, like Pauline's, represents the tragedy of those who live

> as if the earth under our feet
> were
> an excrement of some sky
>
> and we degraded prisoners
> destined
> to hunger until we eat filth. . . .   (*Collected Earlier Poems* 271)

Williams's poem suggests that to free ourselves from these chains we need, in Claudia's words, to have "all of [our] senses engaged" not in what lies above but in what is before us: "The lowness of the stool made for my body, . . . the smell of lilacs, the sound of the music, . . . the taste of a peach . . ." (21).

To explore the tragedy of failing to make this engagement, we look at Pecola's trip to buy candy (40–43). We ask students to characterize Pecola's feelings both before and after her encounter with the shop owner. When Pecola sets out for Mr. Yacobowski's store, she is filled with affection for herself and her immediate world: the "sweet, endurable, even cherished irritation" (40) of the coins in her shoe; the dandelions that others call ugly "because they are so many, strong, and soon" (41); the Y-shaped crack in the worn-smooth concrete perfect for skating. These are "the familiar and therefore loved images" of her world (41). But at the candy store she can't make Mr. Yacobowski see what she wants; she has once again been told that the way she sees is wrong. It is not surprising, then, that on the way home she finds the world beneath her feet has turned to excrement: she looks at the dandelions and discovers, "They *are* ugly. They *are* weeds" (43). Like Elsie, Pecola has been forced to deny her authenticity—the special conditions of her own loves and hates. Instead of finding a self (personal and racial) in anger and love, she experiences false "orgasms" by consuming Mary Jane candies, their wrappers illustrated with the ideal blond-haired and blue-eyed child (43). Her failure is reflected in the personal (and sexual) tragedies of Geraldine and Soaphead Church—sections we go on to discuss in some detail. Claudia's success, in contrast, comes from resisting the authoritarian appeal of the transcendent ideal, whose mechanism of dispersal is illustrated most forcefully in movie technology.

Marjorie Perloff writes, "Once the site of all that was radical, exciting, and above all *new*, . . . by the early 1970s modernism found itself under attack as a retrograde, elitist movement" (154). Published in 1970, *The Bluest Eye* engages precisely this conflict. Pecola wanders in a wasteland produced by the elitist demands of a white cultural ideal. But Claudia makes things new, creating a landscape in which the values of self and race are not subject to external authentication. This message is one that students find profoundly affecting.

NOTES

[1]Cholly's failure as a father (he rapes his daughter partly from twisted love) can similarly be approached through the Platonic allegory. Cholly sets out to look for his father (Samson Fuller), but he finds a man, not a hero; the shock of this discovery triggers a symbolic rebirth into the "godlike state" (126) that makes him dangerous—to himself and his family. The problem is not that Samson is a foul-mouthed wastrel but that Cholly has no way of measuring failure or success except against an ideal notion of absent and impossibly perfect paternity. Claudia, in contrast, makes a god of her father, but one who serves survival in a real and threatening world. In winter he is a "Vulcan guarding the flames," and he has the physiognomy of a natural force: "His eyes become a cliff of snow threatening to avalanche; his eyebrows bend like black limbs of leafless trees" (52).

[2]Scott and Cary Nelson, among others, redefine the modernist canon to include women, blacks, proletarian writers, and others. See Perloff, "Modernist Studies."

[3]Since Morrison's interest in the classic texts of white authors is not as overt as, for example, Ellison's in *Invisible Man*, it is useful to mention that the first section of *Playing in the Dark* begins with an epigraph from Eliot's "Preludes" and the third with an epigraph from Williams's "Adam."

[4]"Critically Eliot returned us to the classroom just at the moment when I felt that we were on the point of an escape to matters much closer to the essence of a new art form itself—rooted in the locality which should give it fruit" (*Autobiography* 174).

Song of Solomon: Modernism in the Afro-American Studies Classroom

Sandra Adell

Toni Morrison once wrote that one objective of her fiction is "to urge the reader into active participation in the non-narrative, nonliterary experience of the text." Therefore, she contends, she deliberately tries to avoid "name-dropping, lists, [and] literary references, unless oblique and based on written folklore" ("Memory" 387). Her ideal reader would have much in common with an illiterate or preliterate one: he or she would have to depend more on knowledge of black culture than on knowledge of literature. He or she would not have to rely on literature to apprehend the experiences that Morrison re-presents. Would that writing and literature were so simple.

Contrary to Morrison's assertions, most of us would agree that while her writing might escape the merely literary, as she defines it in "Memory, Creation, and Writing," it is nevertheless very literary. In fact, one problem with teaching *Song of Solomon* in Afro-American studies, particularly to undergraduates at a large Big Ten university, is that the students come from many disciplines and often have little background in literature and almost no experience with black culture. They enroll in the courses for a variety of reasons. Some of them simply want to complete the ethnic studies requirement and the literature requirement with a single course; others believe they won't have to work hard to earn a satisfactory grade; and a growing number of students, both black and white, take our classes to escape what they feel is the oppressiveness of traditional academic disciplines. I am sure that there are other reasons for our high enrollments, but my point is that, almost without exception, students take our classes believing that knowledge of the American and European literary traditions is unimportant for the study of Afro-American literature, that Afro-American literature is somehow different and that this (black) difference will render it easily accessible. They quickly find out, however, that difference does not imply accessibility or an estrangement from the general traditions and conventions of literature. It often implies instead a reordering of those traditions and conventions that makes possible new themes and new forms of literary expression. *Song of Solomon* helps illustrate this point excellently.

Song of Solomon is arguably the most literary of Morrison's novels. Its themes are embedded in a complex network of allusions to Greek and West African mythology that many students find difficult to apprehend. Structurally, it appropriates from modernism techniques of narrative discontinuity that challenge students accustomed to more linear and ordered narratives. I therefore find it helpful to present an overview of the development of the novel as a literary genre and to show how modernism, by emphasizing discontinuity and fragmentation and by invoking the magical, the supernatural, and the beliefs and cultural practices of non-Western societies, attempts to disorder and disrupt traditional modes of Western art and literature. This introduction leads naturally to a discussion of how Morrison meets the modernist challenge to "make it new."

Let us take as an example the novel's title. Some students will immediately recognize it as the title of a book in the Bible, but few will have read that book. The Song of Solomon is one of the shorter books of the Bible; in *The New Scofield Reference Bible* it is only six pages long (Scofield 705–10). Students could be asked to read the Song of Solomon and formulate for classroom discussion a question about the significance of using the title of what most biblical scholars consider a lyrical love poem to title a novel in which love seems to have long since withered away. More important, students should be encouraged to reflect on how the title might undermine Morrison's attempts to avoid striking what she calls a "literary posture" by invoking not only the Judeo-Christian tradition but also the Hebraic and Greek traditions ("Memory" 387). The exercise is by no means intended to make light of Morrison's achievement. Her winning the Nobel Prize in literature speaks for itself. What the assignment should yield is a deeper understanding of the complex relation between Morrison's texts and those of the Western literary tradition.

Morrison's interpretation of the archetypal myth of the questing hero offers another opportunity for students to reflect on how *Song of Solomon* refines, reorders, and revises certain canonical texts to accommodate her imagination and her vision of the realities of African American culture. For example, I present Milkman Dead's quest for the gold he and his father, Macon, believe is hidden in Hunters Cave as a displacement of the mythic quest for the golden fleece. Like Jason and the Argonauts, Milkman is as motivated by a spirit of adventure as by the desire for gold. The prospect of going wherever he wants and of finally escaping the unforgiveness that infects the relationships of all the Deads motivates Milkman to plan with his friend Guitar to slip into his aunt Pilate's house late one night and steal the heavy green bag they believe contains the missing gold. Their plan succeeds, but they do not get away undetected. At one window of the moonlit house stands the figure of a man. At another window Pilate watches and wonders, as Milkman and Guitar sneak away, why they wanted the bag, for as they find out when they are arrested, all it contains are some rocks and what Pilate thought were the remains of the white man Macon had killed years ago in the cave.

An important thematic strand for discussion of *Song of Solomon* is Morrison's depiction of the ancestral figure. The three characters who emerge as ancestors are Pilate; her father, Jake, later named Macon; and the midwife Circe. Each of the three possesses a generosity of spirit that Morrison seems to suggest is the mainstay of the community and of communal values. They also possess a special knowledge that enables them to serve as intermediaries between the material and the spiritual worlds. Milkman's father, Macon, stresses this point when he says to his son, whom he had forbidden to visit Pilate, "Pilate can't teach you a thing you can use in this world. Maybe the next, but not this one" (Signet-NAL, 55). Morrison's fictional ancestors and ancestral figures possess mystical powers and a knowledge of the spiritual world that eludes those conditioned by Western logic. They make things happen. They interpret for their people things and events that defy practical reason and understanding. But more important for Morrison, the ancestor links two cultures: the Afro-American and the African, as Macon reminds us when he tells Milkman, "If you ever have a doubt we from Africa, look at Pilate. She look just like Papa and he looked like all them pictures you ever see of Africans" (54).

Pilate also inherited from her father the ancestral properties that helped sustain her when, as a young woman, she found herself ostracized because of her navelless belly. One of those properties is the ability to communicate with her dead father. After she and Macon convince the policemen that Milkman and Guitar have committed no crime, he by paying them off and she by playing the fool, Pilate tells Milkman and Macon that she had the bones because her father, who often came to "see" her, had appeared to her shortly after her daughter Reba's birth and told her, "You just can't fly on off and leave a body" (209). Thinking that he was referring to the dead white man in the cave, Pilate returned to it and collected the bones because "Papa told [her] to, and he was right, you know" (210).

Pilate's posthumous relationship with her father offers an opportunity to introduce into class discussion what John Mbiti describes as the spiritual realm of many West African societies. In this realm, death is regarded as a process by which a person is removed from the physical world but continues to exist, in the collective memory of the people, in one of two dimensions of time: the Sasa and the Zamani. *Sasa*, a Swahili word, suggests a "sense of immediacy, nearness and 'now-ness'"; *Zamani* refers to "the period beyond which nothing can go. Zamani is the graveyard of time, the period of termination, the dimension in which everything finds its halting point. It is the final storehouse for all phenomena and events, the ocean of time in which everything becomes absorbed into a reality that is neither after nor before" (28–29). In this cosmology there is no future or hereafter; the dead dwell in personal or collective immortality, but always in the present.

Personal immortality is guaranteed as long as survivors remember the departed and recognize them by name should they "appear," as those who dwell in the Sasa period are wont to do. According to Mbiti, recognition by name is important, for it ensures that the departed remain alive, as "living-deads," and active in the spirit world. When they are no longer remembered and recognized, usually after the last people who knew them have departed, they become completely dead as far as family ties are concerned and enter Zamani and collective immortality. They lose contact with the family, and whatever traces of their names survive do so only in genealogies, folktales, and myths (32–34).

In this anthropocentric cosmology, Pilate's father, Jake, would be considered a living-dead; he is still in the process of dying and therefore resides in both the physical and the spiritual worlds. His presence is all the more immediate because Pilate, although she does not know it until Milkman returns from his journey and tells her, has been carrying her father's remains around for the past fifty years and not those of the white man Macon killed in the cave. Jake does not have far to travel when he finds it necessary, on behalf of his daughter, to intervene in the physical world. He has been with her all along, suspended by a piece of wire between the realms of the living and the dead until his grandson comes searching for some little bags of gold.

Milkman's odyssey begins in earnest two days after he and Guitar are arrested for riding around in a car with a bag of human bones. For two days, burdened with shame for contriving to steal his aunt's "inheritance," Milkman finds temporary relief by drinking until he is "swaying from light buzz to stoned" (213). An encounter with his sister Magdalene (called Lena) finally brings him out of his stupor and to the realization that it is time for him to leave, to "go solo" and seek out the gold. His first stop is Danville, where he is eventually directed to the midwife Circe.

The Circe episode can easily be used to help students understand literary allusion and intertextuality. Here, M. H. Abrams's definition of *allusion* as an explicit or indirect reference to a "well-known person, place, or event, or to another literary work or passage" is useful (8–9). I explain to my students that intertextuality refers to the intersection of literary texts and traditions. I point out the allusion in the first sentence of the Circe episode in which Morrison invokes the tale of Hansel and Gretel. I then explain that the tale is one of two texts that enframe the episode. The other is the *Odyssey*, which, like the Bible, subtly enhances the intertextuality of Morrison's text. The *Odyssey* traverses *Song of Solomon* from beginning to end and links it to every preceding text in the Western literary tradition. Milkman is as "charmed" as Hansel and Gretel by the strange house before him with its "sweet, spicy perfume" of ginger and a promise of goodies and gold; and like Odysseus and his fellow voyagers, Milkman finds it impossible to resist Circe's magical appeal. The woman standing at the top of the wide spiral staircase in the ramshackle Butler house personifies all the witches he has ever dreamed about, and when Milkman reaches Circe's bony embrace he remains there, enchanted, until a swarming "pack of golden-eyed dogs" breaks his spell (241–43).

Many of my students are so intrigued by the episode that I often assign a project requiring them to do a bit of research on the figure of Circe in classical myth. Barbara Walker's *The Woman's Encyclopedia of Myths and Secrets* and Edith Hamilton's *Mythology* are useful starting points. What I hope they will discover is that in Greek mythology Circe is also often identified as Omphale of Lydia, goddess of the omphalos or umbilicus, whose sacred navel stone marked the center of the world. I can then discuss how Morrison rewrites that myth by making the absence of the umbilicus the mark that cuts Pilate off from the world. Circe, the immortal midwife, provides Milkman with one of the clues he needs to complete the genealogy that would reconnect Pilate and her "Sugarman Song" to the song of the children of Shalimar: the name of his grandmother, Sing. Susan Byrd helps him fill in the remaining gaps, so that when he finally begins to pay attention to the children's endless round, he has no doubt that the flying African is none other than the father of his grandfather, Jake.

Children's ring games are often the repositories of myths, folktales, and genealogies. A project my students have found entertaining and informative is to research the tale of the flying African in children's games and songs. I recommend Virginia Hamilton's collection of black American folktales, *The People Could Fly*, as a starting point because it includes an excellent version of the tale and a useful bibliography of African American folktales and rhymes. In Hamilton's version of the tale, some of the Africans who ended up as slaves once had wings and knew how to fly. When they were captured, they had to shed their wings in order to fit on the crowded slave ships. What they didn't give up, however, was the magical power that once enabled them to rise on the air. They kept their magic a secret "in the land of slavery" until one day, when a young woman named Sarah and her baby were brutally beaten by the slave driver, an old man named Toby decided it was time for them to go. He gave the signal, said the magic words "Kum . . . yali, kum buba tambe," and Sarah, "with the child held tightly in her arms . . . rose just as free as a bird" (170). The next day, old Toby repeated the magic words, and one by one all the slaves who once could fly joined hands in a "ring-sing." But "they didn't shuffle in a circle. They didn't sing. They rose on the air." With Toby in the lead, they flew away, but they left behind all "poor souls" who could not fly. Toby just didn't have time to teach the others to fly (171).

The song the children of Shalimar sing helps clarify, in Milkman's mind, what his grandfather really meant when he said to Pilate, "You just can't fly on off and leave a body." Jake was not referring to the bones in the cave; he was lamenting that his father had flown away and left him behind. What remains to be questioned is whether, in her rewriting of the tale, Morrison is subtly criticizing the flying Africans' decision to leave the others behind. In any event, according to Virginia Hamilton's version of the tale, "The slaves who could not fly told about the people who could fly to their children. When they were free. When they sat close before the fire in the free land, they told it. They so love firelight and *Free-dom*, and tellin" (172). And now Morrison, who so loves "tellin," has retold this tale and the many others embedded in *Song of Solomon* in such a way that her text is a veritable exercise in the study of literature. For students in Afro-American studies *Song of Solomon* provides many opportunities to reflect on the representations of black culture in fiction. But the effect of the novel reaches far beyond the Afro-American studies curriculum. *Song of Solomon* is race-specific in its focus on the experiences of a particular group of black people living in the United States; it is a great work of fiction because these people and their experiences are unforgettable. The work offers a myriad of interpretive possibilities, and this inexhaustibility ensures *Song of Solomon* a place among the world's great books.

Flying Home: Folklore, Intertextuality, and *Song of Solomon*

James C. Hall

Although students grew up on a diet of gravity-defying cartoon characters, they are often perplexed at Toni Morrison's use of the flying motif in *Song of Solomon*. This is especially true when they encounter Milkman's final leap toward Guitar, freedom, and possibly death, a willful decision that many readers—not only undergraduates—find a disruption of the novel's realistic or naturalistic narrative. I suggest a strategy that contextualizes the flying motif as part of an African American folkloric tradition and embraces readerly wonder and disillusion as aesthetically and pedagogically constructive. My central goal when teaching Morrison to undergraduates is to transform my students into rereaders of her novels. Instead of attempting to clarify or close their experience of the novel, I want to encourage their wonderment so that they are drawn back to the text—as am I—over and over again.

Many commentators have, of course, focused on the folkloric content of Morrison's work and the motif of flight. Grace Ann Hovet and Barbara Lounsberry provide the most comprehensive survey of flight in Morrison's corpus; they assert that *Song of Solomon* is Morrison's most "affirmative exploration of flight," in which she explores the possibilities of a flight that signifies "identity, community, and creative life" (121). Gay Wilentz suggests connections between Morrison's novel and other contemporary African American novels like Ishmael Reed's *Flight to Canada*, Richard Perry's *Montgomery's Children*, and Paule Marshall's *Praisesong for the Widow* ("If You"). Jacqueline De Weever examines *Song of Solomon* in an essay that is Eurocentric in orientation but also extremely suggestive of the great diversity of folk and mythic texts to which the novelist made direct and indirect reference. For De Weever, the novel "is the story of the making of a song, of a search for ancestors who inspired the song, told in the manner of the folk tale" (131). Susan Blake's "Folklore and Community in *Song of Solomon*" remains the most suggestively analytic of essays on the folkloric content of the novel. Blake contends that, in "basing Milkman's identity quest on a folktale, Morrison calls attention to one of the central themes in all her fiction, the relationship between individual identity and community" (77). There are a number of other worthwhile commentaries (in particular, see Foreman; Hemenway; G. Jones; Mason; and Skerret). While acknowledging these commentators' valuable and careful documentation of *Song of Solomon*'s relation to the folk tradition, I would like to explore a further ramification of this scholarship: its application in the classroom. Instructors can make considerable use of the motif of flight, the specific African American folktale on which it is based, and the general tradition of African American folklore. Below I briefly sketch how I maximize these possibilities in my teaching.

I believe strongly that centering student writing in the literature classroom facilitates critical thinking and democratic involvement. I therefore provide background and interject secondary texts, literally, in dialogue with my students. I try to let them set an agenda for their learning, while I function as a resource and an experienced reader. This method is consistent with the novel's resistance to closure and to authoritative gestures. Morrison concretely contributes, we might say, to the "teachability" of the novel by precluding easy solutions and assured master narratives.

Students have little difficulty recognizing the preoccupation of the text with flight. In addition to the important scenes that open and close the book—Robert Smith's failed flight with homemade wings and Milkman's surrender to the air—students note the descriptive and symbolic language of flight (or overcoming), the copious ornithologic imagery (peacocks, eagles, buzzards, etc.) in the text, the presence of actual flyers (the 332nd fighter group), and even the punning in Pilate's name. In general they recognize that Morrison is committed to our awareness of the motif and that all these elements force us to reread Robert Smith and prepare us for Milkman's leap. However, this recognition does little to ease many students' anxiety at Morrison's stretching and challenging the boundaries of realistic narrative. Her presentation of the fantastic works to disrupt the usual interpretive process, causing readerly discomfort. Again this difficulty is greatest at Milkman's surrender, paradoxically at the instant we are most convinced of a victory. As Milkman attempts to ride the air toward Guitar, undergraduate readers often feel abandoned, left behind like the children of Solomon.

One way in which I try to make familiar the theme of flight, and by extension the special character of Morrison's narrative, is by placing it at the nexus of rich and complex African American representations. Some of them have clear or direct African or European sources, while others seem to be products of the African American (or perhaps New World) imagination. I wish to give my students access to the text's immense resonance, an access that demands some introduction to *Song of Solomon*'s intertextuality and intracultural exploration of the idea of flight. An openness to and an awareness of this resonance do much to lessen the anxiety associated with the narrative's challenge to the conventional. The most important topic through which to elicit complex reading is African and African American folklore.

Both the indeterminacy and the comprehensibility of *Song of Solomon* are related to Morrison's choice and creation of a variant of the tale of the flying Africans. Blake argues convincingly that Morrison's source for the tale was *Drums and Shadows: Survival Studies among the Georgia Coastal Negroes* (United States), which contains just five variations on the story of African slaves (occasionally a single slave) who, determined to get home, simply up and fly away. Popular collections of African American folklore also offer differing versions of this compelling tale (Brewer; Dorson; Lester). By exposing students to these variations, I immediately introduce the literary-critical idea of interpretation and the literary-historical fact of individual artistry within tradition. Blake further contends that Morrison's choice of a more individualistic version of the tale—Solomon flies away leaving both his immediate family and the community of slaves—reveals the novelist's attempts to negotiate a contemporary politics of moral agency and self-determination. When I introduce this body of folklore—and not incidentally questions of control, authorship, and value—students begin to sense that Morrison is systematically preparing the reader's experience. At this point, complex foregrounding of African American folk thought is not necessary (although the teacher should be familiar with the work of Lawrence Levine, Patricia Turner, and Alan Dundes). The emphasis in class should be on shared knowledge about folk storytelling, especially its variability, improvisation, democratic sensibility, and simultaneous commitment to entertainment and to edification. We talk about what readers expect when interpreting a text clearly identified as folklore and about why and how Morrison's novel mediates between the folk and the literary. We might also discuss the pleasure of reading or hearing folk texts and how *Song of Solomon* is or is not pleasurable to read. At some point we must consider whether to adopt or reject what the text teaches. Often students challenge whether the folk tradition has a democratic sensibility, especially on feminist grounds if they have read *Song of Solomon* alongside Zora Neale Hurston's *Their Eyes Were Watching God*.

Continuing in this vein, I am inclined to begin nonsystematically to map for students the visibility of flight in a variety of African American cultural artifacts. We might begin by commenting on how and where spirituals use flight imagery. This premodern context can be extended by considering the image in the poetry of George Moses Horton and Paul Laurence Dunbar. (Think of the possibilities in teaching Dunbar's "Not They Who Soar," for instance.) In mapping the territory of this century, we examine musical, visual, and kinetic arts. I like to use Romare Bearden's reflections on the beginnings of the lindy hop, a dance commemorating Charles Lindbergh's flight across the Atlantic (Schwartzman 62), with a recording of the African American bandleader Lionel Hampton's immensely popular tune "Flying Home." (A look at Malcolm X's thoughts on dancing to Hampton at the Savoy Ballroom could further enhance the discussion.) I prefer to hand out these texts and intertexts as extra reading (or listening or viewing); without my prodding, students inevitably reintroduce them into conversations. More substantially and systematically, one could compare canonical texts, noting, as have many commentators, the interplay between Morrison's novel and Ralph Ellison's seminal short story "Flying Home." Some explanation of the differences between Ellison's and Morrison's varieties of modernism, and further differences in their attitudes toward the relation of fiction and society, can do much to help students comprehend *Song of Solomon*. The rich intertextual ground of the novel begins to move students toward a historical reading of the flight motif and a necessary suspension of disbelief. Observing this ongoing cultural conversation, this dialogic construction of flight, allows students to appreciate once again the folktale as a democratic form.

The teacher can productively introduce many other texts, especially those that suggest a variety of cross-cultural influences and Morrison's revision of the European tradition. Introducing the myth of Icarus and Daedalus, for instance, can further student speculation about the audience for Morrison's novel. As I suggest above, De Weever's article helps alert students to Morrison's comprehensive rethinking and retelling of the Brothers Grimm, but one might also consider Robert Hayden's excellent poem "O Daedalus, Fly Away Home" as another fine example of African American exploration of the Greek mythic inheritance or, again in the *Autobiography of Malcolm X*, the titling of chapter 15 "Icarus." At the other end of the cultural spectrum, one might draw students' attention to popular cultural phenomena like the groundbreaking television series about the civil rights era, *I'll Fly Away*; the prevalence of the image of flight in spirituals and gospel music; the African American children's book by Virginia Hamilton, *The People Could Fly*; the cultural currency of the Tuskeegee Airmen; or, finally, the ubiquity of Air Jordans. A central part of this mapping must be the realization that flight is not a wholly positive image. The instructor may wish to emphasize the historical restrictions that have generated the yearning to fly.

This intertextual web cannot assuage students' understandable discomfort or disbelief over the actions of Robert Smith or Milkman Dead; it does, however, provide a foundation for considering Morrison's choices as novelist. In particular, it helps the class meditate on the attractiveness of a motif and tradition with weak ties to the conventions of realism. By considering the oral basis of folkloric conservation and transmission, readers are led to earlier occurrences of the story, its resilience, and the possibility of contemporary improvisations on the same theme. The task of reading and understanding *Song of Solomon*, then, is directly parallel to Milkman's struggle. We are attempting to unravel the meaning of the tale. Furthermore, by directing student attention to the history of reading and literacy (and its repression), especially in the context of slavery, we as teachers can underscore the possibilities of oral narrative and raise questions about Western privileging of the written text.

Talking about the centrality of the oral is not an extratextual approach. The emphasis or strategy I suggest does not rely exclusively on the folktale of the flying Africans. Indeed, a close reading of Morrison's text reveals that the most important action in the novel is usually communicated through storytelling as opposed to the direct presentation of dramatic action, with the exception of Milkman's journey-quest (which itself might be based on oral epics like the *Odyssey*). Sometimes, as with Ruth and Macon's account of Ruth's father's death, we even read variant accounts of events, and Guitar is always trying to educate Milkman by telling stories, as Pilate had done.

My preliminary remarks on the appropriateness of a dialogic pedagogy in teaching Morrison's work are even more pertinent to an examination of the general context of folklore and storytelling, to which I turn now. Morrison has suggested as a framework for understanding her work, in addition to the redemptive act of "rememory," a recognition of the audience's desire for narrative.

> I am not experimental, I am simply trying to recreate something out of an old art form in my books—the something that defines what makes a book "black." And that has nothing to do with whether the people in the books are black or not. The open-ended quality that is sometimes a problematic in the novel form reminds me of the uses to which stories are put in the black community. The stories are constantly being retold, constantly being imagined within a framework. And I hook into this like a life-support system, which for me is the thing out of which I come.
>
> (qtd. in Mason 564)

On the one hand, Morrison foregrounds the use of stories in the African American community—as heuristics, as entertainment, as subversive communication—while, on the other, she explains the attractiveness of the commitment to the oral mode. Oral improvisation allows for individual accomplishment within tradition, which, when performed within a society that denies the value of black creativity and black humanity, becomes a claim for being itself. Students do need help in coming to terms with Morrison's unique vision, perhaps even her idiosyncrasy. But with a knowledge of a complex tradition in which the motif of flight is a central trope, students can discover that Morrison's violation of realistic convention does not affront but instead honors the ancestors and, more important, invites entrance into the conversation, surrender to the text. Her idiosyncrasy has more to do with her profoundly social concerns than with narrative fireworks or postmodern skepticism. The reality of those concerns and the kinds of dialogue that the text thus invites demand a commitment by the instructor to let the meaning emerge, perhaps even find its own wings.

Tar Baby: **Philosophizing Blackness**
Madelyn Jablon

In my fifteen-week advanced seminar on Toni Morrison, we discuss her first six novels in chronological order. Although we cover *Tar Baby* right after mid-terms, it is the high point of the course. After *The Bluest Eye* and *Sula*, which introduce Morrison's central themes and motifs, *Song of Solomon* and *Tar Baby* allow us to examine these themes and motifs more closely and carefully, as Morrison herself seems to do.

We begin preparing for *Tar Baby* with our closing observations about *Song of Solomon*, in which we focus on heritage and cultural identity. Students interpret Milkman's journey as evidence of the need to know one's heritage and history; this knowledge is vital to Milkman's well-being. The session prepares students for the more complicated presentation of history in *Tar Baby*. Discussion commences with this question: Does Morrison argue here as she did in *Song of Solomon* for the necessity of knowing and participating in one's heritage? Is that knowledge a prerequisite for the characters' well-being?

Students want to say yes. They want to believe that truths are absolute and constant. They scrutinize Jadine's behavior for evidence. Everyone has a stone to throw: everyone cites a shortcoming. Students condemn Jadine for being a modern woman who has lost touch with her heritage. They criticize her for allowing her aunt and uncle to wait on her, for preferring Margaret's company to her family's, for allowing Valerian to finance her education. They criticize her preference in men, food, education, and vocation. Students argue that she, like Milkman, is fully assimilated into mainstream American culture and that this novel, like its predecessor, teaches the importance of knowing the past. I compliment them on their observations and note that scholars such as Barbara Christian and Trudier Harris have assessed Jadine's character similarly. I recommend Eleanor Traylor's "The Fabulous World of Toni Morrison: *Tar Baby*," a humorous critique of Jadine, whom Traylor identifies as "the carcinogenic disease eating away at the ancestral spirit of the race"; she identifies "Jadinese" as "the disease of disconnection" (146).

I ask students to pursue the same question concerning Son. While students are adept at identifying Jadine as a product of assimilation, they need help recognizing Son as her antithesis, a representative of black nationalism. Students need to recognize him as a trickster, a character rooted in African American folklore—both as an embodiment of mythic past and as a gifted storyteller. They need to recognize his preference for Eloe, his refusal to fill out college applications or look for work, and his celebration of fraternity as part of a nationalist agenda.

Once students are comfortable recognizing characters as representatives of divergent political philosophies, we discuss Morrison's purpose. Some students consider Son a mouthpiece for Morrison, who they say is arguing for national-ism. Others remain silent. They understand that the relationship between Ja-dine and Son, the love affair reminiscent of Janie and Tea Cake's in *Their Eyes Were Watching God*, is destined to fail because of political differences, but they are uncertain about who is "right," about what politics Morrison advo-cates. We turn to the closing chapters for an answer. Students who saw Son as the embodiment of an ideal confront his flaws: his hypocritical and negligent treatment of Alma, the limitations of fraternal feelings that encompass only men, his refusal to compromise his beliefs to survive. We discuss the futility of his joining the chevaliers. Students realize that Morrison is looking skeptically at the nationalist politics that is a theme of her earlier novels. At the same time, they acknowledge the value of Jadine's politics. The first black model on the cover of *Elle* is changing the world. Most important, they realize that Morrison does not ask the audience to choose between assimilationism and nationalism. She illuminates the strengths and weaknesses of each and recommends nei-ther. Deborah McDowell notes that "Morrison confuses binary oppositions" and that her fiction demands a "shift from an either/or orientation to one that is both/and, full of shifts and contradictions" ("Self" 80). This quotation is an appropriate description of politics in *Tar Baby*.

The discussion of politics stops here because we begin to see the strategy McDowell describes at work on other levels. Students realize that Morrison's real concern isn't advocating a political platform but rather suggesting a way of thinking preferable to Kierkegaard's dichotomy of "either/or." We recognize how the novel's structure supports this premise. Students outline several chap-ters on the board. They note that there are six characters around whom the novel is organized like a perfect hexagon. In chapter 2 readers are invited to move through the house at nighttime, from room to room, visiting its inhabi-tants. First we visit Jadine, who lies awake recalling the unsettling episode with the woman in the yellow dress and the enigmatic story of the chevaliers. Next we visit Valerian, who dreams of incoherent messages that he must deliver. Insomnia is visiting Margaret, who is hoping for the dream that will dispel her "occasional forgetfulness" (NAL, 46). Onodine dreams of drowning and touches Sydney's back for reassurance while he dreams of Baltimore in 1921. It is a "tiny dream he had each night that he would never recollect from morn-ing to morning. So he never knew what it was exactly that refreshed him" (51). Morrison repeats the pattern in her descriptions of the characters' responses to Son and the Christmas dinner. Students consider whether democracy and egal-itarianism are attributes of a narrative in which no character is favored. This narrative strategy is consistent with the philosophy that allows Morrison to sus-pend judgment and present characters as different as Jadine and Son without making one good and the other bad. The characterization is not one or the other but both.

At this point I find it helpful to contextualize Morrison's approach histori-cally by referring to W. E. B. Du Bois's double consciousness, James Weldon

Johnson's ex-colored man, and Houston Baker's poetics of blackness (*Workings*). Students discover that seeing beyond the either-or dichotomy is characteristic of black philosophy. Morrison's narration allows her readers to experience what it is to think black—to see everyone's thoughts and recognize that they are all valid, even if they are contradictory. This feature is what makes the novel good to teach. The students learn to accept differences—even contradictions—without choosing among them or ranking them. They may apply this perspective to their own lives and learn to value African American culture for teaching them a way of thinking they can use.

Next, students discover how elementary library research can enrich their appreciation of the novel. We begin by discussing two versions of the tar-baby story. I use a version by Joel Chandler Harris (*Nights*) and one by Langston Hughes and Arna Bontemps, but any of the many variants will work. I supply background information on the oral tradition and the role of the storyteller. We discuss authorship and improvisation and examine the relationship between a griot and his or her audience. The versions of the story I use end differently. Harris's concludes with the rabbit successfully ensnared by the tar baby and awaiting his unhappy fate. In Hughes and Bontemps's account Brer Rabbit uses reverse psychology to outsmart Brer Fox. He begs the fox to burn him at the stake, to hang him, or to eat him—to do anything but throw him in the briar patch. The fox throws the rabbit into the briar patch, and this version concludes with Brer Rabbit scrambling away, crying, "Whup-pee, my God you couldn't throw me in a better place! There where my mammy born me, in the briar patch" (2).

I introduce relevant biographical information, including an overview of Morrison's career as writer, scholar, researcher, and historian. Then students write a paper explaining how the different versions of the story influenced her. Did one version serve as a blueprint, or did all contribute to her story? Each student answers differently, but they all respond to two questions: Who is the tar baby? and What occurs after the novel ends? Students who believe Morrison was influenced by Harris's version usually identify Son as the rabbit and Jadine as the tar baby. They imagine Son's continued search for Jadine as evidence of his ensnarement. Students who prefer this ending read Son's departing "lickety-split" as indicative of a successful escape (264). Equally thought-provoking but less frequent are the essays that cast Jadine as the rabbit and Son as the tar baby. While he finds freedom by joining the chevaliers, she finds freedom on a transcontinental flight that returns her to her briar patch in Paris.

After students have handed in their essays, we discuss these possibilities. Two or three students let earlier discussions of the book influence their answers, arguing that Morrison was influenced by both versions. Like Stephanie Demetrakopoulos, they argue that Son and Jadine are each other's tar babies and that both escape or fail to escape ("Creation" 136). Because of our earlier discussion of politics and philosophy, students can understand how both characters can be tar babies. Students recall their discussion of *Song of Solomon*'s conclusion, in which they were divided over what happened after the novel ended. Some believed that Milkman fell to his death; others believed that he flew back to Africa. I invite students to recall our discussion of this ambiguity. Was Morrison testing readers to see if they had learned the lesson that Milkman does? Students who believe he becomes part of the myth of flying Africans pass the test because they, like Milkman, have learned to appreciate and use African American heritage. Students consider the ending of *Tar Baby* as a similar test. If they believe Son has joined the chevaliers, they believe in the vitality of his cultural inheritance. If they believe he continues his search, they relinquish belief in the stories of the past when the novel ends. Both novels hold up a mirror in which readers can see their own beliefs. It is important to assure students that there are no incorrect answers to the assignment. For an instructor to make such judgments would be to ignore Morrison's views on contradiction. Morrison takes this idea as far as she can by including both versions of the tale as well as an inconclusive ending.

The students in this class have completed an elementary course in literary theory and are familiar with reader-response criticism. We conclude our discussion of the novel with a reference to this theory as a means of understanding the open-endedness of *Tar Baby* and *Song of Solomon*. Selected passages from Morrison's "Unspeakable Things Unspoken: The Afro-American Presence in American Literature" illustrate her view of the audience's role. Morrison identifies her readers as "co-conspirators" (23). Students discuss their readings as acts of co-conspiracy, and they view the class as a collective of co-conspirators. This discussion is a point of entry for our consideration of *Beloved*.

Although I teach *Tar Baby* in an advanced seminar, I have tried many of these techniques in courses on African American literature and courses on contemporary American literature, and they have worked equally well there. I teach the novel frequently because I think it is important. It allows students to consider a philosophy that celebrates difference, one that acknowledges and accepts contradiction.

Using History as Artifact to Situate *Beloved*'s Unknown Woman: Margaret Garner

Angelita Reyes

> I fall, I swoon! I look at the sky.
> The clouds are breaking on my brain;
> I am floated along, as if I should die
> Of liberty's exquisite pain
> In the name of the white child waiting for me
> In the death-dark where we may kiss and agree,
> White men I leave you all curse-free
> In my broken heart's disdain!
> —Elizabeth Barrett Browning,
> "The Runaway Slave at Pilgrim's Point"

In *Beloved* Toni Morrison is not as concerned with recording historical facts as she is with constructing meaning and emotional *truth* out of them. She creates the interior motivations of women like the fugitive slave, Margaret Garner, who in 1856 asserted her right to freedom by escaping her owner's plantation. During the escape she killed her young daughter so that the child would not return to slavery.

When students and general readers learn that Morrison's *Beloved* is based on a historical incident, they often assume the entire narrative is based on documented facts, which they initially perceive as objective truth. Morrison's worldview, however, places truth in the realm of interior motivations and speculations about disremembered black women whose autobiographical narratives will never be known. In *Jazz* Morrison re-creates a 1920s incident in which a young Harlem woman was fatally shot by her lover. *Beloved* is a creative dialogue with the Margaret Garner story. Morrison says of her work in general that "the crucial distinction for me is not the difference between fact and fiction, but the distinction between fact and truth. Because facts can exist without human intelligence, but truth cannot" ("Site" 113). Thus discussing *Beloved* not only as a multifaceted literary text but also as a historical artifact that renders images in text avoids the debate over whether Morrison accurately records the facts of history. Yet through knowing the raw historical facts the reader can understand Morrison's artistic commitment to exposing possible truths of individual black women's experiences.

Before *Beloved* Margaret Garner was one of American history's unknown fugitive slave mothers; although the story of her escape and the murder of her child was sensationalized in 1856, it was quickly forgotten. *Beloved* is a twentieth-century creation of the imagination that, like the literary and journalistic artifacts that immediately followed the Garner tragedy, valorizes and remembers the tragedy as spiritual redemption. Over a century after the Garner incident Toni Morrison is one of the poets who Frederick Douglass prophesied in 1856 would "gather inspiration from this offering of blood to the goddess of Freedom; History will hand down her name to the last generation. Yes, MARGARET, THE SLAVE MOTHER, will furnish an inspiring theme for the painter's pencil, and the poet's song" (qtd. in "Beauties"). Could Margaret Garner have imagined that poets would be inspired by her desperate effort to protect her children?

The Douglass quotation can lead to a lively class discussion on the role of the artist as prophet of social change and deliverer of awareness and often unpalatable truths. Students are often fascinated with how fiction may be unintentionally prescient. For example, Elizabeth Barrett Browning's 1848 poem "The Runaway Slave at Pilgrim's Point" depicts the story of a slave woman who is raped, becomes a fugitive, and gives birth to a "white" child. She murders the child. Like Morrison, Browning based her poem on a real-life incident, which took place in Jamaica. The poem was considered ferocious in 1848 when it was first presented. Ann Parry says that even our contemporary literary critics have labeled or dismissed the poem as "melodramatic," "unintentionally ludicrous," and "too blunt and shocking" (117).

The child that Garner, herself a *mulata*, killed was "white," the press coverage of 1856 consistently noted. But no reporter of that day discussed the issues and problematics of rape and miscegenation. Morrison, however, deals with them in *Beloved*. Indeed, such children were the products of ritual rape aboard the slave ships before they docked in the Americas. The French named the ritual rape *la pariade*, and the practice became established during the centuries of the Atlantic slave trade. How do we understand a truth that is stranger and more unpalatable than fiction?

Morrison as the poet re-creates Garner's story out of literary inspiration as one to pass on, to tell to others, and as one to *pass* on, to give up and bury. The double entendre is an important device to discuss because it is part of *Beloved*'s terminal refrain. As Paul D finally says, "Sethe . . . me and you, we got more yesterday than anybody. We need some kind of tomorrow. . . . You your best thing, Sethe. You are" (Knopf, 273).

Many accounts of the Garner story (con)fuse fiction and reality. By pointing that out, instructors can lead their classes to discuss Morrison's ideas of historical evidence and truth. If truth is more significant than fact, should the facts be dismissed? What does Morrison mean by stating that facts can exist without human intelligence, but truth cannot? What constitutes justifying a murder that arises out of the paradox of a mother's love (for her child) and hate (for slavery)? Is each generation's response to history a more profound nexus of truth and intelligence? Is the mother's act the result of intuitive truth and intelligence? At the time of her flight Margaret Garner was pregnant and only twenty-one years old.

At this point in the discussion students who don't know will want to know the facts of the Margaret Garner story. Knowing the story helps readers view

Sethe's story as one of reconciliation and spiritual redemption. It places her fictional story next to the truth of the silent stories that can never be heard.

On the night of 27 January 1856 seventeen slaves—men, women, and children—fled from Kentucky to Ohio. (For an in-depth study of the case, see Reyes, "Rereading.") The fugitive group had taken advantage of the unusually cold winter, which enabled them to cross the frozen Ohio River on a horse-drawn sleigh. Because they realized that such a large group of blacks traveling together would cause suspicion, they decided to break up into two groups. One group of nine soon established contact with the local Quakers and continued their flight to Canada through the Underground Railroad.

The other eight, the Garner family, included the four Garner children, Mary, Silla (Pricilla), Thomas, and Samuel; an elderly man, Simon Garner; Mary Garner, Simon's wife; Simon, Jr., Margaret Garner's husband; and Margaret Garner. The children ranged in age from about thirteen months to ten years old. While hiding in the home of a manumitted relative outside Cincinnati, they were apprehended under the infamous Fugitive Slave Act of 1850, which stated that any escaped slave could be seized by a white person in any state and returned to the slave owner. During the violent apprehension Margaret Garner attempted to kill her four children by cutting their throats with a knife, but the older children ran into a back room. She succeeded in killing her three-year-old daughter. Garner later referred to the girl as "the little . . . bird" (*Commercial*).

Despite the efforts of local and national abolitionists, including the American Anti-slavery Society, and despite national and international attention, after a month of complicated court proceedings the federal Fugitive Slave Act was sustained. The Garner family was actually kidnapped to Kentucky and back into slavery. The boat carrying some of the Garners farther south to be sold had a collision, and Margaret Garner fell or jumped into the Ohio River with one of her children. Although Garner was rescued, the child drowned. The Louisville *Courier* reported that Garner welcomed the death because another of her children had escaped slavery. Garner was sent to Arkansas and soon after died in slavery.

Students are rudely awakened into the reality of American slavery by learning that a fugitive slave woman actually murdered her three-year-old daughter rather than have the child returned to slavery. This information allows for more discussion of social and historical questions, especially in conjunction with contemporary debates over race, class, and gender and over popular media bias: How did the 1856 newspapers respond to the infamous tragedy? How did black abolitionists respond? Was Garner heroic? What constitutes heroism? Wherein lie the boundaries of male definitions of heroism and gender-oriented resistance? What are the similarities and differences between nineteenth-century and contemporary newspaper reporting of a sensational crime? In today's media lexicon, the Garner case received gavel-to-gavel coverage.

Knowing the Garner story, a reader of *Beloved* might assume that many of the 1856 reports would denounce Garner as inhuman. On the contrary, in the newspaper accounts Garner was a heroic black mother, and the supporters of slavery kept quiet for a while. It must be remembered that her deed, although not the first of its kind, occurred at a time of rising antislavery activity, and the incident embarrassed the Southern cause.

Decidedly, abolitionism gained momentum in bringing to the international forefront the plight of slaves in the United States on the eve of the Civil War. England had already abolished slavery in the West Indies. Haiti had fought for its independence from France. The United States and Brazil were the last bastions of legal slavery in the Americas. Introducing this history to students expands their thinking about nineteenth-century democracy and the meaning of freedom. In addition, during the debate over slavery, Americans recognized that neither side condoned murdering one's children as a response to slavery. Morrison responds to such a sentiment in *Beloved* when it is said of Sethe, "She ain't crazy. She love those children. She was trying to outhurt the hurter" (234). Morrison, however, explores how Sethe hurts as deeply as she loves her children. The community of former slaves leaves Sethe alone after she serves her time. They will not condemn her, but neither can they condone the murder.

In the aftermath of the national debate over Anita Hill and Clarence Thomas, how are the issues of both race and gender still central to African American women? Should race and gender be considered separately, as many responses to the Hill-Thomas hearings indicate? Who should tell the stories? Students need to understand the ramifications of the exploitation of black women since the outset of American history.

The "true" story of Margaret Garner leaves many readers unsettled, disturbed, and even defensive if they are white American readers who feel guilt for the legacy of slavery—the continuing injustices of American racism. These issues can become sensitive and cloud the focus on Morrison's objectives. Thus the teacher should redirect attention to the novel to emphasize how Morrison's envisioning of truth and hope in *Beloved* is based on reconciliation. For although Margaret Garner did not succeed in fleeing from slavery, Sethe does.

Morrison writes novels because, as she has said, we no longer sit by the hearth to pass down stories; no matter how much bigger than life or discomforting her stories may be (such as Sethe's killing of Beloved and the rape of Pecola in *The Bluest Eye*), she makes them discomforting in order to open up avenues for discovery, investigation, and reconciliation. Hence we see how Morrison uses biblical allusion to highlight the theme of reconciliation. Students would know that the epigraph to *Beloved* taken from the New Testament appears to signify loss and rejection: "I will call them my people, which were not my people; and her beloved, which was not beloved" (Rom. 9.25). But Morrison's meaning transcends what the reader initially perceives. The reader must examine the rest of the biblical passage to discover that it signifies conciliation, endurance, and hope:

> And it shall come to pass, that in the place where it was said unto them, Ye are not my people; there shall they be called the children of the living God.   (Rom. 9.26)

Students can also be made aware of previous approaches to slave history. Most slavery studies rely on official records and the accounts of the slaveholding class because, except for a limited number of slave narratives, individual slaves did not leave accounts of their motivations and thought. Civil War clubs continue to reenact and strategize battles with no thought of the war's failure to erase the blight of American racism. The study of American slavery often rendered unheroic black women and men nameless or as generic types such as Uncle Tom, boy, Aunt Jemima, Aunt Sarah, or Jezebel. Thus the experiences of "named" black women and men during slavery must be reconstructed from history and created from literary imaginations. In the new historiography, scholars and students of slavery in the Americas now emphasize searching out those individual voices. However, the experiences of female slaves were different from those of bondmen. How did women seek to reconstruct their lives during and immediately after slavery? What personal circumstances affected their choices? How was gender informed by slavery, motherhood, and miscegenation? Morrison has said, "The [newspaper] clipping about Margaret Garner stuck in my head. I had to deal with this nurturing instinct that expressed itself in murder" (Clemons 75).

The following appendixes are three nineteenth-century responses to the Garner incident. Reading these accounts can help place the Garner incident in its historical context and help readers create their dialogue of reconciliation. And in doing so we remember the unknown Margaret Garners whose stories can never be written and place their legacies next to *Beloved*.

APPENDIX 1: THE SLAVE MOTHER OF CINCINNATI

. . . And what deed of noble heroism ringing through the world, what proud action, showing that the brave man tramples on life as on a dishonoured burden when the oppressor would clutch at his liberties, is like this stern deed of the poor ignorant black woman, done among her enemies in a dark corner of this land? Think of it! The slave-mother, with her children, after long tasting of the cup of servitude, at length flees desperately away to a free State; she is hunted; her den of refuge is found and surrounded; she is liable to be caught, and, perhaps with a slight punishment, to be held in those pleasant patriarchal relations of which we hear so much from Southern apologists. She belongs to a race remarkable for its affectionate and kindly disposition; she herself is described as a woman "of gently and amiable expression of countenance." What does she do? She takes on her knee the young girl-babe. The poor black has a mother's heart. That wee face, the cunning hands, the sweet smile, the crowing, the embrace, have endeared her to the negro woman as they do to the white woman, perhaps even more. She has probably dreamed, too, of the future of the days when the comely daughter should hold up and honour the aged mother. The slavehunters are thundering at the door! She must choose for the innocent girl. On the one side, Slavery—its nameless wrongs eating into the soul—its heart-agonies—its degradation—its unrewarded toil—its prostitution and shame; on the other Liberty! She chose as the noble of all ages have chosen—as you, reader would choose for your babe! She draws the sharp knife across the infant's throat! She seizes another child for the same end—she gashes and stabs the child of her own womb! She hopes, as we hear in the evidence, "to kill them and then to kill herself." It is not frenzy, though done in an inspiration; it is the noblest instinct. She is arrested in the act, and now, as all know, is on trial in Cincinnati for her freedom, while claimed as a criminal for murder by the State authorities. An important question arises between the State and the Federal powers; but for this, we do not care. This fearful event speaks to the civilized world of far more important things. That mother's hand, dripping with the life-blood of her babe; those low voices saying in the prison cell, "We will walk singing to the gallows, rather than go back to slavery," tell all base apologists and all selfish supporters what American slavery is. They say, in tones that thrill every heart where this fearful story goes, "The Negro is a MAN!—Liberty is to him as sweet as to us. He takes death before servitude!"

. . . And now we are to present to the world the disgraceful spectacle of a United States officer seeking to execute a law so barbarous that, to escape from it, the opposing counsel is glad to convict his clients of murder of their own children! A law is claimed to be based on the Constitution of American Liberty, which leads to infanticide and whose legitimate results are considered by its victims as incomparably worse than death on the gallows! But on this, words are useless. After such an event, one is ashamed of his country. We walk about as if it were a disgrace to be an American! We seem to be in sackcloth, and with bitter tears, and yet with faith, we pray, *"How long, O Lord! how long!"*

—C. L. Brace
National Anti-slavery Standard
1 Mar. 1856

APPENDIX 2: A VISIT TO THE SLAVE MOTHER WHO KILLED HER CHILD

Last Sabbath, after preaching in the city prison, Cincinnati, through the kindness of the Deputy Sheriff, I was permitted to visit the apartment of that unfortunate woman, concerning whom there has been so much excitement during the last two weeks.

I found her with an infant in arms only a few months old, and observed that it had a large bump on its forehead. I inquired the cause of the injury. She proceeded to give a detailed account of her attempt to kill her children.

She said that when the officers and the slave-hunters came to the house in which they were concealed, she caught a shovel and struck two of her children on the head, and then took a knife and cut the throat of the third, and tried to kill the other—that if they had given her time, she would have killed them all—that with regard to herself she cared but little; but she was unwilling to have her children suffer as she had done.

I inquired if she were not excited almost to madness when she committed the act? No, she replied, I was cool as I now am; and would much rather kill them at once, and thus end their sufferings, than have them taken back to slavery and be murdered by piece-meal. She then told the story of her wrongs. She spoke of her days of suffering, of her nights of unmitigated toil, while the bitter tears coursed their way down her cheeks, and fell in the face of the innocent child as it looked smiling up, little conscious of the danger and probable sufferings that awaited it.

As I listened to the facts, and witnessed the agony depicted in her countenance, I could not but exclaim, O how terrible is irresponsible power, when exercised over intelligent beings! She alludes to the child killed as being free from all trouble and sorrow, with a degree of satisfaction that almost chills the blood in one's veins. Yet she evidently possesses all the passionate tenderness of a mother's love. She is about twenty-five years of age, and apparently possesses an average amount of kindness, with a vigorous intellect, and much energy of character.

The two men and the oldest children were in another apartment, but her mother-in-law was in the same room. She says she is the mother of eight children, most of whom have been separated from her; that her husband was once separated from her twenty-five years, during which time she did not see him; that she could have prevented it, she would never [have] permitted him to return, as she did not wish him to witness her sufferings, or be exposed to the brutal treatment that he would receive.

She states that she has been a faithful servant, and in her old age she would not have attempted to obtain her liberty; but as she became feeble, and less capable of performing labour, her master became more and more exacting and brutal in his treatment, until she could stand it no longer; that the effort could only result in death, at most—she therefore made the attempt.

She witnessed the killing of the child, but said that she neither encouraged nor discouraged her daughter-in-law—for under similar circumstances she should probably have done the same. The old woman is from sixty to seventy years of age; has been a professor of religion about twenty years, and speaks with much feeling of the time when she shall be delivered from the power of the oppressor, and dwell with the Saviour, "where the wicked shall cease from being, and the weary are at rest."

These slaves (as far as I am informed) have resided all their lives within sixteen miles of Cincinnati. We are frequently told that Kentucky slavery is very innocent. If these are its fruits where it exists in a mild form, will someone tell us what we may expect from its more objectionable features? But comments are unnecessary.

P. C. Bassett,
National Anti-slavery Standard
15 Mar. 1856

APPENDIX 3: THE SLAVE TRAGEDY AT CINCINNATI

Bright the Sabbath sun is shining through the clear and frosty air.
Solemnly the bells are calling to the house of praise and prayer;
And, with hearts devout and holy, thither many wend their way,
To renew to God their pledges—but I cannot go to-day.

For my soul is sick and maddened with that fearful tale of woe,
Which has blanched the cheeks of mothers to the whiteness of the snow;
And my thoughts are wandering ever where the prison walls surround
The parents and their children, in hopeless bondage bound.

Oh, thou mother, maddened, frenzied, when the hunter's toils ensnared
Thee and thy brood of nestlings, till thy anguished spirit dared
Send to God, uncalled, one darling life that round thine own did twine
Worthy of a Spartan mother was that fearful deed of thine!

Worthy of the Roman father, who sheathed deep his flashing knife
In the bosom of Virginia, in the current of her life!
Who, rather than his beauteous child should live a tyrant's slave,
Opened the way to freedom through the portals of the grave!

Well I know no stronger yearning than a mother's love can be
I could do and dare forever for the babe upon my knee!
And I feel no deeper sorrow could the light of life eclipse,
Than to see death's shadows settle on its brow and faded lips.

Yet (oh, God of Heaven, forgive me!), baby sitting on my knee,
I could close thy blue eyes calmly, smiling now so sweet on me!
Ay, *my* hand could ope the casket, and thy precious soul set free;
Better for thee death and Heaven than a life of slavery!

And before the Judge Eternal, this should be my anguished plea:
"They would rob my child of Manhood; so, uncalled, I sent it Thee!
"Hope, and Love, and Joy, and Knowledge, and her every right they crave;
"So I gave her what they left her—her inheritance—the grave!"

And the Lord would judge between us, oh ye men of stony heart!
Even 'gainst the strong and mighty, for the weak He taketh part;
Think ye, hunters of His children, bowed beneath your iron rod,
With your heel upon their heart-pulse, this ye do unto your God!

But the day of vengeance cometh—He will set his people free,
Though He lead them, like his Israel, through a red and bloody sea;
For the tears and gore of bondmen, staining deep the frighted sod,
And the wailing cry of millions riseth daily up to God!

Mary A. Livermore
National Anti-slavery Standard
16 Feb. 1856

Jazz: Morrison and the Music of Tradition

Craig Werner

The title of Toni Morrison's sixth novel clearly signals the importance of African American musical aesthetics to her literary voice. In this Morrison is hardly unique; at least since James Weldon Johnson's preface to *The Book of American Negro Poetry*, writers and critics have recognized the presence, the sound, of African American oral traditions in texts by Paul Laurence Dunbar, Langston Hughes, Zora Neale Hurston, Ralph Ellison, Alice Walker, and countless others. In teaching *Jazz* (as well as *Tar Baby* and *Song of Solomon*), I have found it useful to present students with a framework for understanding African American musical aesthetics through the interrelated gospel, blues, and jazz impulses. Such an understanding helps generate discussion of Morrison's relation to a range of cultural ancestors and traditions. Below I sketch the approach to African American music I have employed in numerous African American studies classes and demonstrate how such frameworks help students understand the elusive narrative voice of *Jazz*.

Grounded in the West African concept of "iwa"—an approach to character that, as Robert Farris Thompson observes, insists on the unbreakable connection between the fate of the individual and of the community—call and response lies at the core of African American musical aesthetics. As Harold Scheub demonstrates in his germinal work on African oral traditions, call and response begins with the call of a leader, who sings a song, tells a story, or describes an image. This call, which provides a communal context for exploration of the individual emotion, itself responds to a tradition that suffuses later stages of the call-and-response process. If the community, as it exists in the ever-changing present, recognizes and shares the experience evoked by the call, it responds with another phrase, again usually traditional, that may affirm or critique the call. In either instance the response enables the leader to go on exploring the implications of the material. Rich with political potential, this cultural form enables both individual and community to define themselves, to validate their experiences in spite of dominant social forces. At its most effective, this process requires individuals not to seek a synthesis, to deny the extreme aspects of their experiences, but to assert their subjectivity in response to other, equally personal and equally extreme assertions of experience. Call and response, then, is African American analysis: a process that, by admitting diverse voices and diverse experiences, supports a more inclusive critique than any individual analysis.

In applying the idea of call and response to teaching *Jazz*, it is useful to focus students' attention on the range of calls to which Morrison responds. Students familiar with either traditional literary analysis or African American music can respond to the musical dimensions of the novel. Students familiar with canonical works may recognize responses to Wallace Stevens's "Thirteen Ways of

Looking at a Blackbird" (Knopf, 153) or understand the story of Golden Gray as an inversion of Charles Bon's search for a father in *Absalom! Absalom!* (143–62). Those grounded in African American literature may hear responses to Jean Toomer's *Cane* (174) or Morrison's own *Song of Solomon* (when "[a] colored man floats down out of the sky" [8]). Discussion of the range of responses in the text can help students understand how Morrison's text calls for readers to develop a new, more inclusive sense of community. To elicit such responses, I have found it effective to present students with texts (whole or in excerpts) to which Morrison responds in *Jazz*. I ask them to identify the responding passages and explore the complexity of Morrison's response. In advanced classes I frequently ask the students to identify calls by focusing on Morrison's responses. In addition to emphasizing the breadth of Morrison's consciousness, the exercise provides the students with a working model of how the call-and-response process operates. Instead of focusing on the individual artist as a genius whose claim to authority rests on originality, the model shifts attention to West African ideas of the artist as transmitter and shaper of a constantly shifting cultural tradition. In addition, the identification of both calls and responses highlights the active participation of the audience in African American aesthetic practices. As Morrison's jazz narrator calls out at the end of the novel, "If I were able I'd say it. Say make me, remake me. You are free to do it and I am free to let you because look, look. Look where your hands are. Now" (229).

Before discussing the implications of Morrison's many responses to her complex literary heritage, it is useful to provide students with more-specific background on the meaning of jazz in African American culture. Ellison, the most insightful and influential theorist of the interconnection between African American music and literature, defines the jazz impulse as a way of defining and creating the self in relation to community and tradition (*Shadow*). As Ellison defines it, jazz—which may be music or another form of cultural expression—allows new ideas to enter the tradition. Ellison writes that

> true jazz is an act of individual assertion within and against the group. Each true jazz moment (as distinct from the uninspired commercial performance) springs from a contest in which each artist challenges all the rest; each solo flight, or improvisation, represents (like the successive canvases of a painter) a definition of his identity: as individual, as member of the collectivity and as a link in the chain of tradition.   (234)

Almost all successful jazz is grounded in what Ellison calls the blues impulse. Before artists can create meaningful new visions for individual and communal use, they must acknowledge the full complexity of their experience. In his classic essay on Richard Wright, Ellison defines the blues impulse as "an impulse to keep the painful details and episodes of a brutal experience alive in one's aching consciousness, to finger its jagged grain, and to transcend it, not by the consolation of philosophy but by squeezing from it a near-tragic, near-comic lyricism" (78–79). Although the blues impulse is rooted in intensely individual feelings, these feelings, for most black American blues artists, can be traced in part to the brutal racism experienced in some forms by almost all blacks. Substituting the less philosophical term *affirmation* for Ellison's idea of transcendence, Albert Murray emphasizes that, especially when the blues artist's call elicits a response that confirms a community's shared experience, the artist becomes "an agent of affirmation and continuity in the face of adversity" (*Hero* 38). Both the individual expression and the response of the community are crucial to the blues. The jazz impulse provides a way of exploring implications, of realizing the relational possibilities of the (blues) self, and of expanding the consciousness of self and of community through continual improvisation.

Although the gospel impulse has received less attention as a literary resource, it grounds the blues and jazz impulses in West African values and cultural forms. The black church—the institutional space furthest removed from the attention and mediation of whites—afforded African American communities relative autonomy to develop means to express their experience in music and speech. Expressing West African values (especially the connection of individual and community and the presence of the spirit in the material sphere) in a Christian vocabulary (employed in part to deflect white suspicion from black gatherings), the gospel impulse resists, though it has always felt the effects of, the European American analytical tradition. Although many whites, because they accept the authority of binary structures (black/white, male/female, mind/body, civilization/savagery, good/evil), behave like devils, the gospel impulse nonetheless holds out the possibility of universal salvation while providing an institutional setting for the communal affirmation of individual experience.

Recognized by numerous jazz and blues musicians as the foundation of African American music, the gospel impulse keeps alive the concept of difference from and within the white world. As Amiri Baraka notes in *Blues People*, both the call-and-response structure of the secular work songs and the AAB form of the classic blues can be traced to sacred forms that encode West African understandings of self, community, and spiritual energy (L. Jones). If the blues impulse can be described as a three-stage process—brutal experience, lyrical expression, and affirmation—then the gospel impulse can be described in three parallel terms from the sacred vocabulary of the African American church: the burden, bearing witness, and the vision of (universal) salvation. Bearing witness to his or her experience of the burden, the gospel artist—possessed by a "spirit" transcending human categorization—communicates a vision affirming the possibility of salvation for any persons willing, as the novelist Leon Forrest phrases it, to "change their name" (73). Whether its components are termed brutal experience or burden, "near-tragic, near-comic lyricism" or bearing witness, existential affirmation or spiritual vision, the blues and gospel process provides a foundation for African American artists' explorations of new possibilities for self and community.

This approach to African American musical aesthetics can be presented to students as a basis for understanding Morrison's adaptation of call and response in *Jazz*. Focusing on the effects of the great migration from the rural South to the urban North, Morrison emphasizes that changes in African American music reflect the community's changing sense of the world to which it must respond. The blues, linking the brutal experiences of the South and the North, continue to teach the newly arrived city dwellers that "laughter is serious. More complicated, more serious than tears" (113). The new music in *Jazz* sounds an urban blues of "clarinets and lovemaking, fists and the voices of sorrowful women" (7). Simultaneously, discontinuously, the new music holds out promises unthinkable in the South: "You would have thought everything had been forgiven the way they played" (196). Morrison portrays a modernist Harlem Renaissance that responds to Ezra Pound's modernist clarion call to "make it new": "At last, at last, everything's ahead. The smart ones say so and people listening to them and reading what they write down agree: Here comes the new" (7). The new music "made you do unwise disorderly things. Just hearing it was like violating the law" (58). Yet Morrison emphasizes the costs associated with this dizzying energy: the loss of the past, of the village self, of the gospel church that Violet leaves in the first paragraph, never to return: "There goes the sad stuff. The bad stuff. The things-nobody-could-help stuff. The way everybody was then and there. Forget that. History is over, you all, and everything's ahead at last" (7). Morrison's image of the "everything," however, emphasizes the isolation where Morrison's characters, destroyed like the tragic jazz artists Charlie Parker and Billie Holiday, sink into "indecent speechless lurking insanity" (179).

Morrison's novel can be discussed as a jazz-inflected response to two calls, one from Virginia Woolf, the other from *The Nag Hammadi*. These two examples can be used as touchstones for broader discussions of Morrison's relations to modernism and Afrocentrism. Both suggest the importance of women's voices to Morrison's response to, and construction of, her tradition.

When I use this approach in the classroom I discuss with my students a set of quotations that serve as originating calls. For Woolf I rely on quotations from Morrison's 1955 Cornell University MA thesis on alienation in the fiction of Woolf and William Faulkner. Contrasting Faulkner's repudiation of characters who choose alienation, which he views as a moral flaw, with Woolf's endorsement of "the objectivity of detachment" ("Virginia" 2), Morrison concludes, "To live in the privacy of self, remain apart from others and share nothing is [Woolf's] conception of an essential independence without which life is meaningless" (7). I present the students with the following passages from Woolf that Morrison quoted and that serve as calls to which Morrison responds: a passage from Woolf's diary describing life as "tragic . . . a little strip of pavement over an abyss"; Woolf's observation that "as the current answers don't do, one has to grope for a new one and the process of discarding the old when one is by no means certain what to put in their place, is a sad one" (5); and a passage from *Mrs. Dalloway* stating that "there is a dignity in people, a solitude; even between husband and wife a gulf; and that one must respect" (8).

In discussing Morrison's response, I encourage students to base their answers on their own experiences; I do not insist that there is one correct conclusion (which would be inconsistent with the aesthetic processes of African American communities). Nonetheless, it is important that the teacher not disavow his or her response. My understanding of Morrison's response—reflected in my crafting of the call through the choice of quotations—is that both Morrison's thesis and *Jazz* reject Woolf's claim to objectivity as a self-protective delusion; the narrator of *Jazz* admits to being "confused in my solitude into arrogance, thinking my space, my view was the only one that was or that mattered" (220).

Although the elusive narrative voice of *Jazz* shifts shape almost continually, it echoes at the outset of the novel several of Woolf's premises. Contemplating the pressure of the city, the narrator recommends self-control as defense against external attacks: "If you don't know how, you can end up out of control or controlled by some outside thing" (9). Aware of how many people, uprooted from their villages, flee first to the city and then to themselves, it describes Dorcas's face as "[a]n inward face—whatever it sees is its own self" (12). Violet's customers seek "the space that need not be filled with anything other than the drift of their own thoughts," though "they wouldn't like it" because it would force them to confront the "seep of rage" (16). Intimating the risk that accompanies any real confrontation with experience, with self or other, Morrison's narrator revoices a recurring (post)modernist theme when she describes the "private cracks" in the foundation of Violet's interior world (22). Echoing Woolf and other psychological modernists such as Ernest Hemingway and Henry James, Morrison describes Violet as she

> wakes up in the morning and sees with perfect clarity a string of small, well-lit scenes. In each one something specific is being done: food things, work things; customers and acquaintances are encountered, places entered. But she does not see herself doing these things. She sees them being done. The globe light holds and bathes each scene, and it can be assumed that at the curve where the light stops is a solid foundation. In truth, there is no foundation at all, but alleyways, crevices one steps across all the time. But the globe light is imperfect too. Closely examined it shows seams, ill-glued cracks and weak places beyond which is anything. Anything at all. (23)

This vision of a world without certainty can be understood either (in high-modernist terms) as a source of alienation requiring a Woolfean withdrawal to the interior or (in jazz terms) as a call to recognize a shared communal experience. Even as Morrison creates a vision that, just as Morrison's thesis does explicitly, implicitly repudiates Woolf's choice, she remains aware that a highly developed sense of interior process is necessary to the call-and-response dynamic, to jazz, in an urban world where many persons, like Violet, respond to their brutal experience by "drowning in it, deep-dreaming" (108).

Morrison's resolution of the social and psychological dimensions of *Jazz* hinges on her recognition of the need to recover understandings of the mysterious wellsprings of human life, understandings that honor the importance of Africa, black women, and the gospel impulse as continuing sources of wisdom in the chaotic modernist world. Seeking a response from his "wild woman" mother (165), Joe calls out to a tree—a fundamental emblem of power in African philosophy—whose response he cannot understand: "'Give me a sign, then. You don't have to say nothing. Let me see your hand. Just stick it out someplace and I'll go; I promise. A sign. . . . You my mother?' Yes. No. Both. Either. But not this nothing" (178). Against the felt reality of this nothing, Morrison's narrator attempts to envision new possibilities: "Now I have to think this through, carefully, even though I may be doomed to another misunderstanding. I have to do it and not break down. Not hating him is not enough; liking, loving him is not useful. I have to alter things." The narrator assumes visionary tones: "I want to be the language that wishes him well, speaks his name, wakes him when his eyes need to be opened" (161).

Nearing the mysterious source of calls and responses, this voice recalls the epigraph to *Jazz*, a quotation from *The Nag Hammadi*, a collection of texts in Coptic (the ancient Egyptian language written in Greek letters) recovered in Egypt in 1945. Morrison quotes from the section titled "Thunder, Perfect Mind," a relatively brief section narrated by a female figure who speaks in a variety of voices, all resounding with her immense generative power:

> I am the name of the sound
>> and the sound of the name.
> I am the sign of the letter
>> and the designation of the division.

These apparently contradictory qualities also characterize the narrative voice in *Jazz*, which resists classification as omniscient (as it seems when recounting the story of Golden Gray) or limited (as when it engages in village gossip or reflects on its inability to envision Joe and Violet's reconciliation). The voice of "Thunder, Perfect Mind," like Morrison's, insists on the ongoing dialogue between interior and exterior, a dialogue that creates, enforces, and, potentially, subverts the terms of the divisions that define human discourse, whatever their manifestation in a specific time or place:

> For what is inside of you is what is outside of you,
>> and the one who fashions you on the outside
>>> is the one who shaped the inside of you.
> And what you see outside of you,
>> you see inside of you;
>>> it is visible and it is your garment.   (302)

In the specific urban context that divides selves and communities in *Jazz*, this African voice provides renewed access to the gospel foundation, the vision of community and possible salvation, lost as the village became city. Morrison's choice of a narrative voice echoing that of a visionary African woman seems particularly significant in the light of *The Nag Hammadi*'s editor's attempts to minimize the African elements of the collection by describing the verses as "originally a Greek literary productivity" (13) and to dismiss the "antithetical, paradoxical" voice of the "Thunder, Perfect Mind" section as "difficult to classify" (296). Asserting a consciousness that does not accept the power dynamic underlying Du Bois's formulation of double consciousness, the text anticipates just such a response:

> Why then have you hated me, you Greeks?
>   Because I am a barbarian among [the] barbarians?
> For I am the wisdom [of the] Greeks
>   and the knowledge of [the] barbarians.
> I am the judgment of [the] Greeks and of the barbarians.
> [I] am the one whose image is great in Egypt
>   and the one who has no image among the barbarians.
>   (302)

Framing her excavation of the multilayered African American past with this invocation of the feminine, African energy that centers, creates, decenters, re-creates the process that shapes meaning, Morrison grounds her jazz vision in the gospel impulse. Acknowledging her own limitations, the narrative voice—at this point, the voice of Morrison's lost villages—echoes the gospel image of the "home in that rock," responding to the wild woman not as destructive nightmare but as "a playful woman who lived in a rock" (221). As she prepares to sound her final call—"Look where your hands are. Now" (229)—the narrative voice provides one of the most affirmative images in Morrison's fiction, one of Joe and Violet at rest: "[T]he mattress, curved like a preacher's palm asking for witnesses in His name's sake, enclosed them each and every night and muffled their whispering, old-time love" (228). A gospel response to blues lives down home and up North, to jazz calls that drive crazy the folks who make those calls possible, to "the voices of the women in houses nearby singing 'Go down, go down, way down in Egypt land . . .' Answering each other from yard to yard with a verse or its variation" (226).

COLORS AND SOUNDS:
LANGUAGE, STYLE, AND TECHNIQUE

Morrison on Morrison:
Using Interviews to Teach Morrison

Terry Otten

D. H. Lawrence long ago warned us to "trust the tale and not the teller." And although we assume his famous remark refers to point of view in fiction, we tend to extend it as well to writers' comments about their own works. Indeed, it is almost a cliché that literary figures are their own worst critics. That is not always true, however, as Toni Morrison demonstrates in her interviews.[1] Though sometimes controversial—as in her 1989 *Time* interview in which she appears to advocate teen pregnancies (Angelo)—she often discusses her fiction and the importance of its themes with extraordinary eloquence and insight. I have used the interviews extensively in undergraduate classes to introduce not only individual novels but also Morrison's formative ideas about the black experience in American culture; the influence of her personal experiences on her work; her acute consciousness of her role as an Afro-American female author; her writing strategies; and her awareness of other Afro-American authors.

I assign interviews for a number of pedagogical reasons. Most important, I find that students usually feel more comfortable and confident responding to Morrison when they have some sense of her as a person and a familiarity with her seminal themes and narrative techniques. Such confidence pays dividends when one introduces students to a writer as complex and rich as Morrison. I ask students to use Morrison's comments as a source of their ideas, I draw on quotations to develop paper topics on individual or multiple works, I employ quotations in examination questions, I assign papers that relate Morrison's views to those of other Afro-American authors, and I direct students to read interviews and to list comments that seem applicable to the novel we are reading.

I certainly advocate using audio- and videotapes to incorporate Morrison's imposing presence and majestic readings into the class experience and discussion (particularly good tapes include the interview with Bonetti; Bridglal; *Profile* [mostly about *Beloved*]; *World*), but I prefer using texts for most assignments. Students watching or listening to a tape without a transcript find it difficult to follow an idea or to retain the power of Morrison's language (and rental or purchase costs can be prohibitive). I consider here only selected written interviews that I have used successfully in mostly beginning-level undergraduate classes.

One set of assignments might address themes in Morrison's novels. After discussing an interview, students might trace specific ideas in particular interviews. Below are a few representative topics, along with related provocative quotations. Because of space limitations I focus below primarily on quotations that apply to more than one novel. Although some of the interviews I cite concern particular novels, most span the range of Morrison's work to the time of the interview.

Love   The theme runs throughout the interviews. Morrison comments, "Actually, I think, all the time that I write, I'm writing about love and its absence . . . [,] how people relate to one another and miss it or hang onto it . . . or are tenacious about love." She continues, "People do all sorts of things under its name, under its guise. The violence is a distortion of what, perhaps, we want to do" (Bakerman 60). Furthermore, "Love, in the Western notion, is full of possession, distortion, and corruption. It's slaughter without the blood" (Tate 123). In an interview with Anne Koenen, she discusses "romantic love" and "blues," especially in reference to *Song of Solomon*, deriding the "notion of love that's the business of the majority culture"; she also contrasts the expansive love of the Afro-American community with "the desperate need to love only one person" and comments on sexual love in her fiction and how she evokes it through language rather than "describes" it (211, 212). Speaking with Gloria Naylor, she observes that "very seldom can the other person bear the weight of all your attention," and she expresses her interest (manifest in *Beloved* and *Jazz*) in exploring how "a woman loved something other than herself so much" (Naylor 574, 584). Elsewhere, she notes that Afro-Americans were attracted to the idea of love in Christianity and that "this very pure, very aristocratic love . . . made them the most civilized people in the world" (Ruas 242). She remarks to Mervyn Rothstein that "mother love," in *Beloved* especially, "is also a killer . . . [because] the precious interior, the loved self . . . is suppressed or displaced and put somewhere else." In the same interview she anticipates writing *Jazz*, which "deals with a woman who sacrifices herself for her lover." To Marsha Darling she describes her intent in *Beloved* to explore how "to love something bigger than yourself . . . and not to sabotage yourself, not to murder yourself" (6).

The Village and the Ancestor   Morrison frequently mentions the "village" (or "tribe" or "neighborhood"), but she addresses the topic at length with Robert Stepto, Thomas LeClair, Koenen, Bessie W. Jones, Charles Ruas, Amanda Smith, and Elsie B. Washington. She says that her writing is "fiction that is really for the village, for the tribe" (LeClair 26). She notes the conflict between the tribe and new urban values, the traditional subversion of the white dominant culture by the Afro-American community, the loss of the village, and the writer's job of preserving the lore of the village. In all her novels, she observes, "there is this town which is both support system and a hammer at the same time" (Smith 50). She frequently refers to the archetypal ancestor figure, embodied in such central characters as Eva Peace, Pilate, Therese, Baby Suggs, and Stamp Paid (see esp. Koenen; McKay; Jones; Washington; Wilson). Useful quotations for class discussion include "Kill your ancestors, you kill all. There's no future, there's no past, there's just an intolerable present" (Koenen 213) and "It's the DNA, it is where you get your information, your cultural information. . . . Our Ancestors are part of . . . an ever widening circle" (Washington 137). (Morrison comments on ancestors indirectly in most other interviews.) Instructors may also assign Morrison's essays "City Limits, Village Values" and "Rootedness" in conjunction with these themes. In "Rootedness" she writes, "If anything I do, [sic] in the way of writing novels (or whatever I write) isn't about the village or the community or about you, then it isn't about anything" (344).

Good and Evil   Morrison gives interesting responses on this pervasive theme in several interviews, especially the interview with Jane Bakerman and the following selected examples. To Stepto she observes, "Sometimes good looks like evil; sometimes evil looks like good—you really never know what it is"; Sula is "a classic type of evil force" (216, 215). Speaking with Claudia Tate, she emphasizes that evil in the Afro-American community is a given, "not an alien force" (129). Elsewhere, she contrasts Sula's supposed wickedness with Hannah and Eva's (Koenen). On her treatment of morality as a writer, she says, "I try to burrow as deeply as I can into characters and I don't come up with all good or all bad" (McKay 420) and "I don't trust any judgment that I make that does not turn on a moral axis" (Jones 137). She notes that the Afro-American community accepts evil as "a natural presence in the world" and does not "tar" or "feather" some "disgraceful" person, whereas the Western "notion of evil" is "to annihilate it" (Ruas 223). On Sethe's killing of Beloved she comments, "It was absolutely the right thing to do, but she had no right to do it" (Rothstein; cf. Eva Peace); "The only person who could judge [Sethe]," Morrison tells Darling, "was the daughter she killed" (5). Morrison makes numerous other observations on particular characters or incidents of seeming evil, such as Cholly's rape of Pecola and Eva's murder of Plum. And in several interviews Morrison discusses the features of black cosmology that invert Western assumptions about good and evil (see Stepto; Tate; McKay).

I have directed students to many other relevant topics in the interviews, such as the use of myth and the supernatural, lore and memory, opposites, sense of place, and naming, as well as general subjects including Morrison's views of current writers, autobiographical elements in her work, and her attitude toward the criticism of her novels. Morrison's reflections on her writing strategies in particular provide a vast reservoir of ideas that help students appreciate Morrison's art and understand individual novels; the following are just a few sample subjects.

Characterization   In the Bakerman interview Morrison notes that symbols can evoke a character (for example, Sula's return is not described by Morrison but rather announced by a plague of robins) and that characters often form complementary pairs, Nel and Sula, for example, and Milkman and Guitar: "each one lack[s] something that the other [has]" (Stepto 216). Characters with grotesque features like Eva and Pilate, she comments, need to "literally invent themselves" (Tate 128). She makes a similar observation to Koenen: "I needed some reason for [Eva and Pilate] to be self-invented" (217). In the same interview she says, "I don't like to do research, but I try very hard to make [a character] organic. . . . My characters are always at some huge crisis situation, and I push them all the way out as far as they will go" (211, 212). She also tells Koenen, "With a character, I do what an actress does: I get inside, I try to see what it looks like and then feel and let them do what I think they'd do" (210). To Nellie McKay, Morrison notes that her characters are "bits" of good and bad— "If you judge them all by the best they have done, they are wonderful. If you judge all by the worst they have done, they are terrible. . . . I need to see how they see the world" (423–24). Sula and Nel, she says, embody "those two desires, to have your adventure *and* safety" (Naylor 577). With Jones, Morrison speaks of characters who represent poles (Macon and Pilate, Son and Jadine), who are "archetypes" (138), and who demonstrate a conflict between outrage and the fear of anarchy (Macon Dead, Jadine, Ondine, and Sydney). Elsewhere she comments extensively on characterization in the novels up to *Song of Solomon* (Ruas) and responds to the charge that her characters are sometimes bigger than life: "I felt I was writing about people who were as big as life, not bigger than life. Life is very big" (Smith 51). Morrison explains why she did little research on Sethe: "I really wanted to invent her life" (Rothstein; see also Koenen; Darling). She insists she is "just interested in *finally* placing black women center stage in the text . . . flawed here, triumphant there, mean, nice, complicated women, and some of them win and some of them lose" (Davis 149). Morrison also treats the relation between her female characters and feminist ideas (see esp. Koenen; Lester; Jones).

Style and Narrative Technique   Morrison discusses style in all the interviews. Here is a limited selection of quotes I have used: "[I want to give] enough of the outline . . . give the language and [the reader] will understand. . . . I didn't want to explain anything" (Bakerman 59); "[writers are like dancers] on stage in their relation to gravity and space and time. [Language] is energetic and balanced, fluid and in repose" (LeClair 25); "[The language] must not sweat" (LeClair 27; also in Bakerman 56); "[Language] has a space that's very biblical and meandering and aural—you really have to hear it" (Wilson 134); "[I leave] holes and spaces . . . the reader can come into" (Tate 125); "[I want] to avoid editorializing abstractions" (Tate 127); "[The language reveals] something underneath much more primitive" in a love scene between Sula and Ajax (Koenen 215); "For a black writer to be didactic is really a cardinal sin. . . . [You should not] go to a book the way you go to a medicine cabinet" (Naylor 579); "We're taught to read [books] like you open a medicine cabinet and get out an aspirin and the headache is gone" (Davis 150); "[The language of Afro-Americans is] full of metaphor and imagery. . . . It has sight and sound" (Jones 140); in the same interview Morrison notes the use of irony in the style of black writers; "I wanted not to have to explain" but to achieve authentic "black language" in "the way words are put together, the metaphors, rhythms, the music" and not to resort to "some kind of phonetic alphabet." She further comments that she likes "writing on the edge, when at any moment you can be maudlin, saccharine, grotesque, but somehow pull back from it" (Ruas 219). "I know if the action is violent," she later remarks, "the language cannot be violent; it must be understated" (222). She also explains that she wants to make her reader "naked and vulnerable" and to experience "a strong intimacy [with characters] that's so complete it humanizes [the reader]" (233). "[I attempt] to make literature—A-U-R-A-L—work because I hear it. . . . the way I hear it is the way I write it" (Davis 148); "[The reader and I] invent the work together. . . . It's a total communal experience. . . . I want somebody to say amen!" (Davis 148).

Endings In several interviews Morrison responds to the criticism that her novels end too ambiguously, obscurely, or negatively; she calls the endings "more vital" than the prescriptive "happy ending" (Wilson 133). "At the end of every book," she tells Koenen, "there is an epiphany, discovery, somebody has learned something that they never would have otherwise. . . . You just know that something has come full circle, something has clicked, a door is shut. Life is like that. . . . Whether it shakes you or quiets you, depends on what the thing was itself" (213, 221). "But," she adds, "I always know the endings. . . . I don't strive for sad endings, and I don't strive for obscure ones. I just know that's it" (221). Speaking with McKay she compares the novels, which share an "open ended quality," to jazz, in which there is "no final chord . . . something [is] held in reserve" (429). In her novels characters "learn something. . . . There is a press toward knowledge, at the expense of happiness perhaps" (424). She comments to Jones, "Order is restored at the end—and the characters have a glimmer of some knowledge they didn't have when the book began. . . . Something important has happened; some knowledge is there—the Greek knowledge—what is the epiphany in Greek tragedy" (135); she also notes "the tragic mode" in her interview with LeClair (28). In the Jones interview she gives particular attention to the endings of *Sula*, *Song of Solomon*, and *Tar Baby*; she observes, "I don't shut the doors at the ends of my books" (135). She focuses on the endings of *Song of Solomon* and *Tar Baby* in the interview with Ruas: "I always know the ending; that's where I start. . . . [The novel] doesn't shut, or stop here. That's why the endings are multiple endings. That's where the horror is. That's where the meaning rests; that's where the novel rests" (224, 225). Elsewhere she notes that her endings are "never like a Western folktale where they all drop dead or live happily ever after" (Darling 6). In reference to *Song of Solomon* she says, "This marvelous epiphany has taken place, and, if I close the door, then it would be misleading to say this thing or that." About that novel and about *Tar Baby* she states, "The reader or listener is in it and [has] to THINK. . . . That's what I mean by participatory—you have to think what do you want it to be" (Davis 149).

Again, these examples illustrate just a few prominent elements in Morrison's writing strategy that Morrison alludes to consistently. The instructor could design class assignments around many of the quotations.[2] Morrison's interviews offer a plethora of topics and quotable passages, constituting not only an essential tool for serious research but also a valuable resource for the classroom.

NOTES

[1] Interviews with Morrison appear in the works-cited section under Morrison's name.

[2] The quotations I have used in class include the following: "It is only by exploration of the past that we can live" (Shange 48); "I like to work, to fret, the cliché" (LeClair 26); "A good cliché can never be overwritten; it's still mysterious" (Tate 120–21); "My mode of writing is sublimely didactic in the sense that I can only warn by taking something away" (i.e., the happy ending) (Koenen 213); "[I write about] what is valuable and what is not, what is true . . . not factual, but true and authentic—and what is not" (Smith 51); "The best things we do often carry seeds of one's own destruction" (Rothstein); "I think what's important about [the literature] is the process by which we construct and deconstruct reality in order to be able to explain it" (Washington 58); "Looking for the easy, passive, uninvolved and disengaged experience—television experience . . . I won't, I won't do that" (Davis 150).

Sula: Imagery, Figurative Language, and Symbols

Elizabeth B. House

Sula is a challenging novel for students. On first reading, the characters seem larger than life, the plot is difficult to define, and point of view and theme are complex and not easily pinpointed. Indeed, undergraduates often voice concern about how even to begin making sense of *Sula*.

This beautiful and original novel can be approached in several ways, but one particularly useful tack is to ask students to study it as if it were a poem. *Sula* is as finely crafted as a sonnet, and careful rereadings—with attention to literary devices such as imagery, figurative language, and symbols—increase students' understanding of the novel's sound and sense.

In preparing to teach any book, I usually begin by creating lists of questions for discussion; I then ask students to write their own. Often our questions overlap, and by comparing lists we begin to define what we want to understand about the work. Thus, before I mention symbols or imagery patterns, the class and I set our goals for understanding *Sula*; we identify questions we wish to answer.

Usually, students have no trouble coming up with puzzling incidents in *Sula*, and typically we pose queries such as the following:

1. Sula does not appear until well into the novel and dies before its end. Why does Morrison choose this structure for a novel entitled *Sula*?
2. Why does Shad inaugurate National Suicide Day? What does he hope to accomplish?
3. A number of characters leave their community, the Bottom, and then return. What effects do their journeys have on them?
4. What do Plum, Shad, and Sula have in common?
5. After BoyBoy deserts her, Eva leaves town and later returns minus one leg but with newfound prosperity. Some people think she let a train sever her leg to gain money to live. If she did, was she justified in doing so? Did she do the "right thing"? What connection does Eva's act have to Sula's behavior when confronted by the Irish white boys? Is there a connection between these acts and Shad's annual "Suicide Day"?
6. Why does Eva set fire to Plum? Why does Sula watch Hannah burn without doing anything to help her? After Chicken Little falls into the water, why don't Sula and Nel try to rescue him or go for help?
7. What are various characters' interpretations of the birthmark over Sula's eyes? What do these observations tell us about Sula and about the persons who make them?
8. Hannah asks Eva, "Mama, did you ever love us?" (67), and Sula overhears Hannah say that she loves Sula, her daughter, but doesn't like her. In Morrison's view, what is love? Who in the novel loves whom? What is your definition of *love*?

9. What effects do Sula's and Nel's families have on their views of the world?
10. The community in *Sula* acts like the chorus in a Greek tragedy. What values does the community hold?
11. On her deathbed, Sula asks Nel, "How you know? . . . About who was good. How you know it was you? . . . Maybe it was me" (146). Who is good, Sula or Nel? What is the town's point of view, Morrison's point of view, your own?

Instead of using strict chronological plot to link events, Morrison relies on figurative language and symbolic patterns to structure and give form to *Sula*.[1] Thus, as the class and I seek answers to the questions we have raised, we examine Morrison's narrative strategies and her use of literary devices.

Sula begins, "In that place, where they tore the . . . blackberry patches from their roots to make room for the Medallion City Golf Course, there was once a neighborhood," and in large part, the novel is about the life and death of this African American community, the Bottom (3). Ultimately, urban "progress" and "renewal" destroy this neighborhood: the golf course replaces blackberry patches, pollution kills the river's nourishing fish, and a tunnel built for commercial purposes collapses and kills many Bottom inhabitants. Also, people who leave the Bottom lose touch with their nurturing roots and are damaged by the competitive, profit-seeking urban world.

One of *Sula*'s main themes, then, is the importance of maintaining links to one's heritage and community. Morrison conveys this idea by using imagery to show conflicts between the Bottom's simple, nurturing life and outside commercial forces of "progress." Among the most important symbolic patterns in *Sula* are those dealing with settings (the rural Bottom vs. the urban outside world), food imagery (nutritious, natural fruits and vegetables linked to the Bottom vs. city-produced, commercially prepared, sweet junk food), and aural images (comforting voices of community vs. the silence of isolation).

Another contrasting imagery pattern Morrison uses in *Sula* and throughout her work is order versus disorder or form versus chaos. Characters in *Sula*, as well as all humans, must decide how much to conform to society's needs for uniformity and how much to rebel and, thus, maintain their individuality. Also, all humans must in some way deal with chaos, the disorder brought about by life's inherent mutability. In biblical terms, there is a time to sow and a time to reap, a time to be born and a time to die. All living organisms go through the natural cycle of creation and birth to disorder and death. In some way, people must accept such changes.

Some of Morrison's characters, such as Eva and Nel, mistakenly believe it is desirable and possible to eradicate disorder, and so they attempt to control life and its mutability in unhealthy ways. Others, such as Sula, make the opposite error, rejecting all order, even that which one must accept to be part of a community. In other novels Morrison describes characters such as Pilate in *Song of Solomon* and Claudia in *The Bluest Eye* who balance form and chaos and live creative, productive lives. In *Sula*, however, no character is able to do so. (I examine Morrison's imagery of food and of order and disorder at greater length in "Artists" and "'Sweet Life.'")

Often the class and I begin discussion of *Sula* with an examination of Shadrack. Shad's ordeals foreshadow many of Sula's dilemmas, and thus one answer to the question of why Sula appears late in the novel is that Morrison prepares for Sula's introduction by delineating other characters' experiences.[2]

War, perhaps the most competitive of all human endeavors, compels Shadrack to leave the Bottom, the community that has nurtured him. Shad's neighborhood is linked to artistic sounds, creations that impose form on life's chaos: "singing sometimes, banjo sometimes" or "the lively notes of a mouth organ" (4). Away from the Bottom, Shad's life is shattered.

As a soldier in France during World War I, Shadrack sees a comrade's head severed in battle and, in horror, watches the resulting "drip and slide of brain tissue" (8). This scene of complete disorder devastates Shad, and he is hospitalized, disoriented and unable to control his hands enough to feed himself.

His perceptions in disarray, Shadrack is convinced that his hands grow chaotically "in higgledy-piggledy fashion" every time he brings them out from under the covers (9). The lonely, confused soldier is grateful when hospital orderlies bind him in a straitjacket, for then "laced and silent" he can try "to tie the loose cords in his mind" and return form to his life (10).

Finally released from the hospital, Shad finds himself on the urban institution's grounds inhaling "a sweetish smell which reminded him of something painful" (11). Shadrack wants to escape the hospital's concrete walks, but, most of all, he wants to return to his home, a place he connects with "someone . . . speaking softly" and remembers as being "on a river which he knew was full of fish" (10). Alone and afraid, Shad cries "soundlessly" (12), and finally a sheriff finds him a ride home in a farmer's wagon loaded with nutritious vegetables, "sacks of squash and hills of pumpkins" (14).

Faced with the problem of how to exist in a world fraught with sights such as the headless soldier, Shadrack "[begins] a struggle . . . to order and focus experience" (14). The result is National Suicide Day, an event whose creation is an attempt to contain death's disorder: "It was not death or dying that frightened him, but the unexpectedness of both" (14). He thinks that if death could be confined to one day, contained within twenty-four hours, humanity could deal with it. Suicide Day becomes a part of the community's fabric, and the minister notes that parishioners who insist on "drinking . . . or womanizing themselves to death" "[m]ay's well go on with Shad and save the Lamb the trouble of redemption" (16).

But order is not so easily achieved. A veteran observer of death, Shad most likely sees Chicken Little drown; thus, when Sula enters his cottage, he believes she is asking him a question he can answer.[3] Shad thinks of the soldier with dripping brains, and as he looks at Sula, he sees "also the skull beneath, and . . . he had said 'always,' so she would not have to be afraid of the change—

the falling away of skin, the drip and slide of blood. . . . He had said 'always' to convince her, assure her, of permanency" (157). Interestingly, years later, as Sula is dying, she remembers Shad's one-word answer, "Always." However, since childhood she has interpreted the word to mean that Shad has "promised her a sleep of water always" (149). Sula and Shad think they have understood each other, but they have not.[4]

When Shad sees Sula lying dead in a funeral home, he realizes that there is no "always" and that Suicide Day has not warded off death and disorder. He understands that "he had been wrong. Terribly wrong. No 'always' at all. . . . It was then that he began to suspect that all those years" of leading Suicide Day "were never going to do any good" (157–58). Shadrack's attempts to control death, to contain disorder, are futile.

In describing Shad, Morrison establishes most of the imagery patterns with which she structures *Sula*. Shadrack leaves the Bottom and suffers irreparable harm in the outside, business-motivated, urban world. The soft voices, music, and simple foods (fish, squash, pumpkins) that he connects with community and home contrast with the concrete, silence, and sweet smell he links to the hospital and outside world. Once the class has examined Shadrack, we are ready to see how other characters contrast or compare with him. The patterns Morrison uses to depict Shad and his experiences illuminate answers to our other questions about the novel and provide us with a template for discussing Plum, Eva, Sula, and Nel.

Plum, Sula's uncle, also fights in World War I and he too returns to the Bottom permanently diminished. Released from his unit, he reenters the United States in 1919 but arrives home a year later: "He wrote letters from New York, Washington, D.C., and Chicago full of promises of homecomings, but there was obviously something wrong." When he finally does appear in the Bottom, he has "a black bag, a paper sack, and a sweet, sweet smile," and it soon becomes apparent that he is a drug addict (45).

Eva, Plum's mother, cannot tolerate her son's behavior, and one night she pours kerosene over him and sets him on fire. When she enters Plum's room, she finds besides the "bent spoon black from steady cooking" (45) other evidence of his unhealthy, city-influenced lifestyle: "There in the corner was a half-eaten store-bought cherry pie. Balled-up candy wrappers and empty pop bottles peeped from under the dresser" (46). The unhealthy, urban-produced sweets suggest the lure, the temptations, of the damaging outside world.

After the class and I discuss Plum's death, we often go back to explore Eva's life when Plum and his sisters were young. BoyBoy, Eva's husband and Plum's father, deserts the family when Plum is a baby. Eva struggles to feed the children, but finally, in desperation, she leaves the Bottom and returns eighteen months later minus one leg but with newfound prosperity. The most prevalent theory about her injury is that she stuck her leg "under a train to collect insurance" (93).

Undaunted by her physical condition, Eva takes control of her life, builds a house of many rooms, and supervises the various people she takes in to live with her. However, she is constricted by hatred for her ex-spouse. Although she has many human interactions, Eva confines herself to an upstairs bedroom for most of her life, and she is repeatedly characterized by images of extreme order, especially ironing. For example, when Nel visits Eva in the Sunnyvale Nursing Home, a place where the rooms are like "sterile green cages," the old woman is "ironing and dreaming of stairwells. She had neither iron nor clothes but did not stop her fastidious lining up of pleats or pressing out of wrinkles . . ." (167).

A central question about Eva is why she kills Plum, the son she loves. Students sometimes point out that when Sula and Nel discuss Eva's finances, Sula says that Hannah had insurance and that "Plum . . . had all that army insurance" (102). However, few students believe that Eva kills Plum for money.

Usually, the class concludes that Eva did place her leg under the train to collect insurance money. She exchanged something living, her limb, for money, something she could control or could use to control her life. But Eva kills Plum because she cannot stand the disorder his drug addiction occasions. She cannot abide the change, the diminishing, that war has brought to his personality. Shad tries to contain life and death with Suicide Day; similarly, Eva believes she can control chaos by taking life and death into her hands.

Students usually agree unanimously that Eva is not justified in killing Plum. However, we always have a spirited discussion about whether Eva did the "right thing" when she sacrificed her leg. In the exchange, I typically ask if connections exist between Eva's act and Sula's slicing off her fingertip to frighten the white boys who threaten her. Then I note the passage in which Nel muses about Sula's being so scared "she had mutilated herself, to protect herself" (101). To avoid impeding the discussion, I save my view for late in the class: Eva's self-mutilation as she sacrifices her leg and murders her own flesh, Plum, are acts of desperation similar to Sula's. However, in attempts to control disorder—the Irish boys' threat, children's hunger, Plum's drug addiction—Sula and Eva cause more chaos by trying to impose order in an inappropriate manner.

Like Shad, Plum, and Eva, Sula is also damaged by her sojourn outside the Bottom. Before she leaves home, the woman is viewed by the town with sympathy, at least partly because of her mother's violent death. (The town believes she stood and watched her mother burn because she was too shocked to move to help her.) However, when Sula returns from her ten-year stay in cities such as "Nashville, Detroit, New Orleans, New York, Philadelphia, Macon, and San Diego" (120), she quickly becomes an outcast in the community. (Robert Grant notes that Sula's ten-year absence between parts 1 and 2 is one of many "gaps, lacks, 'missing' subjects, and ambiguous psychic space, all of which must be filled and interpreted by the reader" [94].) She turns Eva out of her own home and warehouses her in the nursing home, seduces Nel's husband, and sleeps willingly with white men.

Morrison is an inspired name giver, and she links Shad, Plum, and Sula by giving each the name of a food. *Sula* is a genus of gannets, goose-like, edible seabirds. Similarly, shad is a fish and plum is a fruit. However, the characters' nurturing qualities, suggested by their names, are damaged by their experiences in the urban world. Like the blackberries that are mutilated to accommodate the Medallion Golf Course, Sula, Shad, and Plum are harmed by losing contact with their community.

On her deathbed, Sula asks Nel one of the novel's key questions, "How you know? . . . About who was good. How you know it was you? . . . Maybe it was me" (146). Morrison makes clear that the answer is not unequivocally that Nel is good and Sula bad. Rather, she hints that the two women are in some ways two halves of a whole; both err in becoming extremes rather than balancing order and disorder in their lives.

When Sula and Nel become friends at age twelve, both are "unshaped, formless things" (53), and they come from dramatically different homes. Nel lives "surrounded by the high silence of her mother's incredibly ordered house" (51) while Sula is "wedged into a household of throbbing disorder" (52).

As an adult, Nel overorders her life and follows too closely society's dictates about how "nice" people must behave. As a child, she had vowed never to let anyone turn her into "jelly" after seeing her imposing mother, Helene, become "custard" when confronted by an abusive white train conductor (22). However, after she marries Jude, Nel becomes one of the women who "[fold] themselves into starched coffins" (122). And after Jude's departure, she "pin[s] herself into a tiny life" (165), and even her love for her children becomes unhealthy, "a love that, like a pan of syrup kept too long on the stove, had cooked out, leaving only its odor and a hard, sweet sludge" (165). Again, Morrison links sweets to nonnurturing behavior.

Conversely, Sula has no order in her life; the woman has "no center, no speck around which to grow. . . . She [feels] no compulsion to . . . be consistent with herself" (119). Thus Sula flouts society to the point that the community will not help bury her after she dies. Even while making love, Sula experiences no real connection with another human: "There, in the center of that silence was not eternity but the death of time and a loneliness so profound the word itself had no meaning" (123). An "artist with no art form," Sula is unable to create a meaningful life for herself (121).

Beginning with the notion that the Bottom is actually high in the hills surrounding the town of Medallion, Morrison uses irony throughout *Sula*. And one of the chief ironies is that as the town's pariah Sula stimulates good behavior in other people. Her return to the Bottom is marked by a "plague" of robins (89), birds usually thought of as harbingers of spring and new life, and the various ways this event can be interpreted are mirrored by the differing interpretations of Sula's birthmark. The mark is interpreted variously as a rose (by Nel [96]), a "scary . . . thing" (by Nel's children [97–98]), a tadpole (by

Shad [156]), a copperhead (by Jude [103]), and Hannah's ashes (by the towns-people [114]), and Morrison uses these points of view to emphasize Sula's complex nature.

Most likely, many teachers have had undergraduate students ask them if they think a writer really intended the images or symbols in a work to "mean something." In several interviews, Morrison clearly details her dependence on such narrative strategies, and thus in answer to such questions I let the author speak for herself. In a *New Republic* interview with Thomas LeClair, for example, Morrison explains, "There are times in my writing when I cannot move ahead even though I know exactly what will happen in the plot and what the dialogue is because I don't have the scene, the metaphor to begin with" (28). Also, she notes in an interview with Mel Watkins in the *New York Times Book Review*, "Once I get the hook, the right metaphor for a scene, I'm all right" (48). When students grasp the importance of literary devices in *Sula*, they have a key for exploring the novel. They better understand how writers construct fiction, and they realize they are able to make sense of *Sula*.

NOTES

[1]Barbara Christian notes that although each of *Sula*'s chapters is assigned a date, the narrative "is not about the particular year for which it is named—rather some crucial event happens in that year which demands background" (*Black Women Novelists* 155). Christian's treatment of *Sula* in this volume remains one of the best critical studies of the novel.

[2]Deborah McDowell argues that Morrison purposely "defers" Sula's presence and thus downplays concepts such as "protagonist" and "hero" ("Self" 80).

[3]Houston A. Baker connects the ritual burial process that Nel and Sula complete before Chicken Little's death with Shad's and Sula's "common knowledge of disorder" (*Workings* 149).

[4]Morrison frequently describes such miscommunication. Similar misunderstandings are central to my argument that in Morrison's fifth novel Beloved is not a ghost but, rather, a real young woman who has survived the Middle Passage ("Toni Morrison's Ghost").

Reading in the Dark: Knowledge and Vision in *Song of Solomon*

Linda J. Krumholz

Milkman Dead's paternal aunt, Pilate, is both his teacher and his "pilot" in Toni Morrison's *Song of Solomon*. She begins her lesson early in the novel when she tells Milkman and his best friend, Guitar, about her birth, her near-death experiences, her father's death, and her father's appearance after his death. The section culminates with Pilate's explanation of blackness:

> You think dark is just one color, but it ain't. There're five or six kinds of black. Some silky, some woolly. Some just empty. Some like fingers. And it don't stay still. It moves and changes from one kind of black to another. Saying something is pitch black is like saying something is green. What kind of green? Green like my bottles? Green like a grasshopper? Green like a cucumber, lettuce, or green like the sky is just before it breaks loose to storm? Well, night black is the same way. May as well be a rainbow.
>
> (Signet-NAL, 40)

Pilate's blackness teems with color, life, movement. It is connected to the spiritual or supernatural forces of life and death, to the womb and the grave, and to the natural forces and growth metaphorically associated with green. In redefining blackness Pilate describes a way of seeing; her lessons help Milkman learn to see in the dark and to accept his blackness. At significant stages in his quest Milkman experiences intense darkness: when he and Guitar rob Pilate's "treasure" (186), in Hunters Cave (254), and on the hunt for the wildcat (276–83). In the darkness Milkman is blinded to externals, and he must find new ways to understand and to survive. Morrison's novel teaches the reader to see or read in the dark since our quest to garner meaning from the novel forces us to duplicate Milkman's efforts to interpret the words and signs he encounters. As Pilate's pedagogy initiates Milkman, Morrison's novel initiates the reader into new possibilities of perception, interpretation, and imagination.

Song of Solomon is an exciting and difficult novel to teach. Its density—its multiple stories and perspectives, its poetic richness, and its allusive threads—stimulates the reader's imagination. But this density can also overwhelm teachers and students who wish to analyze and engage with the work in a short time. In this essay I offer an approach to teaching this novel to undergraduates in five fifty-minute periods. My outline should be taken as suggestive rather than prescriptive, since the title of the course, the level of the students, and the interests of the teacher will necessarily shape approaches and emphases. My basic strategy is to shift back and forth between classes that focus closely on a scene or chapter and classes that treat issues more generally. The common thread of the discussions is Milkman Dead's quest for knowledge and personal meaning, which becomes Morrison's means of praising, criticizing, and revising concepts of black manhood and the relationships among black men, black women, and black children. Milkman's quest also contains ideas about how education works, how we learn to create and imagine ourselves, and how we develop our sense of meaning—personal, communal, spiritual, and political.

In the first class (which covers chs. 1–4) I establish a framework for reading the novel; I combine a brief introduction with a guided discussion. First I introduce the idea of the quest as a literary and epic form in which individuals (usually cast as heroes) seek out personal or communal meaning, and I discuss the particular relation of African American men and women to literary and historical quests. By connecting quests to education, the teacher can lead students to make connections between Milkman's learning process and their own reading and learning processes: what does Milkman learn and what do we learn as he learns? I also ask the students to look for mysteries, secrets, and riddles that arise and are solved throughout the novel.

Our subsequent discussion focuses on the first scene to establish what happens, what characters are present, what themes and riddles are set up, and how the scene relates to the birth of the hero, Milkman. For example, the names Dead and Bains, Doctor and Not Doctor Street, Mercy and No Mercy Hospital raise issues about the health and survival of the African American community in this northern Michigan city in the 1930s and suggest that Milkman's quest might connect to ailments in the community. The naming and renaming of the streets where the first scene is set also establish both the power struggle between blacks and whites and the humor and irony with which the black people maintain their definitions and knowledge. The scene involves a variety of mysteries: the significance of Robert Smith's flight, of Pilate's song, and of the scene itself as a precursor to Milkman's birth. Mention of mysteries and secrets within the family and the allusion to Corinthians's secret at the end of chapter 4 can anticipate the discussion of family dynamics in the next class.

In the second class (which covers chs. 5–9) I widen the focus to the various characters, their relations to Milkman, and their roles in Milkman's education and quest for meaning. The teacher may find it useful to contextualize the discussion by describing the ways we learn who we are from our family, friends, school, community, and religious institutions and from the media (and to ask students to think what these contexts would be for a black man growing up in the United States in the 1930s to 1960s); it may also help to discuss more specifically the role of family stories in shaping our sense of identity. (See Stone for an elaborate discussion of the power of family stories.) To facilitate discussion I divide the students into five groups, each of which discusses one character (Guitar Bains or Pilate, Hagar, Macon, or Ruth Dead). I ask the groups to report to the class on how the relationships between their characters and Milkman shaped Milkman's education and development. To tie together the reports, the teacher may point out contradictions between stories (like those of

Ruth and Macon or of Pilate and Macon) and conflicts between interpretations (like those of Milkman and Hagar or of Milkman and Guitar), all of which emphasize Milkman's complex and ongoing process of creating his sense of himself and the student's similar process of making meaning from the text. I conclude this discussion by asking what the students think Milkman still needs to learn to improve his sense of himself and his attitudes toward others as his quest continues in part 2.

In the third class, after the students have completed the novel, I shift the focus to chapter 11 and the lessons Milkman learns on his first days in Shalimar, his ancestral home. I discuss the chapter as Milkman's ritual of initiation into black manhood, analyzing the three main parts of his ritual—the "cock" fight with Saul, the hunt with the older men, and the skinning of the cat—and Milkman's new awareness. The "cock" fight can be connected to the recurring symbol of the peacock and to Lena's condemnation of Milkman's "little hog's gut" (218), and the class can then discuss Milkman's cockiness, his flaunting of masculine privilege, and his self-centeredness up to this point. The hunt section contains Milkman's central revelations, which can also be read as a symbolic death and rebirth (at Guitar's hands); Morrison's presentation of Milkman's transformation in the woods (278–84) warrants detailed attention, through which the class can discuss what constitutes Milkman's new vision— his new ability to see in the dark.

The skinning of the cat also has numerous symbolic and thematic implications, as the skinning process is juxtaposed with Milkman's recollection of Guitar's words *Everybody wants a black man's life* (285). Morrison's description of the evisceration reverberates with the history of the lynchings and brutalization of black men. At the end of the scene Milkman's initiation into black manhood is complete; he casts off "the heart of the white men" (269) and receives the heart of a lion (286). In the final scene of the chapter, when Milkman returns each gift reciprocally in his lovemaking with Sweet, we see how Milkman's new vision precipitates new behavior. The focus on these details can open up a more general discussion of manhood and blackness and their relation to the concepts of black manhood Morrison has constructed for Milkman. Blackness, in Morrison's novel, is also a way of knowing, a spiritual perception, a mode of survival, and a shift in values from Macon Dead's quest for acquisition to Pilate Dead's rainbow of possibilities.[1]

On the fourth and fifth days the discussions can range more widely through the novel. At the beginning of the fourth class I ask the students to write down all allusions to flight in the novel and to hazard some interpretations of the various images of flight. Our discussion centers on the list we compile on the board. We then tie the various representations of flight to Milkman's process of learning about his heritage, to his ability to interpret the "song of Solomon," and to his actions in the enigmatic final scene. This exercise inevitably raises the central contradiction contained in Milkman's quest and the imagery of flight— the tension between freedom and connectedness. We conclude our assessment of Milkman's quest and Morrison's revision of black manhood with a discussion of Hagar's death and Milkman's role in it.

In the final session we address the complexity of the novel and the reasons that Morrison encourages multiple interpretations. I write key phrases on the board: "Sing, Sing," "You just can't fly on off and leave a body" (148), "Song of Solomon," and "Milkman Dead," so that we can develop the multiple interpretive possibilities and the ways in which Morrison keeps alive contradictory interpretations. For example, Pilate's more literal and spiritual interpretations of the first two phrases (she sings and carries a dead man's bones) could be superseded by Milkman's knowledge of their historical implications (Pilate's father was married to Sing, and Pilate's grandfather flew off and left his family behind). But in the end, when Milkman accepts the box of Hagar's hair and sings to Pilate at her death, he has accepted Pilate's interpretations of her father's ghost's words.[2]

One might also interpret Milkman's name differently at different points in the novel. In part 1, the meaning of Milkman's name seems evident—Milkman Dead is a pampered mama's boy, suckled too long, and he is the inheritor of a dead culture, dispersed and useless, in which murder is the only solution. But in the spiritual and supernatural context of part 2, we can reinterpret his name with greater complexity. We discover that a connection to one's dead, one's ancestors, is the essence of a vital cultural heritage. We also learn that men must recognize their responsibility to nurture future generations. And (in a lighter vein) isn't the milkman a deliverer for his people? The various readings suggest that meaning is not inherent but created—you make a name for yourself.

With these multiple frameworks in place, the enigmatic concluding scene of Milkman Dead's flight is open to many interpretations. The symbolism of flight elucidates Morrison's treatment of the black male hero's quest. In *Song of Solomon*, Morrison uses flight in its most common association, to signify freedom, and at first *freedom* retains its most common definition in United States usage, escape and individual independence. In part 2, Milkman's airplane ride begins his quest. In his first opportunity to fly solo (as the soloman?) he feels freedom from the bonds of his family, friends, and past errors. But this flight seems mundane in comparison with the many wingless flights in the novel: Robert Smith's ominous flight that opens the novel, Milkman's great-grandfather's flight from slavery, and the flights of Pilate, Milkman, and Guitar in the final pages. Just as Milkman's quest shifts from one for gold to one for knowledge, his quest for freedom changes from the freedom obtained through the solitary power of money to the freedom gained through connections to others, imaginative engagement, and love. This type of flight is signified by Pilate, when Milkman realizes, "Without ever leaving the ground, she could fly" (340).

Milkman's great-grandfather Solomon's flight strengthens the association of flight with freedom while highlighting the ambivalence of this connection. Solomon, as in many African American stories of flying Africans, becomes a powerful symbol of freedom by flying from slavery home to Africa. But the power of his flight is diminished by Sweet's question, "Who'd he leave behind?" (332), and by the echo in Ryna's Gulch, which recalls the grief of Solomon's wife and of the twenty-one children left fatherless. Read in the light of Solomon's flight, Morrison's epigraph—"The fathers may soar / And the children may know their names"—seems contradictory. How can the fathers soar without leaving their children fatherless and their lovers loveless? This central question in the novel is the basis of Morrison's redefinition of freedom and of her reconsideration of the African American male quest.[3] Milkman achieves his flight at Solomon's Leap after he learns to embrace his connections with others; rather than a flight of escape, it can be seen as a flight of commitment.

Flight is also associated with the power of imagination. After Milkman's birth, presaged by Robert Smith's flight, the first thing we are told about Milkman is that "when the little boy discovered, at four, the same thing Mr. Smith had learned earlier—that only birds and airplanes could fly—he lost all interest in himself. To have to live without that single gift saddened him and left his imagination . . . bereft" (9). In part 2, Milkman's imagination blossoms as he engages the natural and supernatural forces surrounding him, which enable him to learn the lessons of the hunt, to hear the preliterate language of the woods, to "see" in the dark, to "read" the history hidden in the song of Solomon, and to learn that he can fly. Perhaps Milkman's final flight is also meant to precipitate the reader's flight of imagination beyond the ending of the book, when Milkman becomes our textual "Dead" to carry with us, as Pilate carries her father's bones.

The image of flight, then, encompasses ideas of freedom, of imagination, and, by extension, of reading. This corresponds to Robert Stepto's assertion that African American literature connects "the quest for freedom *and* literacy" ("Teaching" 18). Stepto argues, "The great gift of the best Afro-American literature to its readers is its historical and linguistic portrait of a culture—once imprisoned by an enforced illiteracy—questing for, finding, and relishing the written word" (23). (In a later article, Stepto amends this statement, adding, "Afro-American literature has developed as much because of the culture's distrust of literacy as because of its abiding faith in it" ["Distrust" 301].) For Stepto, Frederick Douglass's 1845 *Narrative*, the paradigmatic male slave narrative, exemplifies the connection by directly connecting Douglass's power over the written word to his struggle for and acquisition of freedom. But what does the connection mean for later generations of African Americans? How do we define freedom and literacy, and how does *Song of Solomon* shape our definitions?

Milkman and Douglass see literacy, as well as its relation to freedom, quite differently. Growing up comparatively wealthy in the 1930s and 1940s in an industrial city in Michigan, Milkman presumably became literate in the public schools. But Milkman's formal education does little to engage him personally— he is spoiled, self-centered, and bored, and he tries to ignore the political and familial stories he is told. Milkman must learn another kind of literacy; he needs to learn to read the signs and visions he sees. Milkman must find knowledge related to his own life to enable his self-creation, knowledge that will inspire his imagination and enable him to see beyond externals to the spiritual and practical knowledge that Morrison describes as the discredited knowledge of black people.

Women and children are essential to Milkman's achievement of flight—his freedom and literacy. The children's song contains his family history, suggesting the children's central role in cultural transmission. The women are, in many ways, the sustenance and ground from which Solomon and Milkman leap—like the promised land, they contain the milk of the mothers and the honey of the lovers (embodied by Ruth and Sweet). Pilate acts as Milkman's pilot, a guide, a mentor, and a model of the desired balance of strength, wisdom, and love. When teaching the novel, instructors might consider whether these representations perpetuate traditional gender roles in hero quests, in which women are helpers and guides, or whether Morrison breaks those traditions. Whether Morrison gives women more active roles and whether she feminizes Milkman in the end—through his attention to children's games, his use of women's gossip to interpret his origins, his mutual caring with Sweet, and his possible self-sacrificing in the conclusion—are central to our assessment of Morrison's redefinition of the hero quest and of black manhood. The questions—of how we define what is feminine and what is masculine and of how these definitions confine our behavior and our judgments—lead right into the question of how Morrison redefines black manhood so that "[t]he fathers may soar / And the children may know their names."

Song of Solomon is a complex and open-ended novel that draws the reader in with mysteries and riddles that ask to be solved. But they are not solved simply, as in a mystery novel; in Morrison's novel the mysteries raise as many questions as they answer—about race and gender; about hero stories and quests; and about how we construct and imagine ourselves through stories, language, and education. In the last class session the teacher may wish to address the context of the discussion: Why is this book being taught? Why is it part of this class and this curriculum? What does Morrison's novel teach us? *Song of Solomon* can provide fresh perspectives in the heated debate over multiculturalism and over what and how we should teach. Few of us can aspire to be ideal pedagogues like Pilate. But Pilate helped Milkman break free of the white ideological shell of his protected existence to see beyond the social encumbrances of wealth and status to the deeper meanings he finds in the dark. In a playful argument Milkman tells Guitar he wants to be an egg, but Guitar argues that he cannot, because eggs are white (115). When Milkman persists, Guitar responds, "Then somebody got to bust your shell" (116). Perhaps that is part of every teacher's job.

NOTES

[1]In her essay "Rootedness" Morrison describes the "discredited knowledge of black people" as a knowledge that "blend[s] the acceptance of the supernatural and a profound rootedness in the real world at the same time with neither taking precedence over the other. It is indicative of the cosmology, the way in which Black people looked at the world. We are very practical people, very down-to-earth, even shrewd people. But within that practicality we also accepted what I suppose could be called superstition and magic, which is another way of knowing things" (342). See also Morrison's *Playing in the Dark*.

[2]Thanks to Gerry Brenner for this line of discussion.

[3]Morrison's feelings about this contradiction are also ambivalent. In an interview with Robert Stepto she admires black men's mobility and describes it as a kind of self-invention. But in an interview with Mel Watkins she explains: "It's a part of black life, a positive, majestic thing, but there is a price to pay—the price is the children. The fathers may soar, they may triumph, they may leave, but the children know who they are; they remember, half in glory and half in accusation. That is one of the points of 'Song': all the men have left someone, and it is the children who remember it, sing about it, mythologize it, make it a part of their family history."

Jazz: From Music to Literature

Anthony J. Berret

In an interview with Thomas LeClair, Toni Morrison said that she was trying to do in her novels "what music used to do" for African Americans. She went on to say that music was the main expressive and stabilizing medium for African Americans over the years but that the complexities of modern technology mean African Americans need more than music for cultural survival and advancement: "The music kept us alive, but it's not enough anymore" (26). Morrison implies that African Americans require not only literacy and verbal skills but also a solid literary culture in which they can find themselves represented and integrated into modern society. Morrison helps build this culture in her novels, and to facilitate the transition from music to literature, she carefully works musical images into her stories.

However, African Americans are not the only Americans for whom music is a crucial element of culture. Morrison's remarks also apply, with some qualifications, to students in general. Contemporary youth and young adults rely on music, especially rock and its derivatives, to define their selfhood and structure their world (Epstein). Music is the main art form of their subculture. So as they try to integrate themselves into a wider culture through formal education, it is worthwhile to encourage them to relate music to the other forms of that culture, especially literature. They could thus bring to literature what they know and like about music, and they could apply to music, even the music of their subculture, some of the analytic skills that they learn from the study of literature.

For these reasons, and because of the novel's title, I take a comparative music-and-literature approach to *Jazz*. I begin teaching the novel by asking students to mark all the references to music they find in the book: *Jazz* is filled with references to bands, musical instruments, lines from songs, dancing, records, and nightclubs. And because the book is complicated, students benefit from having something to look for as they read it. Of course, the assignment is an exercise in literature, but it prepares the way for a musical approach by demonstrating that music is an important theme in the story.

What I expect students to produce from this first exercise is not just a list of references or images but perhaps, with the help of the teacher or group discussion, some patterns in these images. For instance, in a passage describing the effects of the city, the tall buildings make the narrator "dream tall" and "feel in on things. Hep . . . top-notch and indestructible . . . I like the way the city makes people think they can do what they want and get away with it." Then "a colored man floats down out of the sky blowing a saxophone." Since this music comes from above, it must have the same emotional effect as the tall buildings. But there is another level to this city: "Below is shadow where any blasé thing takes place: clarinets and lovemaking, fists and the voices of sorrowful women."

Still, "It's the bright steel rocking above the shade below" that inspires hope: "The people down there in the shadow are happy about that" (Knopf, 7–8). Morrison divides musical instruments into brass and clarinets. The golden brass instruments express the clean, bright, uplifting emotions of joy, freedom, and self-control, while the clarinets, which are black and called "licorice sticks," express the dark and low-down emotions of grief and uncontrollable passion. On the beautiful spring day near the end of the story, when Felice comes over to Joe and Violet's house with an Okeh record and lifts them out of their doldrums, young men on the rooftops blow tunes

> like the light of that day, pure and steady and kind of kind. . . . The clar-
> inets had trouble because the brass was cut so fine, not lowdown the way
> they love to do it, but high and fine. . . . That's the way the young men on
> brass sounded that day. . . . [W]hen it was clear that they beat the clar-
> inets out, they turned their backs on them, lifted those horns straight up
> and joined the light just as pure and steady and kind of kind.   (196–97)

Joy and sorrow, expressed by brass and clarinets, are further supported by images of high and low, light and shadow. This basic contrast in the novel includes images of the upper and lower parts of the human body and images of racial identity. These patterns show that Morrison integrates music carefully into the novel, they differentiate the various emotions, and they illustrate how the emotions can be expressed through images.

A main purpose of teaching *Jazz* is to help students respond intelligently to music both in writing and discussion. Literature can provide them with models, especially a novel like *Jazz*, in which the main characters articulately respond to music. Joe Trace, Alice Manfred, and Dorcas graphically describe how music affects them. I suggest assigning three students to give brief but detailed reports on how these characters respond to music. For instance, when Joe Trace comes to New York from the South in 1906 with his wife, Violet, he is nervous and scared, until he feels the rhythm of the train under him. This rhythm causes him to stand up in the aisle and tap back at the tracks, joining the train and Violet in a dance of hospitality and acceptance. The city is dancing with both of them, "proving already how much it love[s] them" (32). Twenty years later, however, that same rhythm induces Joe to do something wild, to love a woman half his age and then to kill her. The city switches him onto a track that he cannot get off, a track that also involves music:

> Take my word for it, he is bound to the track. It pulls him like a needle
> through the groove of a Bluebird record. Round and round about the
> town. That's the way the City spins you. Makes you do what it wants, go
> where the laid-out roads say to. All the while letting you think you're
> free.   (120)

For Joe music is at first caring and hospitable, but then it becomes controlling and destructive. Morrison demonstrates the effect of music by sound and rhythm patterns: "Round and round about the town"; the assonance in *through-groove-Bluebird, makes-laid-say*, and *go-road*. Rhythmic and phonetic repetition can be welcoming and soothing, but it can also signal irresistible control.

Alice Manfred recognizes this compulsive and harmful aspect of music. She fears the new music because it appeals to her baser instincts: "Songs that used to start in the head and fill the heart had dropped on down, down to places below the sash and the buckled belts" (56). At first she thought the wild music was an indirect expression of rage over racial injustice and violence, but then she begins to see it as an evil in itself: "It was the music. The dirty, get-on-down music the women sang and the men played and both danced to, close and shameless or apart and wild. . . . It made you do unwise disorderly things. Just hearing it was like violating the law" (58). She admits that there is a "complicated anger" in it, "something hostile that disguised itself as flourish and roaring seduction. . . . It faked happiness, faked welcome," but made her so angry that she made a fist in her pocket and wanted to smash windows or crush the world "for doing what it did to her and everybody else she knew" (59). She tries to control herself, however, by recalling the regular drumbeats of a silent and disciplined march up Fifth Avenue to protest incidents of racial violence. These drums are the only link she can find between the statements printed on banners and leaflets and the sufferings of her niece Dorcas and other victims of racism. They are a "rope" that helps her control herself and hold her life together (58). She grasps this rope with one hand but still makes a fist with the other: "It was impossible to keep the Fifth Avenue drums separate from the belt-buckle tunes vibrating from pianos and spinning on every Victrola" (59).

Dorcas loses her parents in a fire during an East Saint Louis race riot, and Alice tries to snuff out Dorcas's fear and anger by keeping "the heart ignorant of the hips and the head in charge of both." But for Dorcas the discipline of the drums is not enough. A symbolic chip of wood from her burnt home smolders deep down in her body, "somewhere below her navel," and she will not talk about it for fear of losing it or putting it out. The drums keep it glowing, but it is fanned most by the wild new music. Dorcas is happy that there is no place in the city where "somebody [is] not licking his licorice stick, tickling the ivories, beating his skins, blowing off his horn while a knowing woman [sings] ain't nobody going to keep me down" (60). She attends dance parties where "fast music suitable for the brightly lit room" eventually turns into "lights-out music," "slow and smoky" (64–65, 66, 67). She begins an affair with Joe Trace, prompted by the "City seeping music that begged and challenged each and every day. 'Come,' it said, 'Come and do wrong'" (67). She wants Joe to take her to high-class clubs where she can be accepted by society and where she can put her hand "under the table drumming out the rhythm on the inside of his thigh, his thigh, his thigh, thigh, thigh" (95). When the affair ends in tragedy,

Alice blames the whole thing on sexy clothes and "race music" (79). Dorcas's deep hurt and anger cannot simply be controlled. They must be projected into wild and sexy music, which leads to wild and sexy behavior.

The student reports on how music affects Joe, Alice, and Dorcas give the class models for responding to literature and music. The descriptions specify the characters' emotions, show whether the emotions are in harmony or conflict with one another, and express the emotions through active images (a record groove, a rope, a fist, a smoldering chip of wood) or through style (the sound and rhythm of "round and round about the town" and "his thigh, his thigh, his thigh, thigh, thigh").

After hearing the presentations, students should be ready to try their own responses to musical pieces. My long-range intention is for students to talk and write articulately about the music they listen to spontaneously. In the classes on *Jazz*, I recommend that students practice with music referred to by the characters. This provides a historical context for the novel and helps immerse students in the novel's setting. The instructor should remind students that 1920s jazz was popular music, that it had a good beat and was easy to dance to, and that it created the same kinds of controversy that rock and rap music do.

I find *The Smithsonian Collection of Classic Jazz* the most available and educative tool for teaching and learning jazz (M. Williams). Along with fourteen sides of recorded music from the different decades and in different styles, it contains a 120-page booklet that includes a history of jazz and a brief critical analysis of each piece. Gunther Schuller's *Early Jazz* can provide further historical and critical background; the pieces I mention below are in the *Smithsonian Collection*.

I suggest that students listen to samples of the music that influenced the characters for good or ill and then write personal responses to a piece, carefully distinguishing the emotions it elicits and trying to determine exactly what in the music causes these emotions. It may be helpful first to play and discuss some pieces in class, then make other pieces available for individual written responses.

Since it has lyrics and since words may be easier to write about than music alone, I suggest starting with W. C. Handy's "Saint Louis Blues" as sung by Bessie Smith, a famous blues singer of the 1920s and one of the first to be recorded. As students listen, it is useful to have them list the emotions that they think are expressed and the words or sounds that express them. I find sadness, despair, jealousy, and anger. I would note how Smith changes her voice to a hoarse rebuke when she repeats "nowhere" after the lines "If it weren't for powder or for store-bought hair / That man of mine wouldn't go nowhere" and encourage students to describe the effects of Louis Armstrong's cornet responses to Smith's lines. Do they cheer her up or just commiserate? In the organ accompaniment I hear a carnival sound that satirizes the city attractions—women with diamond rings—that pull Smith's man away from her. Violet has an experience like this when Joe runs after Dorcas. Could Violet also sing this song?

Next, we move from a blues song to a blues instrumental, Louis Armstrong's "West End Blues," for example. The piece begins with Armstrong's trumpet solo played without a beat, then provides a strong beat that Armstrong and the band follow for the rest of the piece. Does the beat confine them or give them the security they need to pour out their hearts in melody? Do the different instruments express different emotions? What effect do Armstrong's vocal responses to the clarinet have? I hear a cry of strength and endurance near the end in Armstrong's long high trumpet note with the beat behind it and in his repetition of high phrases after the note. The piece seems to end with calmness and relief.

As an example of the fast dance music played in Harlem in the 1920s and affecting the lives of the characters in *Jazz*, I suggest Jelly Roll Morton's "Black Bottom Stomp." The beat is emphasized to different degrees throughout the piece and is most pronounced when the tom-tom joins in for the final chorus. There are also changes of beat, notes played off the beat, and mixtures of different beats. The speed and diversity permit and encourage every type of wild self-expression. Each instrument gets a solo, and toward the end some players improvise together. Group improvisation is what makes 1920s jazz seem so free and chaotic. This is no doubt the type of music that Alice Manfred found licentious and compulsive. I ask students if the song's beat, off-beat notes, and free solos captivate the listener to the point of uncontrollable bodily and emotional reactions. The same question can be asked of Fletcher Henderson's "The Stampede." The cornet and trombone play their solos with reckless abandon, and the orderly, harmonious, and repetitive responses of the reed ensemble seem to urge them on, to say, "Yeah! Do it! Do it!" almost like congregational amens after the phrases of a preacher. It is indeed a stampede, a wild, compulsive run.

After students respond to these or other pieces, I have them share their responses in small groups. As a final exercise, the whole class discusses the effects of music. How powerful and influential can music be? Is it legitimate to call music violent? dirty? addictive? Can it cause crime? Should it be censored? Questions like these were asked about jazz in the 1920s (Ogren 123–25, 156–61), are raised by Morrison's novel, and are applied to rock and rap music today.

Jazz can be covered in four classes. In the first class my students share and discuss their lists of music references and discover and analyze the image patterns of the novel. In the second class they report on how music affects Joe Trace, Alice Manfred, and Dorcas. In the third they listen to jazz selections of the time and practice responding to them. And in the last class they share their written responses to a 1920s jazz piece and discuss the effects of music, applying their conclusions to the present.

"Laundering the Head of Whitewash": Mimicry and Resistance in *The Bluest Eye*

Gurleen Grewal

A lyrical and courageous first novel, *The Bluest Eye* is uncomfortable reading for many students. Tackling domination in its various forms and confronting racially marked class positions in the United States, *The Bluest Eye* is a challenging novel to teach in any course. Diane Johnson's review of Morrison's first two novels should signal to teachers the complexity of the terrain covered in *The Bluest Eye* and the very different assumptions that readers bring to the novel. According to Johnson, since the novels are about black people who victimize one another, they only confirm Morrison's white audience's stereotypes about black people. Francis Beale amplifies that statement: "In attempting to analyze the situation of the Black woman in America, one crashes abruptly into a solid wall of grave misconceptions, outright distortions of fact, and defensive attitudes on the part of many" (90).

Since the teacher's business is to facilitate the examining of attitudes, our task is to make sure students understand the complex relations of cause and effect in *The Bluest Eye*. For surely the novel goes well beyond replicating stereotypes—the black man as rapist (Cholly Breedlove), the black woman as mammy (Pauline Breedlove), or the black family as fragmented. Rather, in confronting these stereotypes, it goes to the heart of the matter: to the race-based class structure of American society that generates its own pathologies. To forestall the quick cognitive closure promoted by stereotypes, it may be useful to have students read James Baldwin's 1955 essay "Autobiographical Notes" alongside *The Bluest Eye*; Baldwin asserts what Morrison dramatizes so powerfully:

> I don't think that the Negro problem in America can be even discussed coherently without bearing in mind its context; its context being the history, traditions, customs, the moral assumptions and preoccupations of the country; in short, the general social fabric. Appearances to the contrary, no one in America escapes its effects and everyone in America bears some responsibility for it.   (8)

In the prologue, through the extended metaphor of an "unyielding" earth, Claudia MacTeer explains her helplessness in the face of her friend Pecola Breedlove's destruction. Beginning with an admission of the adult narrator's childhood guilt—"For years I thought . . . it was my fault. I had planted them [marigold seeds] too far down in the earth" (Washington Square, 9)—the novel ends with the narrator broadening the "I" to a "we," implicating members of a certain "well behaved," "licensed" class: "All of us—all who knew [Pecola]—felt so wholesome after we cleaned ourselves on her. We were so beautiful when we stood astride her ugliness. . . . Her poverty kept us generous" (159). "All of us" might also include the readers and students in the classroom.

A neglected but valuable supplement to *The Bluest Eye* is *The Black Woman*, a collection of black feminist essays edited by Toni Cade Bambara and, like the novel, published in 1970 (Cade). In fact, there are remarkable parallels between the themes of *The Bluest Eye* and several essays in the collection, including Beale's, Cade's, and Gwen Patton's. Another complementary text is Audre Lorde's *Sister Outsider* (1984), especially the essays "The Transformation of Silence into Language and Action," "Age, Race, Class, and Sex: Women Redefining Difference," and "The Uses of Anger: Women Responding to Racism." In some courses instructors might ask students to draw on these essays in their written responses.

If this novel is taught in a women's literature or women's studies course, it is important to note that the novel's complex portrayal of race, class, and gender forestalls alignments based on gender alone; the oppression of Cholly, the poor black man who rapes his daughter, Pecola, certainly complicates matters. The prologue forewarns against a metaleptic reading that takes the effects as causes: only nine-year-olds may be excused for thinking "that it was because Pecola was having her father's baby that the marigolds did not grow" (9). At the outset, a series of parallel statements, turning from the literal to the figural, place Cholly in a predicament similar to the MacTeer sisters':

> We had dropped our seeds in our own little plot of black dirt just as Pecola's father had dropped his seeds in his own plot of black dirt. Our innocence and faith were no more productive than his lust or despair. What is clear now is that of all that hope, fear, lust, love, and grief, nothing remains but Pecola and the unyielding earth. Cholly Breedlove is dead; our innocence too. The seeds shrivelled and died; her baby too.   (9)

Even as the text indicates the black male's part in consigning the poor black girl/woman to her role as the mule of the world, Morrison is careful to prevent a reading in which Pecola's father is the arch-villain.

Published at the end of a decade of black cultural nationalism, the novel makes clear the necessity of raising the politicized slogan "Black is beautiful" in opposition to the white monopoly on value. However, the novel goes beyond that affirmation to a demystification of social processes: it is able to grasp the way individuals collude in their own victimization by internalizing a dominant culture's values. The novel's handling of the theme of miseducation, of identities formed through mimicry of dominant models inimical to the characters' interests, origins, and cultures is ultimately enabling. A "tragedy of cultural mutilation" (Christian, *Black Women Novelists* 149), *The Bluest Eye* is also the portrait of a black woman artist as a young girl arriving, through internal struggle, at an emergent consciousness. Further, the representation of the united MacTeer family balances the afflicted Breedlove family: a supportive, working father; a resistant black woman as mother and culture bearer; and a spirited narrator who resists and eventually writes her way out of subjection.

A remarkable feature of *The Bluest Eye* is the foregrounding of its challenge to dominant culture. The Dick and Jane preface and the prologue establish what is certainly the hallmark of Morrison's writing, which in her own words is "the ability to be both print and oral literature" ("Rootedness" 341), that is, to combine the layered quality of metaphoric writing (Roland Barthes's "writerly text") with the direct appeal of the narrating voice that engages the reader as listener (a speakerly text). Through its preface the novel marks its own entry as a writerly text into the print literature of a dominant culture. The arrangement of the three typographically distinct versions of the primer is a trope on writing itself. A richly suggestive metaphor that illustrates and encapsulates the primary thematic conflict in the novel, it also represents literature as the contested ground of representation, since the three versions suggest the conflictual or revisioning field of intertextuality. Morrison's account of the conditions under which Pecola was made invisible could be discussed in the context of Ralph Ellison's preoccupation with the invisibility of the black man (*Invisible Man*) and Richard Wright's indifference to the muteness of the black woman; we may recall Wright's concern in *Native Son* with "how Bigger was born" (vii) and his apparent disregard of how Bigger's girlfriend Bessie was killed (by Bigger). Morrison's first novel, then, begins in a highly self-conscious mode, drawing battle lines of representation.

The introductory inscription of competing texts is followed by the voice of the narrator juxtaposing one aberrant event of 1941 ("there were no marigolds" [9]) with another ("Pecola was having her father's baby" [9]), establishing Pecola as the marigold nipped in the bud. From the cultural images of the Dick and Jane text we are led to consider the natural images of seed, flower, and earth. Both are "nursery" metaphors involving inculcation and cultivation. Instructors might ask students to engage with the novel's two structuring principles: nature and culture. While one cannot alter nature, culture and the cultural text (the primer) are open to interrogation and change, even though they appear natural or normal. This move toward a critique of culture is central to *The Bluest Eye*.

While Claudia's first-person narrative lets us see the possibilities of individual and perhaps collective resistance, the omniscient third-person narratives portray subjection. Within them unfold the several condensed biographies, each opening into a particular history: Pauline's, Cholly's, Soaphead Church's, and Geraldine's. Even as black men (Cholly and Soaphead) and petit bourgeois black women (light-brown Geraldine) are implicated as Pecola's oppressors, the novel's symmetry of content and structure makes the reader see them all as an extended black family, caught in different kinds and degrees of self-negating identifications. The novel achieves this "unity" by structuring the narratives after the Dick and Jane primer.

The novel opens with a visually disorienting mimicry: three inscriptions of the Dick and Jane text, one "original" and two "copies." The primer is replicated with increasing typographical distortion, so that the last text is practically illegible. I let students offer their interpretations of the three versions before volunteering mine. The double-spaced first text with its capitalized proper nouns and standard punctuation may be read as the normative "type" of self-formation in the dominant white culture. The second text, which is single-spaced and which lacks privileging signs of capital letters and meaningful marks of punctuation, attempts to reproduce the first text. The third text reproduces the word order of the first, without spacing, capital letters, question marks, or stopgaps; in its disorder, however, it still obeys the order of the first. Here, in brief, is an allegory of class formations and of the first text/world's authorizing of third text/world identities. The first text/world has set itself as the norm against which the third text/world is judged.

Morrison weaves a black story corresponding to each motif in the Dick and Jane text so that Dick and Jane's house corresponds to the Breedloves' poor, storefront house, while Pauline and Cholly and their children, Sammy and Pecola, correspond to and contrast with Mother, Father, Dick, and Jane. Ironically, in the place of the pet cat and dog are the black bourgeois characters, Geraldine (who loves her cat to excess) and the West Indian pedophile, Soaphead (who hates his landlady's dog to excess). Formally, the method by which the singular, homogeneous Dick and Jane text organizes multiple, heterogeneous identities attests to the force of an ideology (of the supremacy of "the bluest eye") through which the dominant culture reproduces its hierarchical power structures. That black subjects consent to reproduction, which leads to psychic violence among them, is also evident from the unintelligible third text. Although Claudia as narrator implies in the preface that she cannot determine why the marigolds did not bloom—"since *why* is difficult to handle"—it is clear that doing so is central to the representation of her truth (9). The entire novel explores the forces that lead Pecola to desire blue eyes. Although Morrison does not use the term *hegemony*, the novel illustrates a hegemonic situation.

As Chandra Mukherji and Michael Schudson point out, "The question to which 'hegemony' is an answer is, 'Why do dominated or oppressed groups accept their position in the social hierarchy?' Gramsci held that, in fact, oppressed groups accept the definition of the world of elites as common sense; their understanding of how the world works, then, leads them to collaborate in their own oppression" (15).

From the beginning of the novel we witness an unfolding drama in which, metaphorically speaking, second and third texts mimic the first. The differences between the second text's mimicking and the third text's mimicking are apparent in the different economic or class situations of Geraldine and Pauline. They both aspire to the norm, the social, cultural, and material privileges of the first text. However, because privileged-class status in America has been historically coded in white terms, the accession of black people to that status is predicated on a disavowal of their race. Whatever the rhetoric of a pluralistic, democratic society, the pressure to assimilate is real. Thus Geraldine's achievement of the security and respectability of class is accompanied by the repression of black "funk." This repression is reflected typographically in the second text. In the third text, there is nothing but irony—the distance between ideal and reality. Pauline Breedlove, who has no means to acquire the material and social privileges of a Geraldine, is nonetheless preoccupied with approximating the trappings of a class position. Her attempts to be Jean Harlow only alienate her further from her home and family. As Pecola's story demonstrates, the socially mandated charade of being something one is not (white) and of not being something one is (black) makes one invisible, while the split mentality it requires equals madness.

I discuss with my classes the novel's use of mimicry as structuring motif and psychological motive and note that the novel grounds the practice of mimicry in the inequalities of race and class and inscribes a spirited resistance to mimicry. I want the students to grasp the wider connections the text makes between capitalism and colonialism, between a hegemonic pattern of inculcation and mental colonization. Linking the predicament of African Americans to others in the black diaspora, the West Indian Soaphead Church is the "mimic man" who enables such a connection.

The presence of Soaphead Church implicates the mimicry of Geraldine, Pauline, and Pecola as part of colonial oppression. Homi Bhabha argues that mimicry is integral to the colonizer's project of disregarding the "cultural, racial, historical difference" of the other and reserving value and priority for its own race, culture, history (129). Colonial education was installed to produce a native elite whose interests would coincide with the colonizers'. Soaphead Church is an example of that product. It is important to see the connections between his story and the other characters', for he is much more than a mere function of plot, that is, an agent to grant Pecola her blue eyes and a substitute for the dog in the Dick and Jane primer. We are told that "his personality was an arabesque: intricate, symmetrical, balanced, and tightly constructed" (131)—

the very words we might use to describe the novel's narrative structure of mimicry. His story, the last of the studies in alienated consciousness, places the other accounts into perspective, for he brings from the West Indies an anglophilia and a consciousness informed—in his case, deformed—by a history of colonization. The connection between colonialism and the institution of the American South was often made during the 1960s by radical analysts of black history. The social critic Harold Cruse explains it thus: "The only factor which differentiates the Negro's status from that of a pure colonial status is that his position is maintained in the 'home' country in close proximity to the dominant racial group" (77).

Soaphead Church (as Elihue Micah Whitcomb is called by black folk in Lorain, Ohio), "a cinnamon-eyed West Indian" with "lightly browned skin," is a descendant of the Enlightenment: "A Sir Whitcomb, some decaying British nobleman, who chose to disintegrate under a sun more easeful than England's, had introduced the white strain into the family in the early 1800's." We are told that Sir Whitcomb's son had a mulatta wife who, "like a good Victorian parody, learned from her husband all that was worth learning—to separate herself in body, mind, and spirit from all that suggested Africa . . ." (132). Elihue's father, a schoolmaster, took on the white man's "strain," or burden, by schooling his son in "theories of education, discipline, and the good life" (133). The effect of "his father's controlled violence" was that Soaphead "develop[ed] . . . a hatred of, and fascination with, any hint of disorder and decay" (134):

> He abhorred flesh on flesh. Body odor, breath odor, overwhelmed him. The sight of dried matter in the corner of the eye, decayed or missing teeth, earwax, blackheads, moles, blisters, skin crusts—all the natural excretions and protections the body was capable of—disquieted him. His attentions therefore gradually settled on those humans whose bodies were least offensive—children. (131)

We are meant to see his eccentricities and alienation (from his body, home, nation) originating in the displacement wrought by the colonial project. Soaphead has failed to enter the ministry and finds himself in the United States sinking into a "rapidly fraying gentility" (135). To compensate for his inadequacy, Soaphead "added the Micah" (142). Ironically, his allegiance to the great works of the masters notwithstanding (we are told he has read his Shakespeare, Gibbon, and Dante), he occupies the place of the trained dog in the Dick and Jane text. Servile to white supremacist values, he finds it perfectly understandable that Pecola should want blue eyes, and he feels gratified at being able to "grant" them to her. Associated with the dog, Soaphead writes a "biting" letter to God that shows him bound to the master's imperial power; after all, his nationalist rhetoric notwithstanding, it is not change in the social structure that he desires but a small portion of that power.

While the novel's structure suggests a similarity of predicament between a colonized West Indian black subject and an African American one—both Soaphead and Cholly are inheritors of complex social historical formations that vex their identities, and both vent their frustrations on the black girl—the difference between Soaphead and Cholly replicates the difference between the second and third texts. Soaphead is the educated colonial gentleman who has internalized the alleged superiority of the colonizer—of his great-grandsire, the Englishman who whitened the race. Cholly is the poor, uneducated black American male doomed to the underclass who thus remains outside the apparatus of education and class privilege. A man of metropolitan learning, the "lightly browned" Soaphead has much more in common with the "sugar brown" Geraldine (68). Soaphead and Geraldine's common identity effects connect the colonies abroad and at home.

Like Soaphead, Geraldine has been thoroughly schooled. Her training, in femininity and docility, opens to her the serving professions useful to the white society she wishes to enter. Educated in "normal schools," she learns "the careful development of thrift, patience, high morals, and good manners" (68). But this virtuous stability is built on repressing her embodied blackness, on "get[ting] rid of the funkiness":

> Wherever it erupts, this Funk, they [southern brown girls] wipe it away; where it crusts, they dissolve it; wherever it drips, flowers, or clings, they fight it until it dies. They fight this battle all the way to the grave. The laugh that is a little too loud; the enunciation a little too round; the gesture a little too generous.   (68)

Her distaste for the physical parallels Soaphead's. "Funk," associated with blackness and sexuality, gives her away and threatens her middle-class composure. In the slave South the construct of purity and femininity that circumscribed white womanhood went hand in hand with the formulation of the black female slave as lascivious other. The pervasiveness of this stereotype makes Geraldine fastidious and vigilant of her own sexuality. Repressing "the funkiness of nature," as befitting a bourgeois economy founded on the exclusion of color, Geraldine comes to occupy the position of the primer cat who "will not play" with Jane/Pecola. Geraldine's distancing herself from her sexuality and her race performs a conservative function, "do[ing] the white man's work with refinement" (68). But Geraldine is at least rewarded with a certain class respectability—a green and gold house with gilded furnishings and a place in society, albeit one that mirrors the position of the pet cat in the primer. There is much greater irony and pathos in Pauline Breedlove's desperate attempts to approximate the white middle-class norm of beauty, distanced as she is from it by her class and race. She ends up negating her daughter while maintaining a social order (the white Fisher household) that recognizes her only as "the ideal servant" (101).

While Soaphead and Geraldine fight signs of corporeal decay, Pauline and Cholly Breedlove fight each other and steadily decay, an inner state manifested by rotten teeth—literally for Pauline and metaphorically for Cholly. Sitting in a cinema mimicking Jean Harlow's hair style, looking at Jean Harlow from a vantage point of assimilation, Pauline erases her identity. Her fallen tooth represents this abject loss of self: it is while taking in celluloid images of romantic love and physical beauty that Pauline bites into a candy that loosens her front tooth. If Pauline's tooth attests to her failure to be that which she mimics, Cholly's "pulled tooth" symbolizes his emasculation (119). Unfathered, unsocialized, and "castrated" early in his youth by an encounter with white men—hunters with flashlights who make a spectacle of his lovemaking with a black girl, Darlene—he is a social derelict, as much outside the system of race, class, and gender privilege as Pecola. His "rape" by white men negates him just as his rape of Pecola negates her.

Morrison's thematic and structural use of the Dick and Jane primer activates the various meanings of priming. A primer is "a person or thing that primes," the verb *to prime* being defined as follows: "to prepare or make ready for a particular purpose or operation"; "to cover (a surface) with a preparatory coat or color, as in painting" (*Webster's New Universal Unabridged Dictionary*). The reader is meant to see the debilitating effect of priming on black subjects: a consciousness turned against itself. In practically all the characters "ignorance" is "smoothly cultivated" and "self-hatred" is "exquisitely learned" (55). There are repeated references to the various characters' miseducation, such as the following passage from Soaphead's letter to God:

> We in this colony took as our own the most dramatic, and the most obvious, of our white masters' characteristics, which were, of course, their worst. In retaining the identity of our race, we held fast to those characteristics most gratifying to sustain and least troublesome to maintain. Consequently we were not royal but snobbish, not aristocratic but class-conscious, we believed authority was cruelty to our inferiors, and education was being at school. (140)

In this rare moment of self-reflection Soaphead admits to his spiritual bankruptcy, an acknowledgment Claudia echoes at the novel's end:

> We courted death in order to call ourselves brave, and hid like thieves from life. We substituted good grammar for intellect; we switched habits to simulate maturity; we rearranged lies and called it truth, seeing in the new pattern of an old idea the Revelation and the Word. (159)

However, the theme of resistance is as important as that of subjection in this novel. If the Dick and Jane text represents the classic *bildungs* theme, the relentless pursuit of a sanctioned identity, *The Bluest Eye* is an antibildungsroman whose project is to disrupt this process of making "adjustment without improvement" (22). Through Claudia's first-person narrative, the consciousness of childhood is given an adult understanding, its utopian energy of uninhibited desire channeled toward political critique. *The Bluest Eye* suggests, along with Toni Cade Bambara, that "you find your Self in destroying illusions, smashing myths, laundering the head of whitewash, being responsible to some truth, to the struggle" (Cade, "Issue" 108). I emphasize that such a contestation entails creation, what Raymond Williams calls "a specific practice of self-making" (*Marxism* 210), in which "active struggle for new consciousness" is

> creative practice . . . the long and difficult re-making of an inherited (determined) practical consciousness: a process often described as development but in practice a struggle at the roots of the mind—not casting off an ideology, or learning phrases about it, but confronting a hegemony in the fibres of the self and in the hard practical substance of effective and continuing relationships.   (212)

Claudia MacTeer, Toni Morrison's alter ego, in her successful emergence from hegemonic constraints, successfully models this idea of creative practice. Depending on the course, the instructor may assign students to write about returning to a site of their childhood or later life and excavating its distortions and sanctioned ignorances. What do they know now that they did not know then? What was the cost of that ignorance or miseducation? Ideally the class will learn to respond with insight and sensitivity to "the anger of exclusion, of unquestioned privilege, of racial distortions, of silence, ill-use, stereotyping, defensiveness, misnaming, betrayal, and cooptation" (Lorde 124), respond to the mixed terrain of their own lives.

An African-Based Reading of *Sula*

Gay Wilentz

> My writing expects, demands participatory reading, and
> that I think is what literature is supposed to do. It's not
> just about telling the story; it's about involving the
> reader. . . . My language has to have holes and spaces so
> the reader can come into it. . . . Then we (you, the
> reader, and I, the author) come together to make this
> book, to feel this experience.
>
> —Toni Morrison

Toni Morrison's comment on her relation to the reader indicates a rapport that
reflects the participatory qualities of African orature, or oral literature (Interview with Tate 125). In numerous interviews Morrison connects her attempt
to interact with the reader to an African worldview she and other African
Americans have inherited. To Thomas LeClair she says that she writes "village
literature" (26), a literature based in African orature and literature, in which
artists both participate in and represent the community.[1] Teaching Morrison's
novels with an understanding of African retentions in the diaspora gives students greater insight into the cultural context of the novels. Moreover, a participatory teaching and learning style, based in African orature, allows students
to contribute their own experiences and integrate the varying traditions that
make up the cultural environment in which they live and Morrison writes. As
a teacher I have found that this style—bringing knowledge to the text while allowing the students space to inform the discussion—blends well with Morrison's aims.

Although a participatory, African-based approach works well with all Morrison's novels, I concentrate here on *Sula* because I teach it most often. *Sula* is
a complex novel with multiple narrative voices, but it is short and appropriate
for undergraduate (sophomore-level and above) and graduate courses. I teach
it in my African American and women's literature courses; it also fits in contemporary American and ethnic literature courses. There are many ways to
read *Sula* in a class, but an African-based reading in conjunction with other interpretations of the work not only enhances understanding of the novel but
also addresses some of its more problematic aspects.[2] In *Sula* this kind of reading explores the alternative reality of the novel, allusions to African traditions
and cultural milieus, and a cosmology that displaces binary oppositions such as
reality/fantasy, science/magic, and good/evil.

It may be useful first to examine the tools for an African-based reading and
to discuss some of the recent resistance to an Afrocentric approach. An Afrocentric approach to literature of the African diaspora exposes what has been
hidden by the dominant culture's discourse. According to Molefi Kete Asante,

Afrocentricity pervades every aspect of African American culture and places "African ideals at the center of any analysis that involves African culture and behavior" (*Afrocentric Idea* 6). Although, in our postmodern society, we may be more interested in decentering (exposing the multiplicity of influences on a work) than in replacing the old center (Eurocentric discourse) with a new one (Afrocentric discourse), the need to comprehend the African aspects of an African-based culture is self-evident.[3] Unfortunately, the media have recently popularized and distorted African-based studies. Critics such as Elliott Butler-Evans have argued that an Afrocentric interpretation is essentialist—simplifying, in this case, Morrison's work. However, an African-based reading, used alongside others, presents the fullest interpretation of the work by uncovering, as Morrison states to LeClair, layers of "that civilization that existed underneath white civilization" (26).

Research documenting African cultural relations and a diasporic approach to literary study have lately flourished. This methodology involves some tools from disciplines such as anthropology and history. Moreover, a developing area of literary criticism that explores African heritage and culture also utilizes this interdisciplinary approach.[4] However, understanding the African context of contemporary African American literature is more than a theoretical engagement; it has important pedagogical implications as well. As I demonstrate with *Sula*, awareness of an African worldview gives students insight into the complexities of the work and into what at times looks like fantasy but is, rather, an alternative reality. Moreover, the often open-ended narrative allows an interrogative approach by the students, reflecting the style of the African dilemma tale, a story that often raises questions about "cultural norms and values" (Bascom 14). The ending of a dilemma tale does not leave listeners with a strict or simple moral; instead, the participants debate the meanings with the storyteller. (For a fuller discussion, see Bascom and the introduction to Abrahams's *African Folktales*, esp. 16–17.) Similarly, students address unresolved issues at the end of *Sula*. Significantly, the discussion increases students' knowledge of and interaction with a heritage historically ignored in academic studies and mainstream society. The process is necessary for all students, since comprehension of America's shared African heritage is not biologically based. Through this approach, non–African American students, especially those raised in the Southeast, deepen their understanding of their own culture, which has been informed by a rich African presence.

The African presence in Morrison's novels has been characterized by the more general literary term *magic realism*. In Morrison's work this alternative reality is connected to an African worldview. Some African critics have balked at the notion of an African worldview since Africa has many cultures and traditions (see Mudimbe; Appiah). However, this concept certainly has validity in relation to African American history because of the intermingling of cultures from west and central Africa during the slave trade. From the different interactions and retentions of traditions during and after slavery, there evolved a worldview alternative and sometimes oppositional to the dominant Euroamerican cultural perspective. (For a reading of the theoretical implications of alternative and oppositional responses to hegemony, see R. Williams, *Problems*.) According to Asante, "Black Americans retained basic components of the African experience rather than specific artifacts" ("African Elements" 21). These "basic components" are part of the African worldview that Morrison evokes in her novels.

Wole Soyinka describes the worldview in African literature as concerned with one's relation to the cosmos, rational and irrational. Morrison describes the writing of *Song of Solomon* in terms similar to Soyinka's: "I could blend the acceptance of the supernatural and a profound rootedness in the real world at the same time with neither taking precedence over the other. It is indicative of the cosmology, the way in which Black people look at the world" ("Rootedness" 342). Although *Song of Solomon* is possibly the novel in which Morrison best incorporates African elements (see Wilentz, "Civilizations"), this worldview is evident in *Sula* as well.

After the framing device that tells us that in 1920 "there was once a neighborhood" (3), *Sula* opens not with the main character, Sula, or even her friend Nel, but with Shadrack, a World War I veteran suffering from what we now call posttraumatic stress syndrome. From the beginning, exposure to Shadrack compels us to accept an alternative worldview. Although his hallucinations of having "monstrous hands" can easily be interpreted psychoanalytically (7), the community's acceptance of both Shadrack and National Suicide Day is less conveniently analyzed as realistic literature. My class and I compare the community's attitude toward Shadrack with the conventional notions of how to treat the apparently insane. The community, which collectively functions as a character (a harkening to the choral presence in much African drama), accepts Shadrack: "They knew Shadrack was crazy but that did not mean that he didn't have any sense or, even more important, that he had no power. . . . Once the people understood the boundaries and the nature of his madness, they could fit him, so to speak, into the scheme of things" (12–13). Rather than lock Shadrack away, the community accepts him for who he is. His role, therefore, in this society corresponds to those of individuals in many African societies who may be considered mad but who are not violent. According to I. Sow, the African concept of madness is based on "the fundamental notion of conflict in the underlying relational networks that give structure to the whole of a person's life" (3); moreover, a cure is always associated with restoring balance between the ancestors and the community, so isolation from the community would be out of cultural context and devastating for the patient. Furthermore, the view among *Sula's* community that the mad person might have power resembles some traditional religions' beliefs about the often eccentric behavior of the priests. (For more on Shadrack as a water priest and on the African elements in *Sula*, see V. Lewis.)

The failure of the veterans' hospital to cure Shadrack and his profound effect on the community of the Bottom reflect another opposition that we address as a class—science versus magic. I find it useful here to ask the class,

What in human experience has science not explained to us? Students give many insightful and varied responses; however, one student always answers that we don't know what happens to us after we die. The comments allow us to examine *Sula's* alternative reality without the ingrained skepticism that usually impedes discussion of the validity of other systems of knowledge.[5] In addition to incorporating the supernatural into the novel, Morrison disrupts our sense of linear time and numerical order, which are among the basic tenets of scientific thought. (For a discussion of the disruption of linear time in relation to history and myth in African American women's texts, see K. Holloway, *Moorings* 100–05.) In the chapter "1923," when strange things begin happening in the Bottom, the opening sentence of the chapter dislodges our sense of structure, because we learn of the "second strange thing" before we have any idea of what the first is (58). The disturbance of the usual numerical order, along with earlier anomalies like the unexplainable indistinguishability of the deweys despite their difference in appearance, invites students—as Coleridge requested—to suspend disbelief.

The acceptance of both the natural and supernatural is part of an African worldview, often dismissed by Western rationalists. In "Rootedness" Morrison addresses the concept of "discredited knowledge" ("discredited only because Black people were discredited"): "We are very practical people . . . but within that practicality we also accepted what I suppose could be called superstition and magic, which is another way of knowing things" (342). In *Sula* a main character who exhibits this knowledge is Eva, Sula's grandmother. In some ways she is an earlier version of the Africanized Pilate in *Song of Solomon*, living in a three-generation women's household that resists assimilation. There is an extended family of a sort, and Eva is the matriarch who keeps things together in opposition to racism and poverty. Like Ajax's mother, she is a conjure woman; she saves her children through the mysterious loss of a leg and learns about what she has not heard or witnessed (like the death of Chicken Little) through conversations with her dead son, Plum. Although Eva is a more controversial character than the loving Pilate, she reflects a West African model of a woman who is resourceful and who is a citizen in her own right (see, e.g., Clarke). Eva passes on much of her resourcefulness to her two daughters, but she can't save Plum from drug addiction. No worldview condones the killing of one's child, but students can better understand this distortion of mother love when it is put in the historical context of slave mothers who committed infanticide rather than have their children live a life of slavery (a subject Morrison further develops in *Beloved*). And because we accept that Plum explains things to Eva from beyond the grave, we may assume that he too has forgiven her (145).

Sula, although confrontational and suspicious toward her grandmother, retains many of Eva's characteristics. Like Eva, Sula is a powerful woman, connected to an alternative reality. Like the story of Eva's leg, Sula's birthmark engenders all kinds of community mythologies. Sula is marked from birth by a configuration on her face that changes with her actions and people's perceptions of her. In many African cultures, a unique marking on a child often indicates the child's relationship to an ancestral figure as well as presages some future event in which the child will participate. (For example, Nat Turner's mother saw his markings at birth as a sign that he was destined for greatness [Greenberg 44].) Vashti Crutcher Lewis comments that Shadrack's perception of Sula's birthmark as a tadpole "links her ontologically" to Shadrack's role as a water priest or spirit (319). We can further read Jude's envisioning of Sula's birthmark as a copperhead as representative of their future betrayal of Nel. Finally, and most revealing, is the community's realization that Sula's birthmark is "Hannah's ashes, marking her [as evil] from the very beginning" (99). One might not fault Sula with somehow prenatally conjuring Hannah's death—as the community implies—since Eva sees it as the "perfection of a judgment" on Eva for burning Plum (67). Instead, in this alternative view of human and natural relations, one might conclude that Hannah's death was inscribed in Sula's birth—possibly explaining why Sula watched her mother die "with interest" (67). The Caribbean writer and philosopher Wilson Harris calls these relations "acausal"—again resisting the scientific notion of cause and effect.[6]

Sula's acausal relation to nature—as exemplified by her return to Medallion with the plague of robins—and her refusal to live according to conventions make her a pariah. However, this does not, at first, affect her friendship with Nel. From the beginning Nel and Sula appear polar opposites, but it is evident early in their friendship that their apparent difference contains a likeness. This implies another ontological shift that reflects an African-based cosmology. Chinua Achebe refers to Igbo cosmological notions of otherness: "Wherever something stands, something else will stand beside it" (*Morning* 161). This African concept of the interrelatedness of ostensible opposites, prefiguring poststructuralist theory, helps us decipher the intricate and complicated relationship between Sula and Nel and begins to make comprehensible Sula's presumed betrayal of her best friend.

Like families in other Morrison novels, Nel's family leads a middle-class existence of conventionality and assimilation, while Sula's family is a loosely constructed African American revisioning of African extended family organization. But the two women's lives intersect in many ways: they share the same dreams, they develop their notions of sexuality conjointly, and together they resist the excesses of each household. Nel keeps Sula focused because she is more "consistent" than her friend (45), and Sula directs Nel away from the destructive aspects of assimilation to which Mrs. Wright is prone. After becoming friends with Sula, Nel stops shaping her nonaquiline nose with a clothespin, and she no longer wants to smooth her hair with the "hateful hot comb" (47). This is both young girls' primary relationship; Sula and Nel share stories, boyfriends, and of course the secret of Chicken Little's death. "Their friendship was so close, they themselves had difficulty distinguishing one's thoughts from the other's" (72). Even Nel's marriage excites Sula, who takes over the preparations for it.

The scene in which Nel walks in on Sula and Jude on all fours is singularly distressing to readers. The way the novel is constructed, Sula's betrayal of Nel seems much greater than Jude's. For students, who often identify with Sula because of her nonconformity and independence, it is a shock. We find it hard to forgive Sula this transgression. In teaching the section, I try to return the students to the novel's structure, away—for the moment—from the valid response of considering how they would feel if it were done to them. We look at Sula's view of the relationship and her inability to understand why Nel was jealous, since they had shared everything else. In their final confrontation Nel asks why Sula couldn't have left Jude alone, since they were such good friends. Sula responds, "If we were such good friends, how come you couldn't get over it?" (125). In class I raise a point only hinted at in the novel, that in a polygamous household, still prevalent in many African societies, Sula and Nel might have been able to share Jude amicably. But more germane is the incident's relation to the Western notion that conjugal relationships are the most important in human interaction. According to Niara Sudarkasa, African-based societies often emphasize consanguinal relations over conjugal. She further states that these extended family networks, because of the African American experience in slavery and afterwards, also included communal relations (39–45). Wilhelmina Manns comments that within these communal relations were "significant others," such as friends, related by neither kinship nor marriage (249). In this light, we may also consider Nel to have betrayed Sula. Certainly, the understanding of the strength of human bonds other than conjugal lends resonance to Sula's last comment to her friend: "How you know . . . about who was good . . . ? I mean maybe it wasn't you. Maybe it was me" (126).

The novel seems to pose Nel and Sula as polar opposites, especially as they grow up—Nel as a good woman, that is, one who acquiesces to the conventions of society (dominant culture), and Sula as an evil woman, that is, one who rejects community mores. This opposition, which Morrison places and displaces throughout the novel (and especially in the above scene), reflects an ingrained binary opposition in Western culture. Melville Herskovits forcefully argues that African Americans as a group have resisted the dichotomy "between good and evil in the realm of the supernatural, but [believe] that both are attributes of the same powers in terms of predisposition and control" (242). According to Herskovits, this worldview is "characteristically" African, and it "contrasts vividly with the European habit of separating good and evil so strongly that the concept of the two as obverse and reverse of the same coin is almost nonexistent" (243). An African-based understanding of good and evil is explicitly articulated by the community in its response to Sula's behavior: "They would no more run Sula out of town than they would kill the robins that brought her back, for in their secret awareness of Him, He was not the God of three faces they sang about. They knew quite well that He had four, and the fourth explained Sula" (102).

The community's acceptance of both Sula and Shadrack reflects a worldview that is an alternative to the binary oppositions in much of Western discourse. The people of Medallion, who live with irrational prejudice and oppression and survive "floods" and "white people" (78), comprehend in their cosmology that since you can't exorcise evil, you had better keep an eye on it. An understanding of these beliefs prepares my students and me for the surrealistic judgment of the tunnel disaster. Through National Suicide Day, Shadrack protects the community by dedicating one day a year to confronting fear and death. Shadrack's ritual connects loosely to ancestor worship rites, and I end my discussion with the function of the ancestor. Commenting on the importance of the ancestor figure in African American literature, Morrison states that, in many works by African American writers, "it was the absence of an ancestor that was frightening, that was threatening, and it caused huge destruction and disarray" ("Rootedness" 343). Daniel Wambutda explains this concept within an African context: "Along with other spiritual forces, [the ancestors] are expected to guard the interest of the community. . . . If offended, however, [they] can also inflict one form of misfortune or another" (132). The community flounders as National Suicide Day becomes a sort of mass suicide, based both in anger at the unfairness of the system and in the rejection of the ancestors whose role it is to protect the community. Sula, despite her power, has no ancestor to guide her (Eva, finally, is no Pilate), and Shadrack, shattered by Sula's death, is unable by the end of the novel to tap into the ancestral presence. Ironically, only the most assimilated (like Mrs. Wright) and those who, through their connection to the ancestors, "understood the Spirit's touch" were saved from the tragedy in the tunnel they were forbidden to build and tried to kill (137–38).

After the tunnel disaster, we return in the final chapter to the novel's present. Through Nel's realization, we learn that the Bottom, as a place that houses a community, is no more; people no longer "drop by" for conversation but stay home and watch television (143). Morrison, like other African American women writers, is committed to passing on the traditions of her culture— once communicated through orature and through dropping by—to neighborhoods everywhere that are no longer places. She thus takes on the role of the African woman (writer) whose position in society is to impart her culture's values and mores to future generations. (For a fuller discussion of the role of the African woman and African American women writers, see Wilentz, *Binding* xxvi–xxxiii.)

A reading of *Sula* in an African context not only presents critical insights into a complex text but also allows students to explore a significant part of our rich African American cultural heritage. An African-based approach broadens the knowledge and cultural understanding students can bring to Morrison's writings, and it enables teachers and students to enter into the special rapport Morrison hopes to find with her readers, a truly interactive and participatory relationship that re-creates the time when "an artist could be genuinely representative *of* the tribe and *in* it" ("Rootedness" 339).

NOTES

I would like to thank my graduate students and friends Kathleen Cusick and Selden Durgom for their comments on this essay as students and beginning teachers.

[1]Many African writers and critics refer to the participatoriness of their art. See, for example, Achebe, "Writer."

[2]*Sula* has been read in numerous ways—for example, as part of an African American women's literary tradition, as a psychoanalytic discourse, as a poststructuralist narrative, and as a lesbian novel. An African-based reading does not discount other interpretations and can coexist with them.

[3]Morrison comments that despite her interest in the African presence, she does not want to "encourage those totalizing approaches to African-American scholarship which have no drive other than the exchange of dominations" (*Playing* 8).

[4]Some of the works outside literary study that I have found most useful are *The Myth of the Negro Past* (Herskovits), *Precolonial Black Africa* (Diop), *Flash of the Spirit* (Thompson), *Africanisms in American Culture* (J. Holloway), *The Black Woman Cross-Culturally* (Steady), and *Women in Africa and the African Diaspora* (Terborg-Penn, Harley, and Rushing). Some contemporary literary critics using this kind of approach are Abena Busia, Chinosole, and Henry Louis Gates, Jr., as well as the critics cited in this essay.

[5]M. Akin Makinde comments wryly about the narrowness of the scientific vision, "Although a scientist may argue that there are good scientific reasons for preferring science to magic, presumably, there would be good magical reasons for preferring magic to science in certain cases and circumstances" (92).

[6]Harris referred to this concept in a seminar at the University of Texas in spring 1983. For Harris's important musings on the multiplicity of cultural visions in the Americas, see *Explorations*.

Songs of the Ancestors:
Family in *Song of Solomon*

Keith E. Byerman

I have found *Song of Solomon* the most difficult of Toni Morrison's novels to teach. Not only does it involve her usual sophisticated, often poetic, style and her own version of magical realism, but it also features her most complex and complicated plot and her most elaborate use of African American folklore. Students often simultaneously express frustration and a desire to simplify the text to interpret it within their realm of experience. I have found that the most effective way to work through the difficulties in the classroom is to focus on the representation of family. This focus allows exploration of all the crucial aspects of the book: structure (the quest motif), characterization and relationships, theme, forms of folk material, symbolic patterns, and social criticism. From the birth of the protagonist, Milkman Dead, on the first page to his replication of his ancestor's flight on the last, the narrative is defined and driven by family.

At the outset we must clearly understand the multilayered meaning of "family" in this text. Morrison offers an analysis of the American nuclear family, a version of the extended family in which several living generations interact, and a family history that reflects an African worldview in that ancestral spirits affect the destinies of the living. The author is also concerned with the ambiguities of family; she seeks to avoid sentimentality and animosity in her portrayals. The families in all her fiction are both loving and deeply troubled; the two characteristics are in fact often indistinguishable. Love destroys as often as it creates, and trouble often leads to the reconstruction of identity and relationships.

Given such complexity, the instructor must take care to avoid oversimplification in the discussion of characters and situations. It is easy, for example, to set up a straightforward moral dichotomy between Macon Dead (Milkman's father) and Macon's sister Pilate; indeed Morrison seems to encourage such a division. Macon's immediate family epitomizes the negative connotations of the term *black bourgeoisie*. Macon himself derives his identity from his possessions; he considers his rental property more important than the people who live in it, and he values his home and car more than he does his wife and children. He will exploit anything and anyone to enhance his wealth and status. His home is in truth a Dead place, where members of the family lead empty, frustrated lives. In contrast, his sister Pilate, with whom he maintains no contact, has created a lively, loving environment despite her lack of money, status, or conventional family structure. She sustains a multigenerational family of women that is also embedded in the African American community. She, unlike her brother, has sought to hold onto remnants of their family history, including a sack she believes contains the bones of a white man her brother killed.

Despite these profound differences, Morrison does not allow us to draw the obvious conclusions. For example, it is worthwhile to explore with students how Macon's materialism is grounded in the childhood trauma of seeing his father murdered by whites envious of his father's success. His response is to secure the greatest possible economic power so as to put himself beyond white control. Tracing a character's full personal history leads students to conclusions very different from the assumptions with which they began. Directed discussion of why Macon is as he is rather than simple examination of what he is can shift the focus dramatically. In fact, Macon's exploitation of others arguably serves as a form of resistance to a deadly racist system. While exploring Macon's history does not turn him into a hero, it does help students avoid reading the book as a simple melodrama.

Careful character analysis leads to similarly complex conclusions about Pilate. A key question is the effectiveness of her love. When Hagar, her granddaughter, falls in love with Milkman, who coldly rejects her, nothing Pilate can do saves the girl from obsession and self-destruction. Ironically, Pilate herself interceded years earlier when Macon wanted his wife Ruth to abort the unborn Milkman. Thus the life Pilate saved in the past destroys the one she loves in the present. Literature students often exhibit both a strong pragmatic instinct and a sentimental or idealistic impulse; instructors can turn this conflict into a useful tension by asking students to consider at length what good Pilate's generous heart does her.

Given the tendency of students (and some critics) to simplify these familial differences into moral absolutes, I have found it helpful to encourage students to talk about what they believe family ought to be and do. They tend largely to agree on certain values: security, nurture, and esteem. But when race is introduced into the discussion, the issue becomes more complex. The African American students I have taught are more likely than white students to come from single-parent, economically marginal families and thus are less likely to idealize Pilate's household or to criticize Macon's. Once the question shifts from what ought to be to what is possibly in a racially and economically discriminatory society, most students begin to see what kind of person Macon feels he has to be to achieve his version of the American dream. And both black and white students from single-parent families understand the limitations of Pilate's family arrangements; their experiences teach them that love and emotional strength do not automatically overcome all the problems of such a household.

In addition, it is useful to refer to other scenes in which the book's African American community itself problematizes the conventional student reading of Macon and Pilate. The community, after all, sees Pilate as the freak because she has no navel. By asking students why such a difference would be significant, the instructor can link family with folk beliefs and values, a connection of central importance to interpreting the novel. The lack of a navel implies the lack of natural family ties. The scapegoating of Pilate reveals the community's commitment to such a natural order. Pilate's abnormality must mean something; there are no accidents in nature. *Song of Solomon* is in part about the construction of meaning in an often disorderly universe. The circumstances of Pilate's anatomy provide a relatively straightforward way to get at that point.

Ambiguities are apparent not only in the present time of the novel but also in its sections concerning the past. Unlike Alex Haley, Margaret Walker, and other recent authors, Morrison does not see the African American past as an undiluted tale of black suffering and heroism. (On Morrison's use of history, see Foreman; Kubitschek; Fabre.) The family legend that Milkman uncovers as he returns to the South and to history is very much a part of the folk tradition. (On elements of folklore in the novel, see Blake, "Folklore"; Byerman; De Weever; T. Harris; Hovet and Lounsberry.) He finds in children's songs and in oral performances the tale of his ancestor, variously named Solomon and Shalimar. It is the folktale of the flying African, versions of which have existed for many generations. Morrison makes the tale a part of Milkman's family history and uses it to explore the ambiguities of the past. One of the first problems I encounter in teaching this section of the novel is encouraging students to distinguish myth from history without diminishing the power of either. They have relatively little difficulty accepting Solomon as mythic and even seeing how such a myth could be useful to African Americans, especially in slavery. But it is harder for them to accept that he is historical as well, that he is Milkman's actual ancestor, since they believe that real people cannot fly. They can link myth and history if the instructor presents Milkman's quest as the solving of a puzzle in which the past is constructed, not given. Milkman gathers information and impressions from his father, Pilate, Circe, and the Shalimar community and shapes them into a meaningful tale. I ask students to piece together the information for themselves and fashion their own explanations from the evidence. They begin to see history not as fixed but as a creation of the observer, made to meet the creator's needs.

Then they must confront the meaning of what Milkman has made. The story Milkman constructs is not only one of heroic magic, in which Solomon one day tires of slavery and so flies back to Africa, but also one in which such magic requires the abandonment of family. Solomon leaves behind his wife and many children to face alone an enslaved future. The very act that ensures a remarkable family history also begins a tradition of family disruption that persists into Milkman's generation. It is important to point out the parallels because classes intrigued by the folkloric magic often resist the connection to the present, in part because it seems to destroy the magic.

Milkman, of course, is the center of the novel. His quest structures the book, his identity is shaped and changed by the events of the story, and his insight gives meaning to this family history. But students must be encouraged to see him not as an isolated individual but as part of a community and a family. It is valuable to suggest that Morrison works against the American literary grain of individualism. Milkman is no Bartleby, Jake Barnes, or even Invisible Man. He is always within a network of relationships, even when he tries to be outside them. Both his positive and his negative qualities are determined by the family. He gets his name—Milkman—from his mother's suckling him long past normal weaning age. He develops an exaggerated sense of self-worth because the family disparages his sisters in favor of him. His few real moments of pleasure come in his Aunt Pilate's house, and it is her granddaughter who initiates him sexually. The early part of the novel can be taught as a bildungsroman, but that traditional approach needs to be contextualized by the role of family in the protagonist's development. His journey south itself begins in a conspiracy with his father to exploit Pilate, then continues as he seeks both family treasure and family name.

The story, then, is made from a family history of violence, greed, and betrayal. But in Morrison's dialectical vision, redemption is possible only through such evil.[1] And just as the negative aspects of Milkman's character are clarified through family, so must his transformation come through them. When he arrives in the family hometown, he finds a community memory of his father and grandfather, and in it he hears a respect for their material possessions and manipulative energy that seems to validate his own desires. But he also finds an incredibly old woman, Circe, who calls into question the morality of his search. She keeps family history, but she contextualizes it through her memory of the injustices committed by whites, including the murder of his grandfather. The episode suggests to Milkman that history is not merely self-serving; therefore discussion should focus more on Circe's moral function than on her almost mythical status in the book. The scene provides another opportunity to make clear Morrison's use of myth to comment on history.

The joining of these two episodes in discussion should point out the emerging ambiguity of Milkman's quest. Milkman still seeks the gold, but the family story has itself begun to take on value as a means of generating the sense of self he lacks. Students should now begin to see the search as a complex of spiraling movements: deeper and deeper into the South, from the city to the town to the village to the cave, and back through the generations. This return to origins is essential to a discovery of the true self.

Symbolic of the changes necessary for self-realization is Milkman's experience in the village of Shalimar. Here his city clothes, city talk, and city values are not privileged; they are in fact seen as making him a white-hearted intruder. Though he believes he is seeking his roots, he must undergo rituals of cleansing and testing before he can decode the tale of history. Some discussion of the initiation theme usually helps undergraduates at this point. It both establishes the tradition Morrison is working in and allows students to see how she revises it. In a hunting ceremony that is a rewriting of similar narratives in Faulkner, Hemingway, and others, Milkman experiences the male initiation rite that he never had and thus is enabled to emerge from his extended, narcissistic childhood. Like Ike McCaslin of Faulkner's "The Bear," he is stripped of all the emblems of the dominant culture and must use his instincts to survive.[2] By learning what he is capable of as simply himself, he learns the value and necessity of family and community. Morrison's revision of this ritual tradition is seen in Milkman's new appreciation and respect for women. Having tested his manhood, he no longer has to prove it through sexual domination.

It is consistent with Milkman's return to basics that he finally realizes the family story he seeks is embedded in the song of the village children. They sing the story of Solomon, who one day discovered his magical power and flew from slavery back to Africa. He left behind a wife, Ryna, and twenty-one children, including Jake, Milkman's grandfather. Ryna, like Hagar, is driven crazy by the abandonment, and her children must be cared for by Heddy, an American Indian. The seemingly random elements of family history can now be presented to the class as a coherent narrative: The men (Solomon, Jake, Macon, Milkman) seek magical or material power; the women (Ryna, Sing, Ruth, Hagar) must suffer for this pursuit; and the children are abandoned because of it. Parts of the story also become community folklore, such as Milkman's name, the stories about his grandfather, and the children's song of Solomon.

Instructors should emphasize the importance of the folkloric aspect of the novel because it indicates the work's larger meaning. The linking of family to folk traditions and to history indicates Morrison's understanding of African American life as creative and in some sense organic. Folklore is not local color; it is integral to the fabric of black experience. It is a means by which people who have suffered and who were denied a history and an identity validate themselves. Milkman supplements Circe's story of white domination and violence by uncovering and creating a tale of an African American past filled with magic, love, moral dilemmas, and tragedy. A man totally absorbed in a self-centered present is transformed into a true son of Solomon.

But discussion cannot stop even here, because with this change also comes a revision of the parable. The class needs to focus on what Milkman does with his new understanding, and this examination leads to the "magical" conclusion. Once a Dead man who escapes responsibility and emotional commitment, the protagonist becomes a Milkman who uses his power to nurture others. He brings Pilate to the cave to rebury the bones, which he now knows are those of his grandfather. He thus relieves her guilt and simultaneously gives his ancestor a proper interment. At this moment she is killed by Milkman's friend Guitar, who believes the quest is still for gold and who, like the white men who killed Pilate's father, values possessions over human life. Milkman responds by offering Guitar the life he needs to take:

> "You want my life?" Milkman was not shouting now. "You need it? Here."
> Without wiping away the tears, taking a deep breath, or even bending his knees—he leaped. As fleet and bright as a lodestar he wheeled toward Guitar and it did not matter which one of them would give up his ghost in the killing arms of his brother. For now he knew what Shalimar knew: If you surrendered to the air, you could *ride* it.   (Knopf, 337)

The natural question for students is the meaning of this final gesture. Is it suicidal? Is it sacrificial? Does Milkman really believe he can fly? Milkman revises the family history by flying into history and responsibility rather than out of it. He incorporates even Guitar the destroyer by naming him a brother and thus a part of the tradition. Destruction becomes a part of the creativity of history. And it does not matter which one of them dies, because the flying is life affirming even if it results in death, since it establishes the connection with the spirit of the ancestors, including now Pilate, who, in a play on her name, leads the way into the spirit world.

Through the use of family in this text, Morrison encourages a rethinking of both the American and the African American past. The point becomes, first, to acknowledge the full humanity of both pasts, in all their ambiguity. To make blacks only invisible persons or only heroic martyrs is to restrict and even deny that humanity. Pain, love, betrayal, abandonment, affirmation, and responsibility are all entangled in history. Then and only then can that story become a guide to the future. It is possible to revise, to transform oneself and reality by embracing the full variety of the self and the community. Even those who intend harm must be embraced as family. The nation, the race, the community, and the self can succeed only through a practice of inclusion that respects difference but does not reify it. What Morrison espouses through the metaphor of family is a true song of Solomon, a new story of love and wisdom.

NOTES

[1]The notion of dialectic is an excellent aid to student understanding. Not merely the presence of opposites but also their constant interaction is crucial to Morrison's vision, as the contrast of Macon and Pilate demonstrates, for example.

[2]It is noteworthy that Morrison did her master's thesis on Faulkner. On Faulkner's influence on the novel, see Duvall; Cowart.

Telling Stories: A Cultural Studies Approach to *Tar Baby*

Marilyn Sanders Mobley

I have not written about being a Negro at such length
because I expect that to be my only subject, but only
because it was the gate I had to unlock before I could
hope to write about anything else. I don't think that the
Negro problem in America can be even discussed
coherently without bearing in mind its context; its
context being the history, traditions, customs, the moral
assumptions and preoccupation of the country; in short,
the general social fabric.

—James Baldwin, *Notes of a Native Son*

The frontiers of a book are never clear-cut; beyond the
title, the first lines, and the last full stop, beyond its
internal configuration and its autonomous form, it is
caught up in a system of references to other books, other
texts, other sentences: it is a node within a
framework. . . . The book is not simply the object that
one holds in one's hands; and it cannot remain within the
little parallelepiped that contains it: its unity is variable
and relative. As soon as one questions that unity, it loses
its self-evidence; it indicates itself, constructs itself, only
on the basis of a complex field of discourse.

—Michel Foucault, *The Archaeology of Knowledge
and the Discourse on Language*

There is really nothing more to say—except why. But
since *why* is difficult to handle, one must take refuge in
how.

—Toni Morrison, *The Bluest Eye*

Whenever I teach a novel by Toni Morrison, I want my students to keep in
mind that the text is written by an author concerned with how culture—particularly American culture—operates. I seek to help them discern the multiple
layers of discourse, signs, and signifiers at work in culture and the ways these
signs and signifiers produce identities, subjectivities, and communities, African
American and otherwise. I first attempt to establish the multiple contexts for
Morrison's work, whether the course is African American Literature of the
Twentieth Century, in which I usually teach one Morrison text; Toni Morrison
in Context, in which I teach all the novels along with work by other writers in

the African American women's literary tradition, such as Zora Neale Hurston, Alice Walker, Paule Marshall, Gloria Naylor, and Marita Golden; or The Novels of Toni Morrison, in which I focus exclusively on the novels. While I avoid reductive readings that suggest essentialist definitions of black texts or black women's texts, I want to point out recurring cultural patterns in African American expression, epistemology, and cosmology; therefore I usually invite the students to think about the African American literary tradition, the African American woman writer's presence in that tradition, and the conspiracy of silence around race, class, and gender that will inevitably both constrain and enable discussion of Morrison's fiction. The recent paradigm shift from literary studies to cultural studies, I note to my students, is of particular interest in African American studies, an inherently interdisciplinary field that has always provided a political critique of representations and discursive practices; and this shift offers additional possibilities for teaching one of Morrison's most challenging novels. Indeed one reason for the difficulty of *Tar Baby* is that it engages the reader to contemplate complex historical, cultural, and political issues, and these issues stylistically complicate reading and understanding in ways that call attention to the rich African American folk, vernacular, and narrative traditions that inform her fiction. Thus a useful way to teach this novel is to invite students to examine, analyze, even revel in the dialogic density of Morrison's prose, in the complexity of the stories she attempts to tell, and in her texts' critique of American cultural practices. In other words, I encourage what Clifford Geertz would call "thick descriptions" of the texture, text, and context composing the layers of discourse and narrative that produce meaning in *Tar Baby*.

I begin by introducing the African American literary tradition as a series of conversations about what it means to be a person of African descent on American soil. I identify five pivotal periods in the series: from the African past to enslavement; from enslavement to Reconstruction; from Reconstruction to the Harlem Renaissance; from the Harlem Renaissance to the Black Arts Movement of the sixties; and from the Black Arts Movement to the present. I explain that the African American literary tradition is informed by folklore, the oral tradition, vernacular discourse, and African epistemology and cosmology. Anticipating the discussion of *Tar Baby*, I quote Morrison's statement, "We don't live in places where we can hear those stories anymore; parents don't sit around and tell their children those classical, mythological, archetypal stories that we heard years ago" ("Rootedness" 340). Like the African griot who memorizes the stories of the village community, Morrison enters the series of conversations with a narrative project to tell stories that have not been told, to tell old stories in a new way, and to speak the "unspeakable things" that have been left unspoken. Although each writer enters into this series with her or his own narrative poetics, to a certain extent each responds to questions of race, gender, class, history, identity, and community as reflected in her or his own cultural moment.

By combining an introduction to African American literary theory, criticism, and culture with an introduction to feminist theory and reader-response criticism, I offer my students a glimpse into the politics of their own reading. The work of such scholars as Deborah McDowell, Nellie McKay, Michele Wallace, Michael Awkward, Mae Henderson, Houston Baker, bell hooks, Henry Louis Gates, Peter Brooks, Steven Mailloux, Inge Crosman Wimmers, and Patrocinio Schweickart informs my teaching of the ideological underpinnings of interpretation. I remind students that their reading or interpretation of a text (as well as mine) is always already informed with these underpinnings; at the same time I hope they remain open to new ways of entering the textual spaces that Morrison consciously and unconsciously creates for her readers. I intend this attention to prepare them not only for understanding the concept of dialogism in Morrison's novels but also for dealing with the inevitable manifestation of heteroglossia—Bakhtin's term for the noisy context of words—in the classroom. As Bakhtin says in "Discourse in the Novel":

> [T]he word, directed toward its object, enters a dialogically agitated and tension-filled environment of alien words, value judgments and accents, weaves in and out of complex interrelationships, merges with some, recoils from others, intersects with yet a third group: and all this may crucially shape discourse, may leave a trace in all its semantic layers, may complicate its expression and influence its entire stylistic profile.   (276)

By foregrounding these layers of tension-filled discourse, I anticipate the ideological and interpretive clashes that emerge in racially and ethnically diverse classrooms because "the habit of ignoring race is understood to be a graceful, even generous, liberal gesture," as Morrison says (*Playing* 9–10). Like Michele Wallace, I am interested in how distinct categories of population read culture differently and reproduce the unequal relations between discourses in the classroom. Although "cultural orphan" is the term Valerian thinks of to criticize his son Michael's propensity for seeking "other cultures he could love without risk or pain," I ask students to consider whether Jadine is a cultural orphan (Plume-Dutton, 145). If she is, what heritage has she lost? What does it mean to keep one's heritage intact? What does her adoption of Valerian's Eurocentric values and attitudes mean for her relation with what the text calls her "ancient properties" (305)? In what way is she on the border of "high culture" while Son is on the border of mass culture, or what Jadine considers "low culture"? How do the sexual politics between Jadine and Son help Morrison tell another story about cultural politics, about racial politics? Because I have had white women students who view Jadine positively and black women students who view her negatively in the same class, I often ask them what constitutes a liberated woman (even if the term seems somewhat dated). It is useful to respond to these clashes, whether over race, gender, or class, by having what I call metadiscourse days—days during which we focus on the use of language itself as a source of tension in our discussions. Even a few moments of metadiscourse help students negotiate difficult feelings and attitudes arising from differing responses to the text, understand what is at stake in the various conflicts that emerge in the text, and perceive the ways in which language is contested terrain, or, to use the words of bell hooks, in which "language is also a place of struggle" (*Talking* 28).

If nothing else, *Tar Baby* is about conflict. As the epigraph states, "For it hath been declared unto me of you, my brethren . . . that there are contentions among you." While it is useful to review the various versions of the African and African American tar baby folktale of the rabbit outwitting the fox, Trudier Harris correctly cautions readers against comparing the folktale and the novel too literally. As she contends, "It becomes increasingly less clear in Morrison's work whose territory is being invaded, who is the tar baby, who is trapped, who needs rescue from whom, and whether or not he (or she) effects an escape" (116). However, a sense of the early forms of the folktale enables students to see how Morrison transforms it into what I call a modern cautionary tale. I suggest that this cautionary tale is a manifestation of Morrison's folk aesthetic in which the folktale gets transformed right before the reader's eyes through "a series of conflicts or disruptions that dramatize the interplay between form and substance, silence and truth, nest and journey, self and other, public and private, mother and daughter" (137). Situating her tale on an island in the Caribbean—Isle des Chevaliers—enables Morrison to foreground and exaggerate the very conflicts that determine the cultural malaise in the United States. Her narrative strategy is analogous to taking a substance out of its familiar habitat and studying it under a microscope.

Yet Morrison is not so much interested in resolving these conflicts as in narrating them. In an interview with Nellie McKay, she explains:

> [T]he way in which I handle elements within a story frame is important. . . . There is always something more interesting at stake than a clear resolution in a novel. I'm interested in survival—who survives and who does not, and why—and I would like to chart a course that suggests where the dangers are and where the safety might be. I do not want to bow out with easy answers to complex questions.   (420)

Therefore, it is interesting to approach this novel by moving from a basic understanding of the folktale to the narrative itself; to the setting, which shapes its cultural and social context; to the central characters, whose lives shape the conflicts around which the narrative revolves; and to the layers of meaning that give texture to the discourse in the novel, which shapes the larger story.

The novel begins with Son's arrival and ends with his departure. Students will probably want to speculate about how it is significant that the island that Son sees from a distance in the opening chapter—the "island that, three hundred years ago, had struck slaves blind the moment they saw it"—is the same island he flees to at the end (8). The historical reference encoded in this description of the island serves as a counterpoint to the ahistorical lives of the occupants at L'Arbe de la Croix. As a stowaway, someone whose very position makes him ahistorical (i.e., out of history), it is fitting that he considers the possibility of being discovered in narrative terms:

> He had nothing in mind to say if anyone suddenly appeared. It was better not to plan, not to have a ready-made story because, however tight, prepared stories sounded most like a lie. The sex, weight, the demeanor of whomever he encountered would inform and determine his tale.   (5)

A sense of history and culture determines Morrison's tale. Moving from Son's arrival to a description of the island to which he flees, Morrison narrates the story of the colonial and imperialist forces that have shaped both the past and present histories of the people who reside there. A phrase from chapter 1—"laborers imported from Haiti" (9)—speaks volumes about the forces that transformed the land, abused the river, and created the swamp "Sein de Vieilles," with its "thick black substance that even mosquitoes could not live near" (10). The privileged lives and lavish house of Valerian Street, the candy tycoon, and his wife, Margaret, the "Principal Beauty of Maine" (11), operate not only to retell a history of class and racial struggle but also to critique it. Beyond Morrison's characteristic attention to place, students should notice the details she uses to describe the Streets: everything from Valerian's preference for reading mail over books "because language in them had changed so much—stained with rivulets of disorder and meaninglessness"—to Margaret's history of abusing her son, reveal much about the forces that shape Jadine's consciousness (14).

By thus engaging students in close readings, I prepare them to answer crucial questions about the protagonist, Jadine. Raised by her Aunt Ondine and Uncle Sydney, then turned over to their employer, Valerian, who finances her education at the Sorbonne, she is considered to have "[e]verything. Europe. The future. The world" (29). One of the first questions I ask students is, To whom does Jadine belong anyway? Students usually understand that this question is less about her literal status as an orphan than about her symbolic status. Like the other characters in self-exile on the island, she exists in a state of liminality, an anthropological concept that is useful for helping students understand being rootless or betwixt and between cultures. Pointing out the sleeping arrangements within the Street household also indicates her problematic relationship to her aunt and uncle and their employers. While she sleeps in a room connected to Margaret's, the servants sleep downstairs, an arrangement that reiterates the power relations in the house.

But at the center of the text, of course, is the conflict between Jadine and Son. Instead of regarding the relationship as purely romantic, a cultural studies approach requires that we examine how and why it develops and then disintegrates. Students should consider Jadine and Son's "reading" of each other.

For example, they first view each other from perspectives born out of cultural stereotypes each has accepted without question. Getting students to discern what the stereotypes are is useful. Jadine and Son each attempt to "rescue" the other on the basis of their assumptions (269). The ways in which the indigenous islanders, such as Therese and Gideon, read Son and Jadine are also important for understanding the various cross-cultural readings that shape the tensions in the characters' interactions. In fact the woman in yellow's reading of Jadine at the beginning of the novel is arguably one of the first instances in which identity, self, and other are introduced as cultural issues.

Reading the text this way may raise other questions, such as how other elements of the narrative fit into the analysis of cultural politics at work in the novel. The Christmas-dinner explosion may be designed to tear off the veneer of cultural cohesion that Margaret and Valerian attempt to maintain. Moreover, the extended passages about Michael, his refusal to join his family, and his exploration of other cultures all pose questions about the silences and secrets that create the illusion of a cohesive family and culture. In addition, the extended references to Valerian, the way of life he left in the States, the one he pursues on the island, and the one he ultimately resigns himself to point to what bell hooks critiques as an exoticism, in which whites view various others (ethnicities) as spice to liven up white culture. That is, Morrison's narrative project in *Tar Baby* is focused not on Jadine alone but on the cultural forces that produce Jadines and, for that matter, Sons as well. The novel reveals how imperialism operates, circulates, and reproduces itself in new forms and places.

The reading of *Tar Baby* that I propose is laden with tension and complications as thick as culture is. It requires students to read the text closely and carefully but also to step outside the text in order to analyze its cultural critique. In other words, the instructor should invite students to see how *Tar Baby* intervenes in contemporary discussions about identity politics, multiculturalism, representation, even tourism and encourage them to examine why these conversations are difficult and why we must engage in them nonetheless. As Stuart Hall says, "[D]angers are not places you run away from but places that you go towards" (285); as Jadine discovers, right before her return to Europe, there are "[n]o more dreams of safety" (290). *Tar Baby* is a disconcerting book to many students. The reading I suggest will make it no less so, but the approach offers students a way through a difficult text and suggests how we might make our way individually and collectively through the difficulties of our own cultural moment.

Teaching *Tar Baby*

Ann Jurecic and Arnold Rampersad

Tar Baby, Toni Morrison's fourth novel, is perhaps the most problematic and probably the least written about and acclaimed of her works. Reviewers and scholars have registered their general uncertainty about the text not only through their widely divergent interpretations and judgments of its artistic merit but also through their relative silence. If the novel perplexes professional critics, students too may have trouble understanding it. Thus in teaching *Tar Baby* one would do well to recognize its controversial aspects that may alienate readers. *Tar Baby* may seem difficult at first because it differs in certain key respects from the rest of Morrison's canon: it is set outside the United States, on a fictional and mythic Caribbean island, and it extensively examines the complicated relations of blacks and whites living close to one another—relations of intimacy and conflict. The novel also makes demands on readers by taking as its foundation the tar baby, the central figure in a folktale that exists in many versions and has diverse origins in African, Asian Indian, and African American cultures (T. Harris 54). An understanding of Morrison's rendering of the tale requires some knowledge of the myth, which many students may not have, and is facilitated further by a basic familiarity with several variations of the myth and a sense of its complex history. Finally, the end of the text has frustrated reviewers and other readers and may frustrate students as well because it offers what seem to be two conclusions. One appears to be for the character Son, the other for Jadine. Unfortunately, they seem to be two irreconcilable resolutions to the conflict involved in constructing the self in relation to issues of race, class, and gender. But the same elements that make the work difficult also make it provocative and thus a particularly rich text to read and to teach.

Morrison's stylized foreign setting is deliberately unfamiliar to the typical reader. The Isle des Chevaliers, described as "the end of the world" (NAL, 9), offers an almost surreal landscape. Luxurious houses sit on the ruins of an ancient rain forest, above a "[p]oor insulted, brokenhearted river" and a swamp called Sein de Vieilles, or witch's tit, "a shriveled fogbound oval seeping with a thick black substance that even mosquitoes could not live near" (10). As in Shakespeare's *The Tempest*, this isle is full of noises. Morrison gives nature there a voice, or many voices; fish, birds, trees, and the river think, speak, and suffer. Indeed, not only the Caribbean setting but also the United States is rendered foreign in the novel. The American homeland is reduced to two discrete islands of culture, Eloe and New York City. Son's home, Eloe, is an isolated haven of black folk culture that nurtures him but threatens Jadine for various reasons, not least of all because the power of women is curtailed there. Jadine, by contrast, is far more at home in New York City, "a black woman's town" (222). Son finds it populated disconcertingly with "a whole new race of people" (217).

While the primary setting may, at first, put off some readers, its essence is recognizably American. It offers readers no escape from "contemporary immediacy," Wahneema Lubiano has asserted, because even there "brand and corporate names so permeate the text that one's nose is rubbed in the 'this worldness' of the story" (329). And L'Arbe de la Croix, the home of the expatriate Street family, evokes the colonial past of America (and France) in the Caribbean. With its explicit stratification of white owners, house servants, and poor workers, the house on the hill is like a plantation. The setting draws attention to the source of the Streets' American wealth in the colonial past. The family made its fortune in the candy business, an industry founded on the exploited land and labor of the Caribbean sugarcane fields. Thus Morrison's depiction of the island ultimately proves a microcosmic portrait of America, with the full spectrum of American history and social problems carefully filtered so that the primary elements of race, class, and gender stand out in sharp relief.

Tar Baby may also strike readers as unusual for its depiction of white culture, a subject Morrison has not often given priority. In her other works, Morrison writes about black culture largely in and of itself, without bringing white culture into the foreground. Occasionally she creates white characters of significance, such as Amy Denver in *Beloved*, whose surname is passed on to the child she helps Sethe deliver. However, in *Beloved* Morrison never allows either this midwife or the plantation owners at Sweet Home to divert narrative focus from the black community. Cynthia Davis asserts that Morrison's general exclusion of white characters from her mythic fiction "allows [Morrison] to treat white culture as 'necessity' without either mythicizing specific acts of oppression or positing present necessity as eternal" (334–35). Morrison's attention to white culture in *Tar Baby* thus may make racial oppression seem mythic or eternal and may estrange readers.

But the major difficulty for some students may be that in *Tar Baby* Morrison writes about race relations that are further complicated by significant—not peripheral—factors of class and gender. The first chapter appears to make explicit a rigid social hierarchy of race and class in which Valerian and Margaret Street, wealthy white Americans, reign, followed by their servants, Sydney and Ondine Childs, who are self-defined "Philadelphia Negroes" (61). At the base are the generically named (and thus without individual identity) Yardman and Mary, Caribbean natives who serve as gardener and laundress for the household. But the introduction of Son and Jadine, the "undocumented" man (166) and the orphaned woman, into this hierarchy reveals that the rules that structure it are complex and sometimes obscure. The Sorbonne-educated model Jadine is Sydney and Ondine's niece, but when she visits she sits at the dining table with the Streets. Son's presence in the Street home also elicits judgments that are not easily categorized. When he appears in Margaret's closet, she accuses him of being a rapist. Sydney and Ondine seem to share her revulsion. Calling the stranger a "wife-raper" (99) and "swamp nigger" (100), they assert that "the man upstairs wasn't a Negro—meaning one of them" (102). Valerian, however, offers Son a guest room and seats him at the family table, where Sydney and Ondine never sit. The relationship between Margaret and Ondine is particularly complex. A working-class past and sense of gender loyalty lead Margaret to seek a friendship with Ondine. However, their relationship is ultimately not a friendship but an uncomfortable blend of familiarity and distance, further complicated by their roles as employer and employee, their differences of class and race, and their shared secret of Margaret's stunning abuse of her child.

Morrison demonstrates how white characters create their privileged identities and dominant status by adopting and adhering to various myths of self-definition. By naming its scion Valerian after an emperor, the Street family evokes a historical representation of power in an apparent attempt to ensure the legitimacy of his authority. (On the Isle des Chevaliers, however, he has competition for his throne from both the emperor butterflies and his laundress, Marie Thérèse, who seems to have been named after the queen consort of Louis XIV of France.) As head of his family's candy-making business, Valerian established himself as the mythically grand Candy King and has retired to his island retreat. Here he had created his own special paradise according to the honored but conventional plantation myth, with himself in the role of benevolent master. Margaret is the candy-colored wife of the Candy King, a pink and white former beauty queen once known as the Principal Beauty of Maine. Readers must recognize that the labels and fictions by which Valerian and Margaret try to define themselves are dangerous not only because they place rigid limits on human identities but also, more important, because they inscribe racism, classism, and sexism within the identities they construct. Valerian's creation of himself as a benign plantation master in a cultivated paradise obscures the history of racial and economic oppression on plantations. Margaret, who embodies the conventional white American ideal of beauty, is insensitive to the racism and sexism that may be inherent in any ideal of physical beauty.

While Morrison investigates the myths by which white characters construct their identities and status, the novel is ultimately more concerned with the myths by which African Americans define themselves. Sydney and Ondine Childs have solidified their own sense of race, class, and cultural role by naming themselves "industrious Philadelphia Negroes—the proudest people in the race" (61). The term "Philadelphia Negro" has its source in the title of W. E. B. Du Bois's landmark 1899 sociological study of the black Seventh Ward of Philadelphia. Many of these blacks worked as servants for whites (*Philadelphia* 136, 428). In adopting the term, the Childses not only create a myth out of African American history that confirms their racial identity but also transform the label to connote the lofty status of a class of black servants who empower themselves mainly by assimilating their white employers' values. Sydney and Ondine create the myth to counter those imposed by white society, but it threatens to entrap them by reinforcing the social boundaries set by the dominant culture. (For a theoretical analysis of countermyths in *Tar Baby* see

Werner, "Briar Patch.") Their choice of the label "Philadelphia Negro" also causes them to cling to an anachronistic social hierarchy. In a study of domestic service appended to Du Bois's study, Isabel Eaton reported that among the most highly paid black servants were those who were, like Sydney and Ondine, butlers and cooks (446–47). The Childses still seem to measure their status according to this scale. Eaton describes yard and laundry work as beneath the better class of servant and recommends hiring such jobs out to lesser servants (502–03). The class prejudice evident in Eaton's description of the Seventh Ward echoes in the Childses' judgment of Yardman and Mary. The dehumanizing myth of the poor black as illiterate, lazy, and anonymous provides a foundation for the Childses' myths of economic and national superiority.

It may appear that above all other characters in the novel, Marie Thérèse Foucault and her nephew Gideon—the black native-born residents of Dominique known as Mary and Yardman—have myth imposed on them as an alien force. To black and white residents of L'Arbe de la Croix, they represent the other. That is, the household members vastly inflate their senses of worth by defining themselves as absolutely different from these workers. But the relation of Thérèse and Gideon to myth is not only that of determined object. The two transform the labels *Yardman* and *Mary* into countermyths. Allowing themselves to be misread as an illiterate man and an anonymous woman, they distance themselves from the dominant culture. Like the countermyths of Sydney and Ondine, however, these myths do not set their creators free. Thérèse and Gideon's acceptance of their position on the margins of society and of their identity as other to the American expatriates does nothing to undermine their oppression and thus may actually reinforce it.

The primary focus of the novel is not on these characters but on Jadine and Son, the culturally ambiguous children who look to the spectrum of available representations of race, class, and gender for those myths by which they can define themselves with dignity. A full appreciation of the two characters and their cultural dilemmas is crucial to comprehending the novel. To gain such an appreciation students will need to understand Morrison's inscription of Jadine and Son into the tar-baby folktale and thus will need to know the tale and its past.

The traditional tar-baby tale has a lengthy history, and scholars have researched its African and Indian origins as well as its many American versions. The tale may be best known through the work of the white writer Joel Chandler Harris. In 1880 Harris popularized the tale in two stories, "The Wonderful Tar-Baby Story" and "How Mr. Rabbit Was Too Sharp for Mr. Fox" (*Uncle Remus*). The tale gained further prominence in popular American culture from Walt Disney's motion picture *Song of the South* (1946).

The many permutations of the story are interesting not only in and of themselves but also because Morrison seems to allude to several of them. Harris's version, which is among the most widely recognized, is an obvious source for Morrison. Harris imposes a frame on the traditional tale: Uncle Remus, an elderly former slave, tells his folktales to a young white boy. In Uncle Remus's narrative, Brer Fox, who is in search of a meal and annoyed at Brer Rabbit for having outfoxed him, creates the tar baby, a "contrapshun" of turpentine and tar, and places it in Brer Rabbit's path. Brer Rabbit meets the tar baby, tries to begin a conversation, and becomes irritated with what he interprets as its refusal to speak. Striking at it, he is completely entrapped in the sticky, black tar. Not until the second story does Uncle Remus complete the tale with Brer Rabbit's escape from the fox. The rabbit frees himself by begging the fox to do anything to him except throw him into the briar patch—which is, in fact, his home. Out of ignorance and cruelty Brer Fox releases the rabbit into the briar patch. Freeing himself, Brer Rabbit finally taunts Brer Fox, "Bred en bawn in a brier-patch, Brer Fox—bred en bawn in a brier-patch!" (*Uncle Remus* 64).

This variation of the tale differs from probably more authentic African American versions that are set during a drought.[1] The first chapter of Morrison's novel, which describes an "exhausted, ill and grieving" river that "slow[s] to a stop just twenty leagues short of the sea," suggests that the author intends to echo this version (9). A version published in the December 1877 *Lippincott's Magazine* contains other elements absent from Harris's tale. Among these are Brer Rabbit's "love for ladies" and the tar baby's appearing to look "like a beautiful girl." The rabbit initially becomes trapped because he kisses the feminine figure and finally blames the "deceitful tar maiden" for his situation (qtd. in Keenan 56). The tar baby in Harris's 1880 stories is also female, as is apparent from the repetition of the phrase "Tar-Baby, she ain't sayin' nuthin'" (58–59), but that is easily overlooked. In an 1893 revision, a translation from Frederic Ortoli's *Les contes de la vielles* entitled "A French Tar-Baby," Harris makes the gender and race of the tar figure—as well as his own racism—more apparent by calling her "Guinea girl" (Keenan 62).

Many elements of these variations of the tar-baby tale echo in Morrison's novel. The history of the tar baby as a signifier of race or gender or both is particularly resonant, but the context of the narrative—who tells the tale, when, and to whom—is also significant to a full understanding of Morrison's work. Angelita Reyes maintains that during the antebellum period slaves told a form of the tale, perhaps inherited from African trickster lore, to educate young slaves to use their intelligence to overcome their masters' power and to conceal their anger behind a mask of humility ("Ancient Properties" 22–23). Hugh T. Keenan maintains that after the Civil War the tar-baby tale served for African Americans as an allegory of their history, of the passage from freedom to entrapment and back to freedom. He analyzes Harris's imposition of the Uncle Remus frame as a device meant to turn the tale into propaganda about the reconstructed South (60–61). Through the figure of the polite young boy, Harris taught his Northern audience that white Southerners were reformed and could be given control over their affairs. White Southerners unhappy with Reconstruction could read this version as representing the struggle of the "unreconstructed south" against the "predatory north" (61). The white Southerner is the rabbit, caught in the tar baby of the "Negro Question." He "distract[s] the Northern fox by asking only to be left alone in his briar patch (local political matters), and finally find[s] himself free by the eventual partial disenfranchisement of the Negro" (61).

Essential to any assessment of *Tar Baby* is an appreciation of it as a reclamation of the myth from this vexed history. Because the tale itself had been an embattled pawn in the cultural conflict of traditional African American and dominant white American culture, it can be read as an allegory of the struggle of those caught between these cultures. The rabbit can be seen as an African American seeking a sense of belonging in either culture; the tar baby created by a fox or a farmer figure may represent temptations of the dominant culture, particularly American materialism. The briar patch may signify traditional African American culture and values or the African aspect of Du Bois's double consciousness. However, that reading of the tale need not be the only one. Brer Rabbit can be seen as encountering any figure or representation that threatens to entrap him. His escape may be toward a firm sense of identity that seems independent of the representations offered by the dominant culture. In the briar patch he appears to find a haven from imposed myth.

Considering the background of the tar-baby tale, Jadine and Son are the two characters in *Tar Baby* who are most clearly caught, like Brer Rabbit, between two cultures. Son overtly positions himself as Brer Rabbit by accusing Jadine of being a tar baby. Once he describes her as a "tar baby side-of-the-road whore trap" (220); he later accuses her of being a decoy created by Valerian (270). Son constructs or envisions Jadine as a feminine tar baby who has accepted the values of white society and who now threatens to ensnare him by luring him into complicity with that society's values and away from his "authentic" home, the traditional black culture in which he was born and bred. (For analyses of Son as Brer Rabbit see K. Holloway, "African Values"; P. Bell; and Hill.) Jadine can also be seen as Brer Rabbit. Marilyn E. Mobley states that Jadine's tar baby is the materialism of the dominant white culture, which tempts her away from the "cultural constructions of race and mothering that are part of her African-American heritage" (763). According to Peter B. Erickson, however, the vision of the African woman in yellow with her "tar-black fingers" (Morrison, *Tar Baby* 46) is Jadine's tar baby, an image of maternity, sexuality, and traditional femininity from which she desires to break free (18). Son could also be seen as Jadine's tar baby. A man of traditional values with a conservative vision of women, he tries to tempt her back into a limited, traditional female role. While Son watches Jadine sleep, he attempts to "manipulate her dreams, to insert his own dreams into her"; these dreams are of "fat black ladies in white dresses minding the pie table in the basement of the church" (119).

By inscribing these characters into the tar-baby tale, Morrison explores some of the cultural choices available to young African American women and men. At the end of the novel Jadine flees into the briar patch of Paris. She seeks to define herself free of the expectations concerning gender, race, and class that she feels overwhelming her on the Isle des Chevaliers and in Eloe. When Son, by contrast, flees into the hills of the island at the close of the novel, he is apparently running toward the mythical horsemen and toward further absorption into a traditional folk culture. He runs from the dominant white culture, from Jadine's rejection of his cultural history, and toward a view of racial identity that emphasizes the power of inherited "ancient properties" and connection with the natural world (305).

It has been difficult for critics to decide on the character for which Morrison feels more sympathy. The ambiguity of Morrison's stance may trouble students. Finally, it seems, neither Son nor Jadine triumphs unequivocally, and neither discovers a cultural choice that is appropriate for them both. In fleeing from family, country, and her African American community, Jadine seems possibly to be denying any value to black culture or traditional femininity. Her life, according to Trudier Harris, "is not about having forgotten her ancient properties; it is a refusal to recognize the existence or value of such properties" (137). Son's escape is equally ambiguous, in part because he remains blind to the oppression of women in his traditional values. And as Keith E. Byerman has observed, Son's escape, like Jadine's, is based on a problematic denial of history. His reclamation of "ancient" values suggests his belief in "the possibility of returning to a prewhite black purity" (215).

The multiple and irreconcilable resolutions to *Tar Baby* have frustrated those seeking a fulfilled "quest for wholeness" in the novel (Coleman 63; M. E. Mobley 763). But in leaving unsolved the problem of how best to define the self in relation to race, class, and gender, Morrison provides "places and spaces so that the reader can participate" (Morrison, "Rootedness" 341). She supplies material for widely divergent analyses of her mythic fiction, thus allowing readers themselves to act as Brer Rabbits while her text serves as a kind of tar baby. The novel places a spectrum of representations of race, class, and gender in the reader's path, tempting engagement and provoking response. While Morrison gives readers room to retreat into familiar cultural positions, to efface contradictions and choose either Jadine or Son as heroic embodiment, she also provides readers space for self-reflection about their stances in relation to these pervasive cultural myths. Students can only benefit from the opportunity for such reflection that this *Tar Baby* offers.

NOTE

[1]Trudier Harris notes that a version of this form of the tale was recorded by Langston Hughes and Arna Bontemps in *The Book of Negro Folklore*. Harris draws on this rendering of the tar-baby tale and analyzes it and Morrison's novel as being "informed by the trickster tradition in African-American folklore" (116). Hugh T. Keenan quotes extensively from a version recorded by William Owens in the December 1877 *Lippincott's Magazine*; it takes a drought and the digging of a well as its context.

Morrison's *Jazz*: "A Knowing So Deep"

Judylyn S. Ryan

> You can start anywhere—Jazz as Communication—since
> it's a circle, and you yourself are the dot in the middle.
> You, me. For example, I'll start with the Blues. . . . Now,
> to wind it all up, with you in the middle—jazz is only
> what you yourself get out of it.
>
> —Langston Hughes

Toni Morrison has frequently discussed the type of participatory reading that her novels are crafted to encourage. She acknowledges that "to have the reader work *with* the author in the construction of the book—is what's important. What is left out is as important as what is there" ("Rootedness" 341). Morrison's self-conscious disposition as an artist opposes the standard view of a reading process in which the reader tries to discover the meaning that the author has carefully hidden in the text. Morrison instead envisions the author and the reader as partners in the dialectical creation of the text and of its meanings, a relation derived from call-and-response forms characteristic of African diaspora oral traditions, particularly in music. Call-and-response structures, inherent in spirituals, the blues, sermons, folktales, and so on, anticipate and require a response that may extend, challenge, revise, clarify, or transform any previous utterance, and they outline a generative sequence in which the response becomes the new call. These structures delineate a performance environment in which creative responsibilities are shared between the lead speaker or singer and the audience, allowing all attentive or informed listeners to become involved. Locating her writing in this tradition of African American art, Morrison concludes, "Having at my disposal only the letters of the alphabet and some punctuation, I have to provide the places and spaces so that the reader can participate" (341).

The prescription for a dialectical collaboration between author and reader, designed in accordance with call-and-response principles, is entirely relevant to a discussion of approaches to teaching Morrison's novels. It recalls and exemplifies the type of liberating pedagogy advocated by the renowned Brazilian educator Paulo Freire.[1] Like the student in Freire's pedagogical paradigm, Morrison's reader must help construct the text. Both approaches reflect a belief that the reader or student must be encouraged to develop and depend on internal sources of knowledge in preparation for long-term social responsibilities as an agent of transformation. *Jazz*, more than any of Morrison's previous works, demands conscious participation from its readers. The novel's ostensible failure to provide answers to the many questions it raises must, therefore, be reconsidered as an opportunity for the reader to enter the text and formulate her or his own interpretation from the many layers of knowing densely configured in this novel. For as Morrison observes, the novel should have "something in it that suggests what the conflicts are, what the problems are. But it need not solve these problems because it is not a case study, it is not a recipe" (341).

I examine the pedagogical possibilities Morrison's works afford us in order to confront and contextualize the disappointment that students may express about the novel's failure to provide a satisfactory resolution. Despite these initial responses, according to all evidence in the text and Morrison's own implicit literary judgment, *Jazz* is her most sophisticated literary work, her magnum opus. Disclaiming any affinities with the likes of Joyce, Hardy, and Faulkner, Morrison confesses, "My effort is to be *like* something that has probably only been fully expressed in African American music" (Interview with McKay 426). The title of the novel perhaps signals Morrison's recognition that she has accomplished that goal. Apart from confirming the indisputable connection between Morrison's oeuvre and African American musical and oral traditions, the title suggests the broad cultural, historical, and social dimensions of this literary project. In the 1963 study *Blues People* LeRoi Jones uses "the music that is most closely associated with [African Americans]: blues and a later, but parallel development, jazz" as the vehicle for examining and interpreting the path to "citizenship" (ix). Jones's thesis is that "if the music of the Negro in America, in all its permutations, is subjected to a socio-anthropological as well as musical scrutiny, something about the essential nature of the Negro's existence in this country ought to be revealed, as well as something about the essential nature of this country, *i.e.*, society as a whole" (ix–x). Almost three decades later, at a reading in New York, Morrison, in explaining her choice of title, concurred with and extended Jones's observation: "Jazz is contested territory, within and without. . . . The United States gets its most important cultural marker from that music." Consequently, these suggestions for teaching *Jazz* illuminate and follow the novel's blue(s)print. They are designed to promote an aural engagement and to identify the many "places and spaces" Morrison creates for the reader, teacher, or student to situate her or his participatory and interpretive performance.

The opening of the novel—including the epigraph—attempts to orient the reader toward sounding the text and language. The instructor may guide students toward this approach by having them sound or speak the first word of the novel, "Sth" (Knopf, 3). The class can then discuss the significance of the novel's opening and epigraph in relation to the definition of *sth* in *Beloved*:

> When [Stamp Paid] got to the steps, the voices drained suddenly to less than a whisper. It gave him pause. They had become an occasional mutter—like the interior sounds a woman makes when she believes she is alone and unobserved at her work: a *sth* when she misses the needle's eye; a soft moan when she sees another chip in her one good platter; the low, friendly argument with which she greets the hens. Nothing fierce or

> startling. Just the eternal, private conversations that take place between
> women and their tasks.   (Knopf, 172)

The students should consider the implications of the passage for determining
the narrator's gender and identity and for identifying the lines of continuity between *Beloved* and *Jazz*. The instructor might ask, How and why does this ob-
trusive and unnamed narrator know so much? Who is the narrator? What is the
connection between the novel's title, the technique used in its crafting, the lay-
ering of interlocking personal histories within the text, and the narrative consciousness that holds them all together?

The question of how to sound or inscribe familiar themes in their oral interactive context is a major concern in the novel. Zora Neale Hurston's story "How
to Write a Letter," retold in *Mules and Men*, provides an illuminating context
for discussing this difficulty:

> The man sent his daughter off to school for seben years, den she come
> home all finished up. So he said to her, "Daughter, git yo' things and write
> me a letter to my brother!" So she did.
>
> He says, "Head it up," and she done so.
>
> "Now tell 'im, 'Dear Brother, our chile is done come home from school
> and all finished up and we is very proud of her.'"
>
> Then he ast de girl "Is you got dat?"
>
> She tole 'im "yeah."
>
> Now tell him some mo'. 'Our mule is dead but Ah got another mule
> and when Ah say (clucking sound of tongue and teeth) he moved from
> de word.'"
>
> "Is you got dat?" he ast de girl.
>
> "Naw suh," she tole 'im.
>
> He waited a while and he ast her again, "You got dat down yet?"
>
> "Naw suh, Ah ain't got it yet."
>
> "How come you ain't got it?"
>
> "Cause Ah can't spell (clucking sound)."
>
> "You mean to tell me you been off to school seben years and can't spell
> (clucking sound)? Why Ah could spell dat myself and Ah ain't been to
> school a day in mah life. Well jes' say (clucking sound) he'll know what
> yo' mean and go on wid de letter."   (40–41)

A discussion of the girl's challenge should pave the way for a discovery and
analysis of the ways in which *Jazz* "sounds" both the mourning of Dorcas's
death—in the conversations between Violet and Alice Manfred—and Joe's
punishment for the murder. The class could compare Alice Manfred's decision not to seek prosecution or punishment for the murderer with the view
expressed in the lyrics of Bessie Smith's "Tain't Nobody's Business." Smith not
only rejects the forms of redress and resolution proffered by the dominant

society but also reiterates and explains Alice Manfred's and African Americans' recourse to other institutions of intervention and resolution—including the blues itself: "the dead girl's aunt didn't want to throw money to helpless lawyers or laughing cops when she knew the expense wouldn't improve anything. Besides, she found out that the man who killed her niece cried all day and for him and for Violet that is as bad as jail" (4). The narrator also reveals, "She would have called the police after both of them if everything she knew about Negro life had made it even possible to consider. To actually volunteer to talk to one, black or white, to let him in her house, watch him adjust his hips in her chair to accommodate the blue steel that made him a man" (74).

Listening to jazz recordings from the 1920s can allow students to enter and interpret the social ambience of the era. King Oliver's, Duke Ellington's, and Fletcher Henderson's bands stand out as exceptional choices. With the instructor's help, students can identify the instruments in a typical jazz band—drums, bass, saxophones, trumpet, trombone, clarinet, guitar, flute, piano, and vibraphone. The instructor should point out how the instruments mimic sounds in the physical urban environment—such as laughter, screams, trains, subways, and moving feet—and how they sound the many emotions in the cultural and sociopolitical environment, as well as how the complex interplay between the instruments produces a polyvocal but unified creation. This musical analysis will prepare the class to recognize and interpret Morrison's narrative strategies and to discover how Morrison creates a polyvocal text that successfully tells and sounds the lives of Violet, Joe, Dorcas, Felice, Sweetness, and other orphans in Harlem.

Since the novel is set in a period variously dubbed the Roaring Twenties, the Jazz Age, and the Harlem Renaissance era, the instructor and students will benefit from a consciousness of the major historical events that helped form 1926 Harlem. The period between the end of Reconstruction and the beginning of the Harlem Renaissance—roughly coterminous with the interval between the events of *Beloved*, set in 1873, and those of *Jazz*—witnessed a rapid escalation of racial violence toward African Americans in the South (which precipitated the great migration to northern cities). Among the developments that provide an interpretive context for prominent aspects of *Jazz* are the abandonment of Reconstruction, with the withdrawal of federal troops from the South in 1877, and the unequal struggle for civil rights that African Americans were left to wage; the development of new and more vicious racial stereotypes (as evidenced, e.g., by D. W. Griffith's 1915 film *The Birth of a Nation*) in conjunction with the passage of Jim Crow legislation and the ascendancy of lynch law; northern industrialization, the demand for labor, and conflicts arising from increased European immigration; the antilynching campaign and career of Ida B. Wells-Barnett, the call for an exodus from southern oppression, and the African American women's club movement; the outbreak of World War I, demands for labor in the North, and African American military participation and patriotism, which African Americans hoped would bring full citizenship rights; Marcus Garvey and the United Negro Improvement Association; W. E. B. Du Bois and the Niagara Movement; and the development of a new cultural consciousness and pride; and the music—jazz—that sprang from the mud and blood of the Delta and traveled west and north with migrating African Americans to Kansas, Oklahoma, Illinois, Ohio, New York, and elsewhere.[2]

The instructor can help convey these connections by having students take turns reading aloud a section of the novel that juxtaposes sound, jazz, and sense, of struggle and survival:

> Now, down Fifth Avenue from curb to curb, came a tide of cold black faces, speechless and unblinking because what they meant to say but did not trust themselves to say the drums said for them, and what they had seen with their own eyes and through the eyes of others the drums described to a T. . . .
>
> . . . [Alice Manfred] knew from sermons and editorials that it wasn't real music—just colored folks' stuff: harmful, certainly; embarrassing, of course; but not real, not serious.
>
> Yet Alice Manfred swore she heard a complicated anger in it; something hostile that disguised itself as flourish and roaring seduction. . . . It faked happiness, faked welcome, but it did not make her feel generous, this juke joint, barrel hooch, tonk house, music. It made her hold her hand in the pocket of her apron to keep from smashing it through the glass pane to snatch the world in her fist and squeeze the life out of it for doing what it did and did and did to her and everybody else she knew or knew about. Better to close the windows and shutters, sweat in the summer heat of a silent Clifton Place apartment than to risk a broken window or a yelping that might not know where or how to stop.   (54, 59)

This reading prepares students to discuss the sociopolitical and economic climate Morrison describes. What is the source of the cold anger—on the faces of the marchers, in the drums, and in the honky-tonk music? How does Morrison position the reader to view Harlem and other urban centers as sites both of sustenance and survival (for "the droves and droves of colored people flocking to paychecks and streets full of themselves" [58]) and of struggle and suffering? How do the music and the characters negotiate the tension between the masking and the manifestation of anger? The class could examine Morrison's comments—here and in *Sula*—on the lack of awareness among European immigrants that positions them to consent to and participate in the disenfranchisement of African Americans, since "their place in this world was secured only when they echoed the old residents' attitude toward blacks" (*Sula* 53). It might further consider Ralph Ellison's observation, "The blues is an impulse to keep the painful details and episodes of a brutal experience alive in one's aching consciousness, to finger its jagged grain, and to transcend it, not by the consolation of philosophy but by squeezing from it a near-tragic, near-comic lyricism" (*Shadow* 78).

That discussion could lead to a conversation about art—musical and literary—as a vehicle for healing, for expressing and reconciling what Du Bois called the "two-ness of being" (*Souls* 5) (i.e., being an African, oppressed nationally, and an American, privileged internationally) and for maintaining the balance, as the blues trope does. Students might compare Langston Hughes's fictional account of the origins of "Bop" in *The Best of Simple*:

> "You must not know where Bop comes from," said Simple, astonished at my ignorance. . . .
>
> "From the police beating Negroes' heads," said Simple. "Every time a cop hits a Negro with his billy club, that old club say, 'BOP! BOP! . . . MOP! . . . BOP!' . . . That's where Be-Bop came from, beaten right out of some Negro's head into them horns and saxophones and piano keys that plays it." (118)

From the examination of *Jazz* and African American music, the class may turn to a number of related cultural and literary issues. For example, the instructor might ask how the novel acknowledges, revises, and celebrates a generation of African American women warriors: "Those who swelled their little unarmed strength into the reckoning one of leagues, clubs, societies, sisterhoods designed to hold or withhold, move or stay put, make a way, solicit, comfort and ease. Bail out, dress the dead, pay the rent, find new rooms, start a school, storm an office, take up collections, rout the block and keep their eyes on all the children" (78). In appropriate courses instructors may also examine intertextual relations—call-and-response dialectics—between *Jazz* and Harlem Renaissance works including Claude McKay's *Home to Harlem*, Nella Larsen's *Quicksand*, Hughes's *Not without Laughter*, and Jean Toomer's *Cane*, as well as other contemporary representations of the period in Ishmael Reed's *Mumbo Jumbo* and Rosa Guy's *A Measure of Time*.

Finally, to bring together these various lines of discussion, the instructor and students might consider the musical, literary, historical, and social dimensions of *Jazz* in relation to Nina Simone's 1970s evaluation of jazz:

> Jazz is not just music, it's a way of life, it's a way of being, a way of thinking. I think that the Negro in America is jazz. Everything he does—the slang he uses, the way he talks, his jargon, the new inventive phrases we make up to describe things—all that to me is jazz just as much as the music we play. Jazz is not just music. It's the definition of the Afro-American black. (qtd. in Taylor 156)

NOTES

Like jazz itself, this essay is the result of a communal performance—discussions with various colleagues and friends about what approaches might work best in teaching *Jazz*. This consultational performance is a typical one for most academicians. I would, therefore, like to thank some of the many "instruments" without whose performance there would be no jazz or *Jazz* and no knowing: Toni Morrison, Bessie Smith, Duke Ellington, Ralph Ellison, Langston Hughes, LeRoi Jones, and Nina Simone; Katherine Bassard, Anthonia Kalu, Estella Conwill Májozo, Nellie McKay, Cheryl Wall, and other birds.

The subtitle of this essay is the title of a short essay by Morrison that appeared in the May 1985 *Essence*.

[1]In *Pedagogy of the Oppressed* and *Education for Critical Consciousness* Freire, a former consultant to Harvard University's Graduate School of Education, analyzes the debilitating effects of a pedagogical tradition founded on a "banking concept" of education, in which the teacher "deposits" information on or in the student. In its stead, Freire recommends a "problem-posing education" in which teacher and student "become jointly responsible for a process in which all grow" (*Pedagogy* 67).

[2]For discussions of these interrelated developments, see Adero; D. Bell; A. Davis; Franklin and Moss; Giddings; L. Jones; and D. Lewis.

CONTRIBUTORS AND SURVEY PARTICIPANTS

We list below the contributors of essays in this volume and all those who participated in the survey that formed the basis for this volume. Their contribution was invaluable, and we are very grateful for the time they took from busy schedules to assist us.

Sandra Adell, *University of Wisconsin, Madison*
Michael Awkward, *University of Pennsylvania*
Anthony J. Berret, *Saint Joseph's University*
Susan Blake, *Lafayette College*
Gerry Brenner, *University of Montana*
Keith E. Byerman, *Indiana State University*
Grace C. Cooper, *University of the District of Columbia*
Angelo Costanzo, *Shippensburg University*
Carolyn C. Denard, *Georgia State University*
Marilyn Elkins, *University of North Carolina, Chapel Hill*
Thomas H. Fick, *Southeastern Louisiana University*
Frances S. Freter, *University of California, San Diego*
Vickie M. Frost, *John A. Logan College*
Eva Gold, *Southeastern Louisiana University*
Gurleen Grewal, *University of South Florida*
Jeanne Gunner, *University of California, Los Angeles*
James C. Hall, *University of Illinois, Chicago*
Sharon P. Holland, *Stanford University*
Karla F. C. Holloway, *North Carolina State University*
Deborah Horvitz, *Tufts University*
Elizabeth B. House, *Augusta State University*
Madelyn Jablon, independent scholar
Ann Jurecic, independent scholar
Lynn Keller, *University of Wisconsin, Madison*
Lynda Koolish, *San Diego State University*
Linda J. Krumholz, *Denison University*
Toni A. H. McNaron, *University of Minnesota, Twin Cities*
Gretchen Mieszkowski, *University of Houston, Clear Lake*
James A. Miller, *Trinity College, CT*
David Mitchell, *University of Michigan, Ann Arbor*
Marilyn Sanders Mobley, *George Mason University*
Linda Buck Myers, *Hamline University*
Linda E. Opyr, *Sewanhaka High School*
Terry Otten, *Wittenberg University*
Rafael Pérez-Torres, *University of California, Santa Barbara*
Joyce Pettis, *North Carolina State University*
Sanford Pinsker, *Franklin and Marshall College*
Deborah G. Plant, *Memphis State University*
Susan M. Popkin, *University of California, Los Angeles*

Arnold Rampersad, *Princeton University*
Angelita Reyes, *University of Minnesota, Twin Cities*
Ruth Rosenberg, *Kingsborough Community College, City University of New York*
Judylyn S. Ryan, *Rutgers University, New Brunswick*
Maggie Sale, *University of California, San Diego*
Gary Storhoff, *University of Connecticut, Stamford*
Claudia Tate, *George Washington University*
Denise Troutman, *Michigan State University*
Mark C. Van Gunten, *University of South Carolina*
Craig Werner, *University of Wisconsin, Madison*
Joseph H. Wessling, *Xavier University, OH*
Roxann Wheeler, *Syracuse University*
Gay Wilentz, *East Carolina University*

WORKS CITED

Abrahams, Roger. *African Folktales*. New York: Pantheon, 1983.

Abrams, M. H. *A Glossary of Literary Terms*. Fort Worth: Holt, Rinehart, 1988.

Achebe, Chinua. *Morning Yet on Creation Day*. London: Heinemann, 1972.

———. "The Writer and His Community." *Hopes and Impediments*. New York: Doubleday, 1988. 47–61.

Adero, Malaika. *Up South: Stories, Studies, and Letters of This Century's Black Migrations*. New York: New, 1993.

Andrews, William L. *To Tell a Free Story: The First Century of Afro-American Autobiography, 1760–1865*. Urbana: U of Illinois P, 1988.

Andrews, William L., and Nellie Y. McKay, eds. Beloved: *A Casebook*. New York: Oxford UP, forthcoming.

Appiah, Kwame Anthony. *In My Father's House: Africa in the Philosophy of Culture*. New York: Oxford UP, 1992.

Asante, Molefi Kete. "African Elements in African American English." *Africanisms in American Culture*. Ed. Joseph E. Holloway. Bloomington: Indiana UP, 1990. 19–33.

———. *The Afrocentric Idea*. Philadelphia: Temple UP, 1987.

Baker, Houston A., Jr. *Blues, Ideology, and Afro-American Literature: A Vernacular Theory*. Chicago: U of Chicago P, 1984.

———. *Workings of the Spirit: The Poetics of Afro-American Women's Writing*. Chicago: U of Chicago P, 1991.

Baker, Houston A., Jr., and Patricia Redmond, eds. *Afro-American Literary Studies in the 1990s*. Chicago: U of Chicago P, 1989.

Bakhtin, Mikhail. *The Dialogic Imagination: Four Essays*. Austin: U of Texas P, 1981.

Baldwin, James. *Notes of a Native Son*. Boston: Beacon, 1955.

———. *Go Tell It on the Mountain*. New York: Dell, 1953.

Bascom, William. *African Dilemma Tales*. The Hague: Mouton, 1975.

Bassett, P. C. "A Visit to the Slave Mother Who Killed Her Child." *National Anti-slavery Standard* 15 Mar. 1856: n. pag.

Beale, Francis. "Double Jeopardy: To Be Black and Female." Cade, *Black Woman* 90–100.

Bell, Bernard W. *The Afro-American Novel and Its Tradition*. Amherst: U of Massachusetts P, 1987.

———. "*Beloved*: A Womanist Neo-slave Narrative; or, Multivocal Remembrances of Things Past." *African American Review* 26 (1992): 7–15.

Bell, Derrick. *Race, Racism, and American Law*. 3rd ed. Boston: Little, 1992.

Bell, Pearl K. "Self-Seekers." *Commentary* 72.2 (1981): 56–60.

Berret, Anthony J. "Toni Morrison's Literary Jazz." *CLA Journal* 32 (1989): 267–83.

Bhabha, Homi. "Of Mimicry and Man: The Ambivalence of Colonial Discourse." *October* 28 (1984): 125–33.

Bjork, Patrick Bryce. *The Novels of Toni Morrison: The Search for Self and Place within the Community*. New York: Lang, 1992.

Blake, Susan. "Folklore and Community in *Song of Solomon*." *MELUS* 7.3 (1980): 77–82.

———. "Toni Morrison." *Afro-American Fiction Writers after 1955*. Ed. Thadious M. Davis and Trudier Harris. Vol. 33 of *Dictionary of Literary Biography*. Detroit: Gale, 1984. 187–99.

Bloom, Harold, ed. *Toni Morrison*. New York: Chelsea, 1990.

Brace, C. L. "The Slave Mother of Cincinnati." *National Anti-slavery Standard* 1 Mar. 1856: n. pag.

Brenner, Gerry. "*Song of Solomon*: Rejecting Rank's Monomyth and Feminism." McKay 114–25.

Brewer, Mason. *American Negro Folklore*. New York: Quadrangle, 1968.

Bridglal, Sindamani, dir. *Indefinable Qualities: A Film on Toni Morrison*. Videocassette. Women Make Movies, 1989.

Browning, Elizabeth Barrett. *The Poetical Works of Elizabeth Barrett Browning*. Introd. Ruth M. Adams. Boston: Houghton, 1974.

Butler-Evans, Elliott. "Beyond Essentialism: Rethinking Afro-American Cultural Theory." *Inscriptions* 5 (1989): 121–34.

Byerman, Keith E. *Fingering the Jagged Grain: Tradition and Form in Recent Black Fiction*. Athens: U of Georgia P, 1986.

Cade, Toni, ed. *The Black Woman*. New York: Signet, 1970.

———. "On the Issue of Roles." *Black Woman* 101–10.

Callaloo 13 (1990): 471–525. Spec. section on Toni Morrison.

Carby, Hazel V. *Reconstructing Womanhood: The Emergence of the Afro-American Novelist*. New York: Oxford UP, 1987.

Carmean, Karen. *Toni Morrison's World of Fiction*. New York: Whitston, 1993.

Christian, Barbara. *Black Women Novelists: The Development of a Tradition, 1892–1976*. Westport: Greenwood, 1980.

———. "Testing the Strength of the Black Cultural Bond: Review of Toni Morrison's *Tar Baby*." *Black Feminist Criticism: Perspectives on Black Women Writers*. New York: Pergamon, 1985. 65–69.

Clarke, John Henrik. "The Black Woman in History." *Black World* 24.4 (1975): 12–26.

Clemons, Walter. "A Gravestone of Memories." *Newsweek* 28 Sept. 1987: 74–75.

Coleman, James. "The Quest for Wholeness in Toni Morrison's *Tar Baby*." *Black American Literature Forum* 20.1–2 (1986): 63–73.

Commercial [Cincinnati]. 30 Jan 1856: n. pag.

Cooper, Anna Julia. *A Voice from the South*. Xenia: Aldine, 1892.

Courier [Louisville, KY]. 10 Mar. 1856: n. pag.

Cowart, David. "Faulkner and Joyce in Morrison's *Song of Solomon*." *American Literature* 62 (1990): 87–100.

Cruse, Harold. *Rebellion or Revolution?* New York: Morrow, 1968.

Davis, Angela Y. *Women, Race, and Class.* New York: Random, 1983.

Davis, Charles T., and Henry Louis Gates, eds. *The Slave's Narrative.* Oxford: Oxford UP, 1985.

Davis, Cynthia A. "Self, Society, and Myth in Toni Morrison's Fiction." *Contemporary Literature* 23.3 (1982): 323–42.

DeKoven, Marianne. *Rich and Strange: Gender, History, Modernism.* Princeton: Princeton UP, 1991.

Demetrakopoulos, Stephanie A. "Maternal Bonds as Devourers of Women's Individuation in Toni Morrison's *Beloved*." *African American Review* 26 (1992): 51–59.

———. "Morrison's Creation of a White World: *Tar Baby* and Irreconcilable Polarities." Holloway and Demetrakopoulos 130–42.

Denard, Carolyn. "Toni Morrison." Hine 815–19.

De Weever, Jacqueline. "Toni Morrison's Use of Fairy Tale, Folk Tale, and Myth in *Song of Solomon*." *Southern Folklore Quarterly* 44 (1980): 131–44.

Diop, Cheikh Anta. *Precolonial Black Africa.* Trans. Harold Salemson. Trenton: Africa World, 1987.

Dorson, Richard M. *American Negro Folktales.* Greenwich: Fawcett, 1956.

Douglass, Frederick. *Narrative of the Life of Frederick Douglass: An American Slave.* Boston: Anti-slavery Office, 1845. Cambridge: Harvard UP, 1960.

———. "The Beauties of Slavery: A Slave Child Killed by Its Mother." *Anti-slavery Bugle* 23 Feb. 1856: n. pag.

Du Bois, W. E. B. *The Philadelphia Negro: A Social Study.* 1899. New York: Schocken, 1967.

———. *The Souls of Black Folk.* New York: NAL-Penguin, 1969.

Dunbar, Paul Laurence. *Lyrics of Lowly Life.* Secaucus: Citadel, 1984.

Dundes, Alan, ed. *Mother Wit from the Laughing Barrel: Readings in the Interpretation of Afro-American Folklore.* Jackson: U of Mississippi P, 1990.

Duvall, John N. "Doe Hunting and Masculinity: *Song of Solomon* and *Go Down, Moses*." *Arizona Quarterly* 47 (1991): 95–115.

Eaton, Isabel. "Special Report on Negro Domestic Service in the Seventh Ward, Philadelphia." Du Bois, *Philadelphia Negro* 427–509.

Ellison, Ralph. "Flying Home." *Best Short Stories by Negro Writers.* Ed. Langston Hughes. Boston: Little, 1967. 151–70.

———. *Invisible Man.* 1947. New York: Vintage, 1972.

———. *Shadow and Act.* New York: Vintage, 1953. New York: Random, 1964.

Epstein, Jonathan S., ed. *Adolescents and Their Music: If It's Too Loud, You're Too Old.* New York: Garland, 1994.

Erickson, Peter B. "Images of Nurturance in Toni Morrison's *Tar Baby*." *CLA Journal* 28 (1984): 11–32.

Evans, Mari, ed. *Black Women Writers, 1950–1980.* New York: Anchor-Doubleday, 1984.

Fabre, Genevieve. "Genealogical Archaeology; or, The Quest for Legacy in Toni Morrison's *Song of Solomon*." McKay 105–14.

Fabre, Genevieve, and Claudine Raynaud, eds. *"Beloved, She's Mine." Essais sur Beloved de Toni Morrison.* Spec. issue of *d'AFRAM Newsletter* 3 (1993): 5–170.

Fisher, Dexter, and Robert B. Stepto, eds. *Afro-American Literature: The Reconstruction of Identity.* New York: MLA, 1979.

Foreman, P. Gabrielle. "Past-On Stories: History and the Magically Real, Morrison and Allende on Call." *Feminist Studies* 18.2 (1992): 369–88.

Forrest, Leon. *There Is a Tree More Ancient Than Eden.* 1973. Chicago: Another Chicago, 1988.

Foster, Frances Smith. *Witnessing Slavery.* Westport: Greenwood, 1979.

———. *Written by Herself: Literary Production by African American Women, 1746–1892.* Bloomington: Indiana UP, 1993.

Franklin, John Hope, and Alfred A. Moss, Jr. *From Slavery to Freedom: A History of African Americans.* 7th ed. New York: McGraw, 1994.

Freire, Paulo. *Education for Critical Consciousness.* Trans. Myra Ramos. New York: Continuum, 1973.

———. *Pedagogy of the Oppressed.* Trans. Myra Bergman. New York: Continuum, 1993.

Gates, Henry Louis, Jr. *The Signifying Monkey: A Theory of African-American Literary Criticism.* New York: Oxford UP, 1988.

Gates, Henry Louis, Jr., and K. A. Appiah, eds. *Toni Morrison: Critical Perspectives Past and Present.* New York: Amistad, 1993.

Gates, Henry Louis, Jr., and Nellie Y. McKay, eds. *The Norton Anthology of African American Literature.* New York: Norton, 1996.

Geertz, Clifford. "Thick Description." *The Interpretation of Cultures: Selected Essays.* New York: Basic, 1973. 3–30.

Giddings, Paula. *When and Where I Enter: The Impact of Black Women on Race and Sex in America.* New York: Morrow, 1984.

Gilbert, Sandra M., and Susan Gubar. *The Madwoman in the Attic: The Woman Writer and the Nineteenth-Century Literary Imagination.* New Haven: Yale UP, 1979.

———, eds. *The Norton Anthology of Women's Literature.* New York: Norton, 1985.

Grant, Robert. "Absence into Presence: The Thematics of Memory and 'Missing' Subjects in Toni Morrison's *Sula*." McKay 90–103.

Greenberg, Kenneth S., ed. The Confessions of Nat Turner *and Related Documents.* New York: St. Martin's, 1996.

Gutman, Herbert. *The Black Family in Slavery and Freedom.* New York: Pantheon, 1976.

Hall, Stuart. "Cultural Studies and Its Theoretical Legacies." *Cultural Studies.* Ed. Lawrence Grossberg, Cary Nelson, and Paula Treichler. New York: Routledge, 1992. 277–94.

Hamilton, Edith. *Mythology.* Boston: Little, 1942.

Hamilton, Virginia. *The People Could Fly: American Black Folktales.* New York: Knopf, 1985.

Harding, Vincent. *There Is a River.* New York: Vintage, 1983.

Harper, Michael S,, and Robert B. Stepto, eds. *Chant of Saints: A Gathering of Afro-American Literature, Art, and Scholarship.* Urbana: U of Illinois P, 1979.

Harris, Joel Chandler. *Nights with Uncle Remus*. New York: Riverside, 1881.

———. *Uncle Remus: His Songs and His Sayings*. Harmondsworth: Penguin, 1982.

Harris, Trudier. *Fiction and Folklore: The Novels of Toni Morrison*. Knoxville: U of Tennessee P, 1991.

Harris, Wilson. *Explorations*. Ed. Hena Maes-Jeinek. Aarhus, Den.: Dangaroo, 1981.

Hayden, Robert. *The Collected Poems of Robert Hayden*. Ann Arbor: U of Michigan P, 1985.

Heinze, Denise. *The Dilemma of Double Consciousness: Toni Morrison's Novels*. Athens: U of Georgia P, 1993.

Hemenway, Robert. "Are You a Flying Lark or a Setting Dove?" Fisher and Stepto 122–52.

Herskovits, Melville. *The Myth of the Negro Past*. Boston: Beacon, 1941.

Hill, Lynda. "An Island, a Vision, the Beauty, and Son." *Black Enterprise* 11 July 1981: 13.

Hine, Darlene Clark. *Black Women in America: An Historical Encyclopedia*. New York: Carlson, 1993.

Holloway, Joseph E. *Africanisms in American Culture*. Bloomington: Indiana UP, 1990.

Holloway, Karla F. C. "African Values and Western Chaos." Holloway and Demetrakopoulos 117–29.

———. *Moorings and Metaphors: Figures of Culture and Gender in Black Women's Literature*. New Brunswick: Rutgers UP, 1992.

Holloway, Karla F. C., and Stephanie A. Demetrakopoulos. *New Dimensions of Spirituality: A Biracial and Bicultural Reading of the Novels of Toni Morrison*. Westport: Greenwood, 1987.

Homans, Margaret. "The Woman in the Cave: Recent Feminist Fictions and the Classical Underworld." *Contemporary Literature* 29 (1988): 369–402.

hooks, bell. *Black Looks: Race and Representation*. Boston: South End, 1992.

———. *Talking Back: Thinking Feminist, Thinking Black*. Boston: South End, 1989.

House, Elizabeth B. "Artists and the Art of Living: Order and Disorder in Toni Morrison's Fiction." *Modern Fiction Studies* 34 (1988): 27–44.

———. "The 'Sweet Life' in Toni Morrison's Fiction." *American Literature* 56 (1984): 181–202.

———. "Toni Morrison's Ghost: The Beloved Who Is Not Beloved." *Studies in American Fiction* 18 (1990): 17–26.

Hovet, Grace Ann, and Barbara Lounsberry. "Flying as Symbol and Legend in Toni Morrison's *The Bluest Eye, Sula, Song of Solomon*." *CLA Journal* 27 (1983): 119–40.

Huggins, Nathan Irvin. *The Harlem Renaissance*. New York: Oxford UP, 1971.

Hughes, Langston. *The Best of Simple*. 1961. New York: Noonday, 1988.

Hughes, Langston, and Arna Bontemps, eds. *The Book of Negro Folklore*. New York: Dodd, 1958.

Hurston, Zora Neale. *Mules and Men*. Philadelphia: Lippincott, 1935. Bloomington: Indiana UP, 1978.

———. *Their Eyes Were Watching God*. New York: Lippincott, 1937.

Irigaray, Luce. *Speculum of the Other Woman*. Trans. Gillian C. Gill. Ithaca: Cornell UP, 1985.

Jacobs, Harriet. *Incidents in the Life of a Slave Girl*. Oxford: Oxford UP, 1987.

Johnson, Diane. "The Oppressor in the Next Room." *New York Review of Books* 10 Nov. 1977: 6+.

Johnson, James Weldon, ed. *The Book of American Negro Poetry*. New York: Harcourt, 1922.

Jones, Gayl. *Liberating Voices*. Cambridge: Harvard UP, 1991.

Jones, LeRoi [Amiri Baraka]. *The Blues People*. New York: Morrow, 1963.

Keenan, Hugh T. "Twisted Tales: Propaganda in the Tar-Baby Stories." *Southern Quarterly* 22.2 (1984): 54–69.

Krumholz, Linda. "The Ghosts of Slavery: Historical Recovery in Toni Morrison's *Beloved*." *African American Review* 26 (1992): 395–416.

Kubitschek, Missy Dehn. *Claiming the Heritage: African-American Women Writers and History*. Jackson: UP of Mississippi, 1991.

Lee, Dorothy H. "*Song of Solomon*: To Ride the Air." *Black American Literature Forum* 16.2 (1982): 64–70.

Lester, Julius. *Black Folktales*. New York: Grove, 1969.

Levine, Lawrence W. *Black Culture and Black Consciousness: Afro-American Folk Thought from Slavery to Freedom*. Oxford: Oxford UP, 1977.

Lewis, David Levering. *When Harlem Was in Vogue*. 1979. New York: Oxford UP, 1989.

Lewis, Vashti Crutcher. "African Traditions in Toni Morrison's *Sula*." *Wild Women in the Whirlwind: Afra-American Culture and the Contemporary Literary Renaissance*. Ed. Joanne M. Braxton and Andrée Nicola McLaughlin. New Brunswick: Rutgers UP, 1990. 316–25.

Lincoln, C. Eric. *Race, Religion, and the Continuing American Dilemma*. New York: Hill, 1984.

Lincoln, C. Eric, and Lawrence H. Mamiya. *The Black Church in the African American Experience*. Durham: Duke UP, 1990.

Livermore, Mary A. "The Slave Tragedy at Cincinnati." *National Anti-slavery Standard* 16 Feb. 1856: n. pag.

Locke, Alain. *The New Negro*. New York: Atheneum, 1968.

Lorde, Audre. *Sister Outsider: Essays and Speeches*. New York: Crossing, 1984.

Lubiano, Wahneema. "Toni Morrison." V. Smith et al. 321–33.

Makinde, M. Akin. *African Philosophy, Culture, and Traditional Medicine*. Africa Series 53. Athens: Ohio U Monographs in Intl. Studies, 1988.

Malcolm X, with Alex Haley. *The Autobiography of Malcolm X*. New York: Ballantine, 1973.

Manns, Wilhelmina. "Support Systems of Significant Others in Black Families." McAdoo 237–49.

Marshall, Paule. *Praisesong for the Widow*. New York: Putnam, 1983.

Mason, Theodore O., Jr. "The Novelist as Conservator: Stories and Comprehension in Toni Morrison's *Song of Solomon*." *Contemporary Literature* 29 (1988): 564–81.

Mbalia, Dorothea Drummond. *Toni Morrison's Developing Class Consciousness.* Selinsgrove: Susquehanna UP, 1991.

Mbiti, John. *African Religions and Philosophy.* New York: Anchor, 1970.

McAdoo, Harriette, ed. *Black Families.* Beverly Hills: Sage, 1981.

McDowell, Deborah E. *"The Changing Same": Black Women's Literature, Criticism, and Theory.* Bloomington: Indiana UP, 1995.

——. "'The Self and the Other': Reading Toni Morrison's *Sula* and the Black Female Text." McKay 77–90.

McKay, Nellie Y., ed. *Critical Essays on Toni Morrison.* Boston: Hall, 1988.

Middleton, David L. *Toni Morrison: An Annotated Bibliography.* New York: Garland, 1987.

Mix, Deborah. "Toni Morrison: A Selected Bibliography." Peterson 795–817.

Mobley, Marilyn E. "Narrative Dilemma: Jadine as Cultural Orphan in Toni Morrison's *Tar Baby.*" *Southern Review* 23 (1987): 761–70.

Mobley, Marilyn Sanders. *Folk Roots and Mythic Wings in Sarah Orne Jewett and Toni Morrison: The Cultural Function of Narrative.* Baton Rouge: Louisiana State UP, 1991.

Mohanty, Chandra. "On Race and Voice: Challenges for Liberal Education in the 1990s." *Cultural Critique* 14 (1989–90): 174–208.

Morrison, Toni. *Beloved.* New York: Knopf, 1987; Plume, 1987.

——, ed. *The Black Book.* Comp. Middleton Harris et al. New York: Random, 1974.

——. *The Bluest Eye.* New York: Washington Square, 1970; Henry Holt, 1970; Pocket, 1972.

——. "City Limits, Village Values: Concepts of the Neighborhood in Black Fiction." *Literature and the Urban Experience: Essays on the City and Literature.* Ed. Michael C. Jaye and Ann Chalmers Watts. New Brunswick: Rutgers UP, 1981. 35–43.

——. Interview. "Toni Morrison: The Art of Fiction CXXXIV." *Paris Review* 128 (1993): 83–125.

——. Interview with Bonnie Angelo. "The Pain of Being Black." *Time* 22 May 1989: 120–21.

——. Interview with Jane Bakerman. "The Seams Can't Show: An Interview with Toni Morrison." *Black American Literature Forum* 12 (1978): 56–60.

——. Interview with Kay Bonetti. *Interview with Toni Morrison.* Audiocassette. Columbia: Amer. Audio Prose Lib., 1983.

——. Interview with Marsha Darling. "In the Realm of Responsibility: A Conversation with Toni Morrison." *Women's Review of Books* Mar. 1988: 5–6.

——. Interview with Christina Davis. *Presence africaine: Revue culturelle du monde noir* 145 (1988): 141–50.

——. Interview with Bessie W. Jones. "An Interview with Toni Morrison." *The World of Toni Morrison.* By Jones and Audrey L. Vinson. Dubuque: Kendall, 1985. 127–51.

——. Interview with Anne Koenen. "'The One out of Sequence': An Interview with

Toni Morrison, New York, April 1980." *History and Tradition in Afro-American Culture*. Ed. Gunter H. Lenz. Frankfurt: Campus, 1984. 207–21.

———. Interview with Thomas LeClair. "The Language Must Not Sweat." *New Republic* 21 Mar. 1981: 25–29.

———. Interview with Rosemarie K. Lester. "An Interview with Toni Morrison, Hessian Radio Network, Frankfurt, West Germany." McKay 47–54.

———. Interview with Nellie Y. McKay. "An Interview with Toni Morrison." *Contemporary Literature* 24 (1983): 413–29.

———. Interview with Gloria Naylor. "A Conversation." *Southern Review* 21 (1985): 567–93.

———. Interview with Mervyn Rothstein. "Toni Morrison, in Her New Novel, Defends Women." *New York Times* 26 Aug. 1987, late ed.: C17.

———. Interview with Charles Ruas. "Toni Morrison." *Conversations with American Writers*. New York: Knopf, 1985. 215–43.

———. Interview with Ntozake Shange. "Interview with Toni Morrison." *American Rag* 1.1 (1978): 48–52.

———. Interview with Amanda Smith. "Toni Morrison." *Publishers Weekly* 21 Aug. 1987: 50–51.

———. Interview with Robert B. Stepto. "'Intimate Things in Place': A Conversation with Toni Morrison." *Massachusetts Review* 18 (1977): 473–89. Rpt. in Harper and Stepto 213–29.

———. Interview with Claudia Tate. "Toni Morrison." Tate 117–31.

———. Interview with Elsie B. Washington. "Toni Morrison Now." *Essence* Oct. 1987: 58+.

———. Interview with Mel Watkins. "Talk with Toni Morrison." *New York Times Book Review* 11 Sept. 1977: 50.

———. Interview with Judith Wilson. "A Conversation with Toni Morrison." *Essence* July 1981: 81+.

———. "Introduction: Friday on the Potomac." *Race-ing* vii–xxx.

———. *Jazz*. New York: Knopf, 1992; Plume, 1992.

———. "A Knowing So Deep." *Essence* May 1985: 230.

———. "The Making of *The Black Book*." *Black World* Feb. 1974: 86–90.

———. "Memory, Creation, and Writing." *Thought* 235 (1984): 385–90.

———. *The Nobel Prize Lecture in Literature, 1993*. New York: Knopf, 1994.

———. "On the Backs of Blacks." *Arguing Immigration: Are New Immigrants a Wealth of Diversity . . . or a Crushing Burden?* Ed. Nicolaus Mills. New York: Touchstone, 1994. 97–100.

———. *Playing in the Dark: Whiteness and the Literary Imagination*. Cambridge: Harvard UP, 1992.

———, ed. *Race-ing Justice, En-gendering Power: Essays on Anita Hill, Clarence Thomas, and the Construction of Social Reality*. New York: Pantheon, 1992.

———. Reading. 92nd Street Y, New York. 19 May 1992.

———. "Rootedness: The Ancestor as Foundation." Evans 339–45.

———. "The Site of Memory." *Inventing the Truth: The Art and Craft of Memoir*. Ed. William Zinsser. Boston: Houghton, 1987. 103–24.

———. *Song of Solomon*. New York: Signet-NAL, 1977; Knopf, 1977.

———. *Sula*. New York: Bantam, 1973.

———. *Tar Baby*. New York: NAL, 1981; Plume-Dutton, 1982.

———. "Unspeakable Things Unspoken: The Afro-American Presence in American Literature." *Michigan Quarterly Review* 28.1 (1989): 1–34. Rpt. in Bloom 201–30.

———. "Virginia Woolf's and William Faulkner's Treatment of the Alienated." MA thesis. Cornell U, 1955.

Mudimbe, Valentin Y. *The Invention of Africa*. Bloomington: Indiana UP, 1988.

Mukherji, Chandra, and Michael Schudson. "Introduction." *Rethinking Popular Culture: Contemporary Perspectives in Cultural Studies*. Ed. Mukherji and Schudson. Berkeley: U of California P, 1991. 1–61.

Murray, Albert. *The Hero and the Blues*. Columbia: U of Missouri P, 1973.

———. *Stomping the Blues*. New York: Vintage, 1982.

Murray, Pauli. *Proud Shoes*. New York: Harper, 1956.

The Nag Hammadi Library. Ed. James M. Robinson. San Francisco: Harper, 1990.

Naylor, Gloria. *The Women of Brewster Place*. New York: Penguin, 1983.

Nelson, Cary. *Repression and Recovery: Modern American Poetry and the Politics of Cultural Memory, 1910–1945*. Madison: U of Wisconsin P, 1989.

Nelson, Dana D. *The Word in Black and White: Reading "Race" in American Literature, 1638–1867*. New York: Oxford UP, 1992.

Ogren, Kathy J. *The Jazz Revolution*. New York: Oxford UP, 1989.

Otten, Terry. *The Crime of Innocence in the Fiction of Toni Morrison*. Missouri: U of Missouri P, 1989.

Parry, Ann. "Sexual Exploitation and Freedom: Religion, Race, and Gender in Elizabeth Barrett Browning's 'The Runaway Slave at Pilgrim's Point.'" *Studies in Browning and His Circle* 16 (1988): 114–26.

Patton, Gwen. "Black People and the Victorian Ethos." Cade, *Black Woman* 143–48.

Perloff, Marjorie. "Modernist Studies." *Redrawing the Boundaries: The Transformation of English and American Literary Studies*. Ed. Stephen Greenblatt and Giles Gunn. New York: MLA, 1992. 154–78.

Perry, Richard. *Montgomery's Children*. New York: Harcourt, 1984.

Peterson, Nancy J., ed. *Toni Morrison*. Spec. issue of *Modern Fiction Studies* 39.3–4 (1993): 461–859.

Plato. *The* Republic *of Plato*. Trans. Francis Macdonald Cornford. New York: Oxford UP, 1967.

"Prime." *Webster's New Universal Unabridged Dictionary*. 1996 ed.

Profile of a Writer: Toni Morrison. Videocassette. Home Vision, 1987.

Raboteau, Albert J. *Slave Religion*. Oxford: Oxford UP, 1978.

Reed, Ishmael. *Flight to Canada*. New York: Avon, 1975.

Reyes, Angelita. "Ancient Properties in the New World: The Paradox of the 'Other' in Toni Morrison's *Tar Baby*." *Black Scholar* 17.2 (1986): 19–25.

———. "Rereading a Nineteenth-Century Fugitive Slave Incident: From Toni Morrison's *Beloved* to Margaret Garner's Dearly Beloved." *Annals of Scholarship Studies of the Humanities and Social Sciences* 7 (1990): 464–86.

Rigney, Barbara Hill. *The Voices of Toni Morrison*. Jackson: U of Mississippi P, 1994.

Sale, Maggie. "Call and Response as Critical Method: African-American Oral Traditions and *Beloved*." *African American Review* 26 (1992): 41–50.

Samuels, Wilfred D., and Clenora Hudson-Weems. *Toni Morrison*. Boston: Twayne, 1990.

Scheub, Harold. *The Xhosa Ntsomi*. Oxford: Clarendon, 1975.

Schuller, Gunther. *Early Jazz: Its Roots and Musical Development*. New York: Oxford UP, 1968.

Schwartzman, Myron. *Romare Bearden: His Life and Art*. New York: Abrams, 1990.

Scofield, C. I., ed. *The New Scofield Reference Bible*. New York: Oxford UP, 1967.

Scott, Bonnie Kime, ed. *The Gender of Modernism: A Critical Anthology*. Bloomington: Indiana UP, 1990.

Shockley, Ann Allen, ed. *Afro-American Women Writers, 1746–1933: An Anthology and Critical Guide*. Boston: Hall, 1988.

Singal, Daniel Joseph. "Towards a Definition of American Modernism." *American Quarterly* 39 (1987): 7–25.

Sitter, Deborah Ayer. "The Making of a Man: Dialogic Meaning in *Beloved*." *African American Review* 26 (1992): 17–29.

Skerret, Joseph T. "Recitation to the Griot: Storytelling and Learning in Toni Morrison's *Song of Solomon*." *Conjuring: Black Women, Fiction, and Literary Tradition*. Ed. Marjorie Pryse and Hortense Spillers. Bloomington: Indiana UP, 1985. 192–202.

Smith, Barbara. "Toward a Black Feminist Criticism." *The New Feminist Criticism: Essays on Women, Literature, and Theory*. Ed. Elaine Showalter. London: Virago, 1986. 168–85.

Smith, Jessie C., ed. *Notable Black American Women*. Detroit: Gale, 1991.

Smith, Valerie, ed. *New Essays on* Song of Solomon. New York: Cambridge UP, 1995.

———. *Self Discovery and Authority in Afro-American Narrative*. Cambridge: Harvard UP, 1987.

Smith, Valerie, et al., eds. *African American Writers*. New York: Scribner's, 1991.

Sollors, Werner, and Maria Diedrich. *The Black Columbiad: Defining Moments in African American Literature and Culture*. Cambridge: Harvard UP, 1994.

Southern, Eileen. *The Music of Black America*. New York: Norton, 1971.

Sow, I. *Anthropological Structures of Madness in Black Africa*. Trans. Joyce Diamanti. New York: Intl. Universities P, 1980.

Soyinka, Wole. *Myth, Literature, and the African World View*. London: Cambridge UP, 1976.

Steady, Filomina Chioma, ed. *The Black Woman Cross-Culturally*. Boston: Schenkman, 1981.

Stepto, Robert B. "Distrust of the Reader in Afro-American Narratives." *Reconstructing American Literary History*. Ed. Sacvan Bercovitch. Cambridge: Harvard UP, 1986. 300–22.

————. *From behind the Veil*. Urbana: U of Illinois P, 1979.

————. "Teaching Afro-American Literature: Survey or Tradition: The Reconstruction of Instruction." Fisher and Stepto 8–24.

Stone, Elizabeth. *Black Sheep and Kissing Cousins: How Our Family Stories Shape Us*. New York: Penguin, 1988.

Sudarkasa, Niara. "Interpreting the African Heritage in Afro-American Family Organization." McAdoo 38–50.

Tate, Claudia, ed. *Black Women Writers at Work*. New York: Continuum, 1983.

Taylor, Arthur, ed. *Notes and Tones: Musician-to-Musician Interviews*. New York: Putnam, 1977.

Taylor-Guthrie, Danille, ed. *Conversations with Toni Morrison*. Jackson: U of Mississippi P, 1994.

Terborg-Penn, Rosalyn, Sharon Harley, and Andrea Benton Rushing, eds. *Women in Africa and the African Diaspora*. Washington: Howard UP, 1987.

Thompson, Robert Farris. *Flash of the Spirit: African and Afro-American Art and Philosophy*. New York: Vintage, 1983.

Traylor, Eleanor. "The Fabulous World of Toni Morrison: *Tar Baby*." McKay 135–50.

Turner, Patricia. *I Heard It through the Grapevine: Rumor in African-American Culture*. Berkeley: U of California P, 1993.

Twain, Mark. *Adventures of Huckleberry Finn*. Berkeley: U of California P, 1985.

United States. Works Project Administration. Writer's Project, Savannah Unit. *Drums and Shadows: Survival Studies among the Georgia Coastal Negroes*. 1940. Athens: U of Georgia P, 1986.

Vlach, John Michael. *The Afro-American Tradition in Decorative Arts*. Cleveland: Cleveland Museum of Art, 1978.

Walker, Barbara. *The Woman's Encyclopedia of Myths and Secrets*. San Francisco: Harper, 1983.

Walker, Margaret. *Jubilee*. New York: Houghton, 1966.

Wall, Cheryl A., ed. *Changing Our Own Words*. New Brunswick: Rutgers UP, 1989.

Wambutda, Daniel. "Ancestors—The Living Dead." *Traditional Religion in West Africa*. Ed. E. A. Ade Adegbla. Ibadan, Nigeria: Daystar, 1983. 129–36.

Warren, Kenneth W. *Black and White Strangers: Race and American Literary Realism*. Chicago: U of Chicago P, 1993.

Washington, Booker T. *Up from Slavery*. New York: Airmont, 1967.

Werner, Craig H. *Black American Women Novelists: An Annotated Bibliography*. Pasadena: Salem, 1989.

————. "The Briar Patch as Modernist Myth: Morrison, Barthes, and Tar Baby As-Is." McKay 150–67.

White, Deborah Gray. *Ar'n't I a Woman? Female Slaves in the Plantation South*. New York: Norton, 1985.

Wilentz, Gay. *Binding Cultures: Black Women Writers in Africa and the Diaspora*. Bloomington: Indiana UP, 1992.

———. "Civilizations Underneath: African Heritage as Cultural Discourse in Toni Morrison's *Song of Solomon*." *African American Review* 26 (1992): 61–76.

———. "If You Surrender to the Air: Folk Legends of Flight and Resistance in African American Literature." *MELUS* 16.1 (1990): 21–32.

Williams, Martin, ed. *The Smithsonian Collection of Classic Jazz (Revised)*. LP. Smithsonian Inst., 1987.

Williams, Raymond. *Marxism and Literature*. Oxford: Oxford UP, 1977.

———. *Problems in Materialism and Culture*. London: NLB, 1980.

Williams, William Carlos. *The Autobiography of William Carlos Williams*. New York: Random, 1951.

———. *The Collected Earlier Poems of William Carlos Williams*. New York: New Directions, 1951.

Wonham, Henry B., ed. *Criticism and the Color Line: Desegregating American Literary Studies*. New Brunswick: Rutgers UP, 1996.

A World of Ideas with Bill Moyers: A Writer's World with Toni Morrison. Videocassette. Public Affairs Television, 1990.

Wright, Richard. *Native Son*. New York: Harper, 1986.

INDEX OF MORRISON'S NOVELS

INDEX OF NAMES

178   INDEX

Modern Language Association of America

Approaches to Teaching World Literature

Joseph Gibaldi, series editor

Achebe's Things Fall Apart. Ed. Bernth Lindfors. 1991.

Arthurian Tradition. Ed. Maureen Fries and Jeanie Watson. 1992.

Atwood's The Handmaid's Tale *and Other Works*. Ed. Sharon R. Wilson, Thomas B. Friedman, and Shannon Hengen. 1996.

Austen's Pride and Prejudice. Ed. Marcia McClintock Folsom. 1993.

Beckett's Waiting for Godot. Ed. June Schlueter and Enoch Brater. 1991.

Beowulf. Ed. Jess B. Bessinger, Jr., and Robert F. Yeager. 1984.

Blake's Songs of Innocence and of Experience. Ed. Robert F. Gleckner and Mark L. Greenberg. 1989.

British Women Poets of the Romantic Period. Ed. Stephen C. Behrendt and Harriet Kramer Linkin. 1997.

Brontë's Jane Eyre. Ed. Diane Long Hoeveler and Beth Lau. 1993.

Byron's Poetry. Ed. Frederick W. Shilstone. 1991.

Camus's The Plague. Ed. Steven G. Kellman. 1985.

Cather's My Ántonia. Ed. Susan J. Rosowski. 1989.

Cervantes' Don Quixote. Ed. Richard Bjornson. 1984.

Chaucer's Canterbury Tales. Ed. Joseph Gibaldi. 1980.

Chopin's The Awakening. Ed. Bernard Koloski. 1988.

Coleridge's Poetry and Prose. Ed. Richard E. Matlak. 1991.

Dante's Divine Comedy. Ed. Carole Slade. 1982.

Dickens' David Copperfield. Ed. Richard J. Dunn. 1984.

Dickinson's Poetry. Ed. Robin Riley Fast and Christine Mack Gordon. 1989.

Eliot's Middlemarch. Ed. Kathleen Blake. 1990.

Eliot's Poetry and Plays. Ed. Jewel Spears Brooker. 1988.

Ellison's Invisible Man. Ed. Susan Resneck Parr and Pancho Savery. 1989.

Faulkner's The Sound and the Fury. Ed. Stephen Hahn and Arthur F. Kinney. 1996.

Flaubert's Madame Bovary. Ed. Laurence M. Porter and Eugene F. Gray. 1995.

García Márquez's One Hundred Years of Solitude. Ed. María Elena de Valdés and Mario J. Valdés. 1990.

Goethe's Faust. Ed. Douglas J. McMillan. 1987.

Hebrew Bible as Literature in Translation. Ed. Barry N. Olshen and Yael S. Feldman. 1989.

Homer's Iliad *and* Odyssey. Ed. Kostas Myrsiades. 1987.

Ibsen's A Doll House. Ed. Yvonne Shafer. 1985.

Works of Samuel Johnson. Ed. David R. Anderson and Gwin J. Kolb. 1993.

Joyce's Ulysses. Ed. Kathleen McCormick and Erwin R. Steinberg. 1993.

Kafka's Short Fiction. Ed. Richard T. Gray. 1995.

Keats's Poetry. Ed. Walter H. Evert and Jack W. Rhodes. 1991.

Kingston's The Woman Warrior. Ed. Shirley Geok-lin Lim. 1991.

Lafayette's The Princess of Clèves. Ed. Faith E. Beasley and Katharine Ann Jensen. 1998.

Lessing's The Golden Notebook. Ed. Carey Kaplan and Ellen Cronan Rose. 1989.

Mann's Death in Venice *and Other Short Fiction*. Ed. Jeffrey B. Berlin. 1992.

Medieval English Drama. Ed. Richard K. Emmerson. 1990.

Melville's Moby-Dick. Ed. Martin Bickman. 1985.

Metaphysical Poets. Ed. Sidney Gottlieb. 1990.

Miller's Death of a Salesman. Ed. Matthew C. Roudané. 1995.

Milton's Paradise Lost. Ed. Galbraith M. Crump. 1986.

Molière's Tartuffe *and Other Plays*. Ed. James F. Gaines and
    Michael S. Koppisch. 1995.

Momaday's The Way to Rainy Mountain. Ed. Kenneth M. Roemer. 1988.

Montaigne's Essays. Ed. Patrick Henry. 1994.

Novels of Toni Morrison. Ed. Nellie Y. McKay and Kathryn Earle. 1997.

Murasaki Shikibu's The Tale of Genji. Ed. Edward Kamens. 1993.

Pope's Poetry. Ed. Wallace Jackson and R. Paul Yoder. 1993.

Shakespeare's King Lear. Ed. Robert H. Ray. 1986.

Shakespeare's The Tempest *and Other Late Romances*. Ed. Maurice Hunt. 1992.

Shelley's Frankenstein. Ed. Stephen C. Behrendt. 1990.

Shelley's Poetry. Ed. Spencer Hall. 1990.

Sir Gawain and the Green Knight. Ed. Miriam Youngerman Miller and
    Jane Chance. 1986.

Spenser's Faerie Queene. Ed. David Lee Miller and Alexander Dunlop. 1994.

Sterne's Tristram Shandy. Ed. Melvyn New. 1989.

Swift's Gulliver's Travels. Ed. Edward J. Rielly. 1988.

Thoreau's Walden *and Other Works*. Ed. Richard J. Schneider. 1996.

Voltaire's Candide. Ed. Renée Waldinger. 1987.

Whitman's Leaves of Grass. Ed. Donald D. Kummings. 1990.

Wordsworth's Poetry. Ed. Spencer Hall, with Jonathan Ramsey. 1986.

Wright's Native Son. Ed. James A. Miller. 1997.